Eat Real Food

or else...

LOTUS

LIÊN NGUYÊN
MIKE NICHOLS, M.D.
CHEF CHARLES VOLLMAR

Many thanks to our friends and families whose reviews and criticism helped make this book a better one.

Published by Golden Lotus Publishing
Palo Alto, CA
Copyright © 2016 Lien Nguyen,
Mike Nichols, Charles Vollmar
All rights reserved.

Cover design and illustration by
CamilleMaiIllustration.com

This book is not intended as a substitute for the medical advice of physicians. The readers should regularly consult a physician in matters relating to their health and particularly with respect to any symptoms that may require diagnosis or medical attention.

Printed in the United States of America
First Printing January 2016
ISBN: 978-0-9862520-1-3

www.EatRealFoodOrElse.com

CONTENTS

Not Another Diet Book!

This book presents a way of eating that is both enjoyable and healthful. It is not a diet book: its focus is on whole body health. It strongly advises to eat (almost) everything. The rules are simple: enjoy the widest possible variety of fresh foods, avoid only one type of ingredients, those high in sugar and low in nutrients.

Eat Real Food proposes:

- A comprehensive system that promotes lifelong health, with nutritional advice based on the broad view of the entire body.

- Very tasty recipes, demonstrating that healthy everyday food can be delicious.

- Explanations about the effects of food on our body, with simple yet scientifically accurate justifications that take into account the findings of the latest research.

- Tools to make informed food choices.

- Perspectives from which to examine the existing diets and the nutritional literature.

Every dietary recommendation makes assumptions about the population's eating behavior. This book is no exception. It assumes that its readers have been bombarded with the established nutritional dogma; that, although they don't follow the rules as much as they think they should, they feel guilty when eating bacon, virtuous when buying low-fat dairy; that they strive to consume record quantities of whole grains and fiber; that they count calories and maybe cook egg-white-only omelets. Even for those who know better, deep down in their subconscious mind lurks the thought that fats cannot possibly be good for you. Such is the power of the media.

The goal of this book is to shatter this current dogma of a low-fat, low-calorie, mostly vegetable-based diet. This is why it so brutally bashes sugar. When it insists on the virtues of fat, it doesn't mean "Live on fat!": it is merely trying to restore some balance in a nutritional world where fats have been wrongly demonized. Given the strength of the beliefs, certain points must be emphasized (with the risk that some people might go overboard in the other direction, there is no way around that).

A reasonable recommendation heard today is to "eat less." And indeed, as a nation we might consume too many calories, but how does this fact apply to you as an individual? It is hard to figure out; most people don't have a way to know when they have eaten enough. By restoring its sensitivity to various hormonal signals, the nutrition system proposed in these pages will empower your own body to tell when it's had enough food.

This is not a textbook either. Although all the views expressed here are solidly backed by scientific fact, we will not engage in a technical paper "shoot-out" against the dogma. Several authors have done so in superb ways (see *Further Reading* in the appendix).

However, throughout these pages, the readers will find pointers that will help them to further explore nutritional science with a critical mind and a different perspective. One can find everything about anything on the internet. What is hype and what is fact? What poses a real health threat and what is merely an inconvenience? Plenty of leads are given here so that the readers who trust themselves to take their health into their own hands can study nutrition and form an opinion, with the whole body in mind, rather than missing the big picture by focusing on a single point.

No doubt that the concepts presented here will evolve and be refined with passing time: there will be progress. But these are our best options in the current state of science.

The first section, *Basics,* constitutes the technical portion of the book:

- **Eating Well / The Ideal Plate / What, When, How Much?**
  These three short chapters present the simple practical rules that are the backbone of our diet. It is indispensable to read them first.

  The other chapters in the section contain the scientific justification of the nutritional principles presented throughout this book.

- **Carbohydrates, Grains, Cereals and Starches**
  Shows that by eating sugar and starches we deprive our body of nutrients: since starches are very calorie-dense, they prevent us from enjoying many other foods. "Slow carbs" and grains are not significantly better than plain sugar.

- **The Hormonal Effects of Food**
  Demonstrates how eating carbohydrates can trigger vicious hormonal cycles leading to hormonal resistance, overeating and, paradoxically, malnutrition.

- **Fats and Metabolism**
  Reports on the scientific findings that fats, animal or vegetal, saturated or unsaturated, are good for us, and explains how saturated fats acquired their bad reputation.

- **Macronutrients and Energy**
  Details how we can generate energy using either carbs, fats or proteins; shows that fat is the preferred way, and that, by eating more fat and fewer carbs, we can train our body to burn a larger proportion of stored fat for energy.

- **Weight Loss - Body Fat**
  Explains how high blood sugar prevents people from burning fat. Although weight loss is not the purpose of this book, it is important to understand why the traditional low-calorie, low-fat diets don't work.

The rest of the book can be leafed through in random order. The sections contain recipes, sorted by categories, together with additional pages about nutrition. We have thought it useful to spread the information that is non-essential to the general comprehension to avoid boring the reader unduly. The observant reader will find the macronutrient that is missing from the first section, general information about cooking oils, vegetable families, sweeteners, drinks, sourcing and a few important topics:

- **Micronutrients**
  Warns about the dangers of focusing on a single nutrient and explains that we are less likely to miss something if, instead of getting lost in the nutrient nomenclature, we choose our food by color.

- **Being a Vegetarian**
  Explains how to get good protein and avoid the trap of the legume and grain combination, dangerous because of the antinutrients contained in the legumes.

- **Nutrition and Exercise**
  Shows that exercise, including high level athletic performance, doesn't require a carbohydrate-based diet, and that it is in fact desirable to switch from a sugar-based to a fat-based energy production.

The **Appendix** at the end of the book provides additional information and scientific explanations. Words in square brackets, such as [cholesterol], refer to the corresponding entry in the appendix. Asterisks in brackets, such as calories[*], refer to the entry for the word preceding the asterisk.

Note: in most recipes, for the sake of simplicity and in order to save space, we are not listing salt and pepper with the ingredients. Season to taste: if you prepare your own food, and in the absence of a particular pathology, there is no need to fear salt.

One frequent comment I receive from my friends, when I indulge in dispensing nutritional wisdom, is that the safest diet is to "eat a little bit of everything."

I suspect this is partially motivated by reluctance to part with their favorite starch. But there is certainly a lot of wisdom in their remark: excessive focus on any particular ingredient most likely results in ill health because our body, in its infinite complexity, needs a lot more than we can comprehend today and for the foreseeable future.

In practice, though, this commendable concept doesn't take into account the efforts of the food industry to make us buy whatever is profitable for them, regardless of its impact on our health. How do we define "a little bit of everything"? A little something from each aisle of the supermarket?

Without nutritional knowledge, we are easy prey for marketing and publicity.

A legitimate criticism of nutritional science is that it changes its mind all the time: first "they" said that starches were fattening; then it was not the starches, but what you put on them that made you gain weight; and now, we've gone full circle, back to starches as the bad guys. To confirm this impression, look at a 1950's cookbook – before Ancel Keys cast in stone the dogma that fat and cholesterol are the cause of heart disease – you'll find recommendations that have similarities with those advocated in this book, for example the absence of mortal fear of animal fat. (The similarity is only up to a certain point though.)

This shuffling back and forth understandably generates the feeling that science is not progressing, but going round and round instead, like a weather vane turning where the wind blows. You'd think that if we can put a man on the moon, we should be able to figure out exactly what food is best for our body.

And indeed, there are a lot of fad diets out there. But, to science's credit, understanding the human body is many orders of magnitude more complex than rocket science. In addition, among medical disciplines, nutrition has a particularly difficult position: it is impossible to rigorously test nutritional theories with randomized well controlled trials, as you would for a new drug; it seems unethical (although not unheard of) to purposefully feed a whole population some given diet with the goal to observe what percentage dies from it. So, what we are left to work with is epidemiology: epidemiology observes various populations and tries to draw conclusions by linking their health data with what is known of their eating habits. This method provides, of course, no proof of causation, it can at best show correlation, that is, association: a recent study found a connection between consuming whole milk and a lower body weight; but if people who drink whole milk are thinner than those who use non-fat, is it because whole milk makes you skinny, or is it that people drink whole milk because they feel they can afford it, being skinny already?

Also, despite appearances, nutritional science is progressing, in part thanks to the availability of new scientific tools: as an example, for a long time there was no easy way to accurately measure a person's insulin level; this impaired the ability to study the effects of sugar and insulin on our metabolism. This is not the case anymore: nowadays, insulin is easily monitored, and its nefarious effects have been proven beyond any doubt.

Another frequent objection is that "everyone is different."

This is true of course: genetics play an important role in how our body deals with food, but suspiciously, it comes up only after we heard something we don't like: we are willing to accept that there are nutritional principles, but when the principles don't suit us, everybody becomes different. Food is a very emotional issue, connecting us to our childhood, to our mother's love. We make leaps of logic to legitimize what we like to eat.

Obviously, it is impossible to prescribe a diet that would apply to everybody and address all the situations and pathologies. However, we must admit that there are some mechanisms that apply to the majority of the human race. It is worth being familiar with these principles: they offer a starting basis from which people can make informed choices depending on their particular physical needs, activity level, cultural heritage, medical problems, finances, available time, taste, environment, etc.

At the same time, it is clear that people have different metabolisms and react differently to foods: some of us should avoid salt, others should avoid legumes, for others it's onions, or kale, or cabbage, peanuts, milk, strawberries... These ingredients are real dangers for those concerned, but if we avoid everything that is a concern for some part of the population, we are left with nothing to eat. A better strategy is to pay attention to our individual response and only eliminate those ingredients that are a problem.

Lastly, there is the nagging suspicion that this is a "low calorie" diet in disguise: by eliminating starches, we might eat less, after all, our stomach only has room for so much broccoli; or maybe, without starches, meals are so unappetizing that they are not worth eating?

First, let's repeat that this is a way of eating for life, not a transitory weight loss diet.

Second, regarding whether life without starches is worth living, I hope the recipes presented here speak for themselves.

Third, that we end up eating less calories might be true or not (in our book, the starches missing from a traditional "balanced" diet are replaced by fats, which, as everyone knows, contain a lot of calories). But the truth is that we don't care: as long as you feel satiated and energetic, as long as you are not craving food, are healthy and feel good about your body, what does it matter if you consume more or less calories than before?

But don't take my word for it. Try and taste for yourself!

Liên Nguyen

Liên Nguyen

Liên was born in Paris, raised in a Vietnamese family, and trained as an electrical engineer. After a career in Silicon Valley, she retired and turned to the only really important matter: food. She has published several cookbooks, which blend culinary topics with culture and history.

Mike Nichols, M.D.

Dr. Nichols is a classically trained physician (Pre-Med U. of Chicago, Med School at Loyola U. of Chicago, Residency at Stanford), with training as a surgeon and with emergency medicine experience.

For the last 20 plus years, Dr. Nichols has been working on a quantitative model of the practice of medicine. Through a combination of software development and integration of heart rate data and other biological markers, he has developed a complete health system called "Quantitative Medicine."

Even though Quantitative Medicine entails more science than the conventional medical model, the goal remains the same: help people achieve a graceful and healthy state.

quantitativemedicine.net

What each person needs in order to attain peak health varies. Sometimes the need is diet modification, sometimes more effective exercise, often it entails dealing with stress and mindfulness, and sometimes even pills. Everybody is different, but appropriate measurements allow understanding of everyone's personal formula. For over twenty years, I have practiced medicine with this point of view, and my patients' results have vastly exceeded all expectations.

☙

Food is, of course, an obvious and important factor in a medical philosophy that treats the body as a whole, rather than a collection of organs.

Eighteen years ago, as I was putting my new clinic together, I realized that to succeed people had to be able to prepare their own food. Thus I began interviewing nutritionists and chefs. At the time, all the nutritionists were heavily schooled in principles that I knew were wrong. Sadly, the chefs, regardless of their creativity, had also been schooled in the same outdated principles exemplified by the "low-fat, low-cholesterol" mantra, which is now well disproven.

When I met Charlie Vollmar, the first thing he declared was "the most important thing about food is that you enjoy it with your family." Boom! This was a chef that understood the human side of eating: someone I could work with on sound nutrition. Real Food is, after all, a matter of going back to our human roots.

Mike Nichols
Dedicated to Anne and Jim Sorden
AMDG

Chef Charles Vollmar

An honors graduate of the California Culinary Academy in San Francisco, following his training at *Chez Panisse Restaurant and Cafe* and *Wente Vineyards*, Chef Charles Vollmar taught at several prominent San Francisco Bay Area cooking schools. He established his company, Epicurean Exchange, in 1999.

As a practicing chef instructor and culinary health educator, Chef Charles Vollmar emphasizes wellness, prevention and lifestyle enrichment. He is interested in all topics relating to cooking, nutrition, fitness and food appreciation.

Epicurean Exchange was a pioneer in the team-cooking concept, using the kitchen as a vehicle for corporate team-building, gatherings and retreats. This continues today, as companies, families and friends gather to cook, celebrate and enjoy quality experiences together.

Chef Charles Vollmar is also a seasoned culinary guide, who leads interactive behind-the-scenes tours presenting the philosophies and practices of local food producers and artisans. He also organizes and guides tours abroad, to explore the various cultures and origins of the food world.

www.epicureanexchange.com

I founded Epicurean Exchange with the belief that awareness, simply applied, adds quality to our life and helps us meet professional and personal goals. My company strives to bring balance, empowerment and enjoyment into people's lives through culinary adventures and education.

For over 16 years, Epicurean Exchange has taught classes on culinary skills and cuisine themes, has designed custom programs for individual and corporate clients, offered workshops, and conducted exclusive gourmet excursions.

The "exchange" takes place in a setting of optimal learning and understanding between like-minded participants, and is offered throughout the greater San Francisco Bay Area.

Charles Vollmar
Dedicated to Doaa, Aidan and Amelia

Words in square brackets [ ] refer to an entry in the Appendix. Asterisks in brackets [*] correspond to the entry for the word preceding the asterisk.

An asterisk without brackets refers to another recipe in this book.

The little hour-glass icons above the list of ingredients only provide an indication of the complexity of the recipe.

Basics

Eating Well

Historically, we looked at food in terms of macronutrients. This classification served a purpose, in particular with respect to energy production. However, as we learn more about the biology of nutrition, it makes a lot of sense to also think in terms of micronutrients.

MACRONUTRIENTS

As package labels show, food is traditionally classified into three categories: fats, proteins and carbohydrates. This is the macronutrient-based approach. An important property of all macronutrients is their capacity to produce energy. Each type of macronutrient also has specific properties:

- **Carbohydrates** are the main components of plants; they include sugars (smaller molecules), starches (long chains of sugars) and dietary fiber[*] (indigestible chains of sugar). Sugars are also present in dairy products. Their reputation is for providing energy rapidly, but in fact they are not uniquely qualified in that respect[energy].

- **Fats** play important structural functions in our body, particularly in cell membranes. We can synthesize most of the fats we need. There are only two types of fat that our body requires but is unable to build: these are called *essential fatty acids* and must be obtained through food.

- **Proteins** are chains of amino acids. They are responsible for the largest array of functions in our body for structure, hormones, enzymes, antibodies... We are able to synthesize many of the 20 amino acids we need; the rest must be supplied by our food and are referred to as *essential amino acids*.

MICRONUTRIENTS

Nutritional science has established that our bodies rely on many substances and chemicals found in our food to grow, repair and regulate themselves. These are *micronutrients, electrolytes and minerals (or elements)*, and they tend to work in small quantities. Even though they are technically classified in different categories, we'll often group them under the term "micronutrients" or even "nutrients" for short.

Nutrients are so numerous that it is impossible to list them all. They include vitamins, but are not, by any means, limited to them.

Vitamins[*] are defined as the micronutrients whose deficiency quickly leads to diseases. You may know that:

- Lack of vitamin B1 leads to beriberi.
- Lack of vitamin C causes scurvy.
- Lack of vitamin D is associated with rickets, etc.

The list of vitamins (A, B, C, D...) is in fact relatively short, and we now know that a much broader array of nutrients (in the thousands) is necessary for optimal health.

Vitamins can be the proverbial tree that hides the forest: by focusing on vitamins only, we expose ourselves to the serious consequences of deficiency in the other nutrients. These effects can build up slowly[glycation], however, they lead to severe ailments such as cancer, cardiovascular disease and immune system malfunction.

PUT A PALETTE OF COLORS ON THE TABLE!

The body is an infinitely complex machine, the seat of countless interactions. Food operates as a whole, and when nutrients are isolated, they don't work as well, or don't work at all.

Given the dauntingly vast quantity of indispensable nutrients, it is impossible, as of today, to offer an exhaustive list of recommended foods. Besides, this would turn meals from a pleasure into an accounting nightmare.

At this point of nutritional knowledge (or lack thereof), our best bet is to consume the widest possible variety of foods, while following three simple guidelines:

1. Seek colored, micronutrient-rich food

With some exceptions, micronutrients are richly colored. Let that be your guide: seek deeply, intensely colored ingredients.

- Look for the blue-indigo to purple-red pigments, as found in berries, eggplants, radicchio, purple cabbage, bell pepper, red onion…

- Find orange-red to yellow nutrients in carrots, tomatoes, pomegranates, berries, squashes…

- And all the shades in between! Train your artistic eye, and soon you'll be able to distinguish subtle hue variations.

Some notable exceptions to the color rule:

- Cruciferous vegetables (such as cauliflower) contain an important class of micronutrients that don't bring much color.

- The allium family (onions, shallots, garlic), revered for its many proven medicinal virtues, is not very colorful either.

2. Seek whole real food

This is food as produced by nature, food that is closest to:

> Pulled from the ground,
> Cut from the flesh,
> Plucked from the plant.

Look for fresh ingredients that received as little processing as possible: humans coevolved with this kind of nourishment for several hundred thousand years and have genetically adapted[*] to it. Keep in mind that, on the evolutionary scale, agriculture is a very recent development!

Industrial processing almost always lowers the nutritional value of ingredients and, willingly or not, introduces chemicals.

3. Seek healthy sources

Consuming foods that have been grown in contaminated soil or with chemical fertilizers and pesticides will lead to elevated amounts of dangerous substances in the body[sourcing].

If buying organic food exclusively is neither practical nor affordable, keep in mind that foods have different capabilities to absorb chemicals, and that ingredients with concentrated nutrition also have the potential for concentrated contaminants.

At special risk are:

- Root vegetables (carrots, turnips, potatoes…)
- Fall berries (blueberries, raspberries, blackberries…)
- Eggs
- Dairy products

So, go the extra mile for these!

The Ideal Plate

For many people, when it comes to diet and nutrition, the first question is:

"How many calories should I eat?"

This is because, as a result of bad eating habits, people cannot hear or trust their body's signals.

With proper nutrition, we can achieve a state where our body reliably tells us when it's had enough food.

Before asking *"How much?"* it is important to focus on *"What?"*, as nutrients have profoundly different effects on our metabolism.

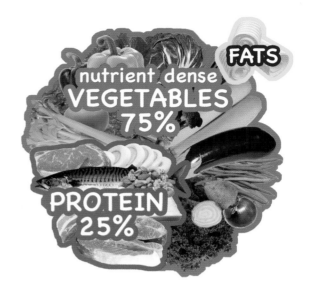

> **The ideal plate contains:**
>
> - **¼ Proteins**
> - **¾ Micronutrient-rich vegetables**
> - **Fats**
> - **No sugars or starches (or cereal)**

Although it is easier to illustrate this concept with volumes (as in the picture above), the proportions are intended in **weight** of cooked ingredients (a cup of raw salad is not the same as a cup of cooked spinach).

The "ideal plate" is designed to provide enough micronutrients and macronutrients. Proteins can be animal or vegetal. They include meat, fish, poultry, eggs, dairy, nuts and seeds.

It is assumed that vegetables are cooked or seasoned with fats. Protein generally comes with built-in fat. Fat is important and greatly contributes to satiety: in the vegetable portion of your plate, half of the calories might come from fat (this is, however, not much in volume).

Try to get all the ingredients from the healthiest, cleanest sources possible:

- Animal proteins come from healthy animals (grass-fed, pastured or wild) whenever possible.

- Vegetables that are particularly susceptible to contaminants should preferably be organic.

On the ideal plate, the protein sets the agenda. This doesn't diminish the importance of vegetables; it simply means that the quantity of vegetables is determined by the quantity of protein on the plate:

Whether you eat a 4-oz steak, a 6-oz fish fillet or a 3-egg omelet, make the vegetable portion of the meal about 3 times larger than the protein portion.

After you have finished your plate, if you want more food, make sure the next serving has the same 3 to 1 proportion of vegetables to proteins.

The quantity of protein required varies from person to person and also depends on the activity for the day. Younger or older people, or athletes, might need more than the general population. However, the "ideal plate" offers a good method for most people.

The exact quantity of fat for cooking vegetables is not important, just use a reasonable amount. The window for "reasonable" is pretty wide: within the context of our micronutrient-rich diet, the body can deal with *excess* fat fairly easily, but it cannot cope with deficiency.

Avoid sugars and starches (or cereals, which are also starches): they trigger unhealthy responses that make our body deaf to our hormonal signaling. This causes, among other things, overeating.

In a well fed society, sugar and starches are useless empty calories.

Of course, we are all different from one another, each with our individual needs for nutrients and energy. The proportions in the plate must be adjusted:

- **For power athletes** in the power building phase, see section *Nutrition and Exercise.*

- **For babies** in the first 18 months of life, fats should be emphasized. Fats are required for organ and brain growth.

- **For children** age 5 to pre-puberty, amino acids are important for their hormone driven growth. Children's level of activity requires more calories in the snack part of their daily meals (see section *What, When, How Much?*). For some, snacks can be as big as the meals.

- **For older adults**, when the hormonal drive to thrive and eat declines (starting between ages 40 to 60) and caloric needs become smaller, the attention to nutrient quality must become even greater.

We are advocating a "nutrient-rich" diet

that strongly limits the consumption of sugars and starches,

promotes the consumption of fats,

and shifts our primary energy source from sugar to fat.

The rest of the chapters in this section are devoted to explaining the reasons behind these principles.

The reader will also find complementary information in the other sections, between and within the recipes.

(See *Table of Contents*.)

What, When, How Much?

Food is one of the pleasures in life. Luckily enough, it also offers a very effective path to health and vitality.

In a society of plenty, focusing on food quality is essential. Routine excessive consumption of unsound ingredients results in health problems. Overeating can be the manifestation of an insatiable search for nutrients that are absent from modern processed food.

Situations where food is scarce, and priority number one is getting enough calories, have very different nutritional issues and need another book all to themselves. But even in those situations, *malnutrition* (lack of proper micronutrients) is an important issue, concurrently with *undernutrition* (lack of macronutrients, that is, not enough food).

In all cases, quality ingredients can be costly. Compromises will be necessary: all the more reason to be knowledgeable about the effects our food choices have on our bodies.

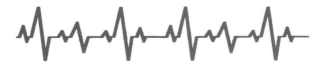

BODY RHYTHMS

Our metabolism follows cycles: seasonal, monthly, weekly, daily... The various phases of a given cycle have specific purposes, and each cycle has an optimal duration that may vary from person to person.

Our digestive system is no exception. The alternating patterns of hunger and satiety that we experience each day are the evidence of the complex periodic processes that regulate energy production and the regeneration of our bodies.

- During the hungry phase, the body scavenges, tearing down nutrients for energy production or cell needs.

- During the fullness phase, the body reconstructs itself, taking care of cell growth, cell reproduction, tissue repair, inflammation control; muscles, ligaments and bones are built.

The tear-down (or catabolic) phase clears the way for the reconstruction (or anabolic) phase.

If the fasting period lasts too long, scavenging becomes indiscriminate, breaking up useful material such as muscle or even brain cells! If satiation is prolonged, excessive blood sugar impairs the functions of our body machinery at the molecular level, causing glycation[*] and the manufacturing of defective cells, hormones or enzymes.

Our eating pattern must respect the natural rhythm of our metabolism. This ensures that we get the right amount of energy and are able to maintain our body in optimal shape.

With these facts in mind, here are additional guidelines for optimal healthy eating:

1. Have the largest meals early in the day.

Meals provide the energy for future activities. Excess food, with respect to the level of physical activity, gets converted into fat[*] and other undesirable by-products. In other words: *Eat for what you will do, not for what you did.*

- Breakfast would, according to this principle, be the main meal of the day. In our culture this is not easy, but at least keep in mind that breakfast is an important meal.

- Lunch is theoretically the second largest meal of the day, after breakfast.

- Dinner is small, since the physically active hours are over by then.

- Snacks are tiny, at set times, and do not constitute a license to munch!

Slight variations are allowed depending on the day's expected level of exertion: eat a little more *before (not after)* more strenuous than usual activities.

2. Each meal or snack consists of:
- ¼ Protein
- ¾ Micronutrient-rich vegetables
- Fats to cook or season with

Build your plate around the protein: for a given quantity of protein, add three times the weight in vegetables. This "ideal" plate is the result of decades of experience and has been shown to provide an adequate ratio of nutrients for most people.

Vary your proteins and vegetables as much as possible in order to benefit from the broadest range of nutrients.

Avoid sugars and starches. Eat fats instead: fat produces energy better than starches, has less harmful consequences and is necessary for the operation of our body.

Consume fruit cautiously: fruits contain a lot of sugar compared to vegetables with similar amounts of nutrients. Consider them a treat and select fruits with a high nutrient to sugar ratio.

3. Rhythm: eat regularly; no skipping, no grazing in between.

To facilitate our hormonal rhythm, we need to eat at regular intervals, allowing "hungry" and "full" periods; we don't want to be eating all day long; we must also avoid going without food for too long. For most people, a cycle of 3 hours is adequate.

- 7:00 am - large breakfast
- 10:00 am - tiny snack
- 1:00 pm - medium lunch
- 4:00 pm - tiny snack
- 7:00 pm - small (but extra tasty!) dinner
- 10:00 pm - tiny bedtime snack

A typical snack is very small (2 to 4 oz) and ideally includes proteins and vegetables like all the other meals: for example ¼ apple with 2 oz of cheese.

You'll know you are not eating enough if you get very hungry before 3 hours have elapsed (being slightly hungry is desirable, though.)

The fact that the "ideal plate" has a large proportion of vegetables doesn't mean that proteins or fats are less important. We need all the nutrients.

You can skip over the next chapters and go straight to the recipes. (They'll taste great either way...) However, these pages provide answers to those who want to understand the facts underlining the nutritional system presented in this book.

Carbohydrates, Grains, Cereals and Starches

With the exception of a few extremes, most people agree that we need to consume a balanced mix of the three macronutrients. The source of disagreement is what ratio of these nutrients constitutes a "balanced diet": opinions on this topic diverge radically.

Plants are mostly carbohydrates and water

At the macroscopic level, carbohydrates are the main constituent in a plant's structure: plants breathe in CO_2, grabbing the carbon atom to build the carbohydrates they need, in particular for their cell walls.

Fruits and vegetables are mostly made of carbohydrates and water. Water content ranges from 75 % (banana, potato) to 95 % (zucchini, cabbage).

> **Carbohydrates** are, by definition, chains of sugar molecules:
> - Short chains (fructose, glucose, sucrose) are what we customarily call "sugar."
> - Long chains, commonly designated as "starch," make up grains and vegetables in general.

It was previously believed that longer sugar molecules took more time to be digested and pass into our blood; hence the notion of "slow carbs" or "complex carbs," as opposed to "fast carbs" in simpler sugars.

And indeed, slow carbs are desirable, but speed has more to do with the fibrous structure of the food than the complexity of its carbohydrate molecule: the sugar from an asparagus goes into our blood slower than that from potato, yam or rice, because it is trapped in fiber, which needs to be broken down first.

All carbohydrates can be divided in 2 categories:

- **Fiber**, which is mostly not digested.
- **Non-fiber**, which is exactly the same as short-chain sugar, as far as our body is concerned.

The macroscopic view

Since all vegetables are mostly made of carbohydrates, fiber (a sub-category of carbs) and water, what then distinguishes one vegetable from another? The answer is mainly in the ratio of macronutrients to water.

Let's compare a cauliflower floret to a potato (the results are similar for raw or boiled):

The potato has almost four times the amount of macronutrients, mostly carbohydrates, as the cauliflower.

This is why you get so many calories from eating grains and starchy vegetables such as potatoes: since water contributes no calories, eating the same weight of cauliflower or potatoes results in dramatically different caloric intakes. If you go trekking, you'll want to carry potatoes in your backpack instead of cauliflower.

Conversely, for the same amount of carbohydrates or calories, you get 3 to 4 times more cauliflower than potato.

A more comprehensive view

The macroscopic view doesn't tell the whole story about the nutritional worth of an ingredient. When we are concerned about the quality of our food, we need to go beyond basic calorie count and examine the value of its micronutrients.

Our food must supply:

- Sufficient energy (i.e. calories) for our daily activity.

- Enough proteins and the full range of essential amino acids.

- The widest possible range of micronutrients, electrolytes and minerals.

- Enough fats and the full spectrum of essential fats.

The next pages show that these properties vary widely from one ingredient to the next and that balancing food is always a trade-off.

Starch is, by definition, a long chain of glucose molecules. It is present in most plants. The chain can be linear (as in amylose) or branched (as in amylopectin).

- By extension, **starches** designate foods containing a large proportion of starch such as potatoes, cassava, wheat, cereals and all the grains in general.

- **Legumes** are a family of vegetables such as lentils or beans that are fairly loaded with carbohydrates, though not as loaded as grains.

75 % carbohydrates

11 % protein

water

Wheat

Grains

Grains are deeply rooted in most civilizations:

- For evolutionary reasons, sugar and starches taste very good! At the dawn of mankind, sugar was a precious commodity; as early humans were in constant need of calories, it is likely that those with a sweet tooth had an advantage.

- Then came agriculture: its development made it possible to feed larger populations with grain, enabling the division of labor and the development of arts, war and political systems. Grains were essential to the development of our civilization.

Not surprisingly, *every culture has its favorite starch:* picture Vietnam without rice, Italy without pasta, France without bread, Germany without potatoes, Morocco without couscous... It is nearly impossible to cook a traditional meal without starch.

- Starches are cheap and convenient. They keep well, sparing us the trouble of replenishing the refrigerator with fresh produce.

- Starches provide a lot of calories. This is important in the parts of the world where many people don't get enough to eat.

- In subsistence cultures, grains and legumes offer an alternative to animal proteins, that can be scarce.

The whole grain controversy

It is now accepted that refined carbohydrates (table sugar, white flour, white bread...) are undesirable: they contain too much sugar, and the refining process deprives them of nutrients. Their excessive consumption leads to obesity and many other ailments.

On the other hand, there is a prevalent notion that whole grains are good for you, whole wheat especially. In whole grains, the bran and germ are not removed, contrary to refined grains.

Many medical institutions emphatically insist that whole wheat[grain] is beneficial to our health (in particular, cardiovascular) with numerous studies as proof. Government recommendations encourage us to consume considerable amounts of whole wheat.

On the other hand, an increasing number of studies argue that, with its high sugar content, whole wheat[grain] is no better than sugar and is linked to serious diseases such as diabetes and Alzheimer's.

Let's start by pointing out that government recommendations[*] are, by necessity, not dictated by scientific truth alone. They can only be a trade off, taking into consideration:

- Practicality.

- The need to provide a diet that is affordable to all.

- Replacing popular nefarious ingredients by supposedly less harmful ones.

- The urgency to fight malnutrition by issuing dietary advice, even though the science is incomplete.

- Political and business reasons.

However, the detractors of whole grain go so far against conventional wisdom that one is tempted to reject them as lunatics. And while the Whole Grain Council defends the grain industry, another industry is built around the "no grains, no gluten" trend.

The research papers from both camps are long, difficult and written in tiny characters with complicated words. Entire books are devoted to either side of the issue.

Even when they are brave enough to undertake the reading of such documents, most people underestimate themselves and don't feel qualified to judge their validity.

The authors have fancy titles, but how can we judge their credentials? How solid are their references? How up-to-date are they with current research? Do they have some investment in advocating their particular cause? Who are they funded by?

It is very easy to cherry pick the evidence in order to prove any point: selectively choose the papers that agree with you and discard the rest. To convince yourself, search the internet for "whole grains are unhealthy," then try "whole grains are healthy."

It is hard to navigate without guidance. However, experts with too much expertise sometimes miss the broad view (or have a vested interest).

Now that you are utterly confused, let's start over and look at grains as scientifically and objectively as possible. Let's reject magic.

Grains and starches *do* possess common properties that set them apart from other foods.

Let's compare starches with non-starchy vegetables, using the following criteria:

- The glycemic index[*] measures how quickly sugar in a given food passes to our blood. The **glycemic load** takes into account the glycemic index, as well as the total amount of sugar in a given serving size, and is a better measurement of how the carbs in the food affect blood sugar.

- **Protein quantity**

- **Protein quality -** In the images below, there is a spoke for each of the 9 essential amino acids, its size proportional to the optimal level for that amino acid in our body.

- **Nutrient quality**, as shown in the images below, is a visual representation of the food's nutritional value, each spoke representing a different nutrient. It can only be a partial representation since the number of important micronutrients is too large to be represented.

- **Fat quality and quantity**, although important, are absent from the tables.

The ingredients are cooked without added salt. Significantly elevated values are highlighted in red.

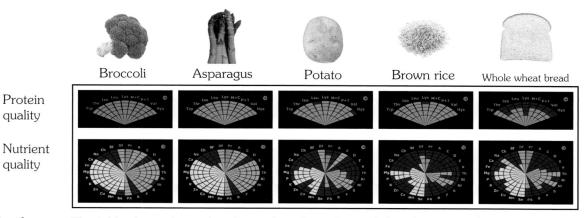

| | Broccoli | Asparagus | Potato | Brown rice | Whole wheat bread |

Nutritional value

The table above shows that the quality of starches is definitely poorer: the protein quality and especially the nutrient wheel are much fuller for the non-starches. The protein quality of wheat bread is especially terrible. (The little graphs in the table are only intended to give the reader an overall idea of the quality of each food, the precise value and name of each spoke are not so important.)

For identical calories

100 Calories[*]

Glycemic load	8	9	10-16	10	8-12
Carbs non fiber	9.4 g	12.7 g	22.1 g	19.4 g	15.5 g
Fiber	9.4 g	9.1 g	2.1 g	1.6 g	2.4 g
Protein	6.8 g	10.9 g	2.2 g	2.3 g	4.9 g

For identical weights

100 g

Calories	35 cal	22 cal	87 cal	111 cal	252 cal
Glycemic load	3	2	9-14	11	19-30
Carbs non fiber	3.3 g	2.8 g	19.2 g	21.6 g	39 g
Fiber	3.3 g	2.0 g	1.8 g	1.8 g	6.0 g
Protein	2.4 g	2.4 g	1.9 g	2.6 g	12.5 g

For a given number of calories, the glycemic loads are similar for all ingredients, which makes some sense because the calories derive from the macronutrients, in this case, mostly carbs.

The non-starchy vegetables provide more fiber and protein than the starches: this is expected since you must eat a lot more of the "non-starches" to get the same amount of calories.

For a given serving weight, the non-starchy vegetables are much lower in calories, sugar and glycemic load, which is expected, since they contain so much water.

The fiber content and protein quantity is similar for non-starches and starches (except for wheat bread, which has a lot more).

Comparison by volume leads to similar results as comparison by weight.

Assuming that you are following a real food, micronutrient-rich diet with the proper ratios of macronutrients, varying your proteins and vegetables as prescribed in the previous pages, you are better off avoiding starches, cereals and grains, whole or not:

- Their protein and micronutrient content is low and can be obtained from better sources. (Whole wheat is an exception in the sense that it has protein, but its quality is poor).

- They are high in calories and fill you up, preventing you from eating more micronutrient-rich foods. It's not only what you eat, but also what you don't eat...

- Satiety[*] comes from a mix of factors: taste, macronutrients, calories and volume of food. For those who want to cut down on calories, eating significant amounts of micronutrient-rich food is a healthy way to do so.

- Starches and grains are high in carbohydrates, which trigger the harmful insulin and sugar cycles. Excess sugar gets stored as fat.

- Many of the micronutrients in grains are not made available to our body because of the presence of phytic acid[bioavailability].

23 g fiber
35 g sugars
18 g protein
(275 Cal)

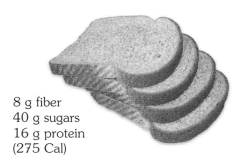

8 g fiber
40 g sugars
16 g protein
(275 Cal)

Food for thought:

- You need a certain number of calories per day. You can get them either from a smaller portion of grains and starches, or from a large volume of other vegetables. Eating grains on a regular basis brings you an incomplete range of micronutrients and, since it fills you up, it robs you of the opportunity to get the various nutrients from all the other vegetables.

- Many vitamins can be absorbed only in the presence of fat. The vegetables must be cooked or seasoned with a variety of fats: vegetal, animal, saturated or unsaturated. Some vegetables, such as broccoli, come with built-in fat, a bonus!

GRAINS ARE NOT A BASIC FOOD GROUP

While the ubiquitous food pyramid, with its sturdy starch base, would have us believe that cereals, starches and grains are a separate food group, they are mostly carbohydrates. They are no more a separate food group than, say, marshmallows or pizza.

The *MyPlate*[*] standard that replaced the pyramid has reduced the recommended proportion of grains, but it still implies that grains are a basic food group. They are not! The indispensable, basic macronutrients are: *proteins, fats and carbohydrates*.

Therefore, a balanced diet doesn't imply that you must include a proportion of starches and grains. It is the food industry, with help from official agencies, which has successfully ingrained this notion in the public's mind.

You don't need to eat all this food in one seating (especially if you are in a hurry or have weak jaw muscles). The pictures on this page are intended to illustrate the huge differences embodied in 275 Calories.

22 g fiber
40 g sugars
17 g protein
(275 Cal)

Reducing our starch consumption is well worth the effort: by getting our nutrition from nutrient-dense vegetables, proteins and fats, we avoid the negative effects of excessive sugar and insulin, and ensure a wide range of micronutrients.

Note that the nutritional system proposed in this book is not a low-carb diet: it is a low-starch diet. We get a fairly large amount of carbohydrates and fiber from our nutrient-dense vegetables.

Don't combine this diet with a low-fat, low-cal or low-carb diet. Don't pick your favorite elements from various diets. This is a whole system that makes sense only if you apply all its principles.

Beyond general principles, different people respond differently to sugar. Pay attention to your own tolerance, which can be higher or lower than average.

But if you must...

You can include a modest amount of whole grains in your diet for variety and pleasure, or if you are one of those few individuals whose metabolism requires more calories and cannot get enough otherwise.

You might need grains because they are cheap, convenient, a part of your culture, and taste good. But if you must eat starches, choose wisely and appreciate them for what they are: a big load of sugar!

- Look for the starches that have the highest nutrition-to-carbohydrate ratio: whole grains are slightly better than refined grains in that respect (but barely).

- Legumes, such as lentils and dry beans, are halfway between the low starch vegetables advocated in this book and the starches: their higher nutritional value somewhat compensates for their sugar content. And here again, some are better than others.

⚠ Beans are rich in *lectins*[*], which at high doses can, among other things, impair the absorption of proteins and nutrients.

⚠ Another reason to stay away from grains are the health problems associated with *gluten*.

Choose legumes over grains, and select those with a lower glycemic load and higher nutrient-to-sugar ratio, such as:

- Lentils
- Split peas
- Mung beans
- Chickpeas
- Peas (fresh)
- Beans

Select whole grains with a lower glycemic index:

- Wild rice
- Amaranth
- Pasta (al dente)
- Raw oats
- Spelt
- Bulgur

The Hormonal Effects of Food

Everybody has heard of hormones and how they govern our lives, especially sex hormones. Less known is the fact that food is tightly connected to a whole system of hormones, with dramatic health implications. We will only talk about a few here, but these are only the tip of the iceberg. Whole books are devoted to the issue. Also see the Weight Loss - Body Fat pages in this book for more discussions about hormones and nutrition.

Sensitivity = Regulation

During digestion, carbohydrates are broken into simple sugars and passed into our bloodstream. The increased blood sugar causes the pancreas to produce **insulin**, a hormone that allows the cells to let sugar in (while insulin also allows the uptake of other macronutrients, its secretion is closely tied to eating carbohydrates). This happens when the cells respond properly to the insulin signal: they are said to be *insulin sensitive*.

The glucose taken away from the blood and into the cells can be burned to provide immediate energy (TCA cycle). If energy is not needed, sugar is stored as *glycogen*. When the glycogen storage is full, which doesn't take much (total capacity is around 2000 Cal), the remaining glucose is stored as fat in fat cells.

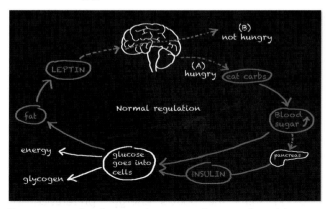

Leptin, or the "satiety hormone," is produced by our fat cells when they have enough fat in store. Our brain recognizes leptin as a signal that we have accumulated enough energy and can stop eating.

This feedback system regulates the amount of food we eat to a proper level: concerning body fat in particular, we need a certain amount, not too much, not too little. Ideally, the process starts at point A (hungry) and stops at point B (not hungry).

Ghrelin, also nicknamed the "hunger hormone," is produced by the empty stomach. Its action on the brain is to increase appetite, the opposite of leptin.

Glucagon is secreted by the pancreas when blood sugar is low: it stimulates the liver to convert stored glycogen back into glucose and to release it in the bloodstream. Glucagon, therefore, has the opposite effect of insulin, and together they work to balance blood sugar.

Resistance = Imbalance

"Resistance" designates a condition where a signal is not recognized by our body. Resistance usually leads to a cascade of disastrous events:

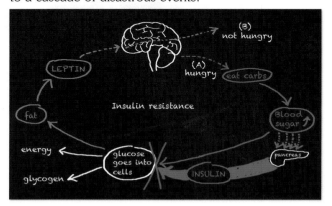

Insulin resistance happens when the cells ignore the insulin message and don't let sugar in. As a result, the blood sugar level stays high; this tells the pancreas to keep producing insulin in an attempt to diminish blood sugar. Eventually, the pancreas maxes out and breaks, losing its ability to produce insulin altogether, a cause of diabetes.

Diabetes can also emerge with the intact pancreas working as hard as it can, but being unable to keep up with the demands of a poor diet; the result is elevated insulin and glucose in the blood.

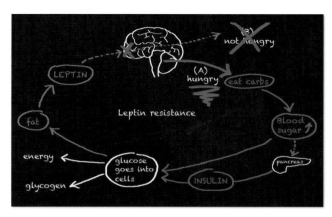

Leptin resistance happens when the brain doesn't hear the leptin signal and keeps urging us to eat. The obvious consequences are overeating and obesity.

What causes resistance?

Various factors can lead to resistance, some of them genetic, others linked to the eating behavior. To mention a few:

- High levels of insulin can lead to insulin[*] resistance.

- Chronically elevated blood sugar can cause leptin[*] resistance (thus blocking the satiety signal and leading to a vicious circle of more eating, more blood sugar and more leptin resistance).

- *Lectins* (present in large quantity in grains and beans) can cause leptin resistance.

- Leptin resistance can lead to insulin resistance: one theory is that the cells that are already full of fat resist the insulin message because they don't "want" to take in more fat.

- Etc., etc.

Many more mechanisms lead to insulin and leptin resistance, with one common cause: the overconsumption of carbohydrates.

Consequences of resistance

Body fat is not necessarily a bad thing in itself. The danger resides in the hormonal side effects of eating carbs. Just to cite the most important:

- Chronically elevated blood sugar is responsible for *glycation*[*]. The body is continually making new proteins, and the manufacturing environment is important: molecules produced in presence of a lot of sugar will be defective. Glycation leads, in particular, to small vessel diseases in the kidneys, eyes, fingertips, toes and brain.

- Chronically elevated insulin is bad in itself: insulin[*] directly increases arterial stiffness, which leads to high blood pressure and atherosclerosis. Elevated insulin also clearly increases cancer risks.

- Elevated insulin impairs the action of glucagon[*], thus preventing the use of stored fat for energy.

- The excessive presence of carbohydrates in the blood shifts the body's energy[*] preference to burning sugar and impairs the burning of stored fat.

Hormones are necessary chemical signals that play an important role. Our food choices have the power to trigger a healthy or unhealthy hormonal response in our body.

We want to make our body as sensitive as possible to the hormonal signals so we can respond to them in a dynamic fashion.

It is very important to manage levels of insulin and sugar in our blood.

Overconsumption of carbohydrates leads to a vicious circle of insulin production, elevated blood sugar and resistance.

Fats and Metabolism

To untangle the controversies surrounding dietary fats, it is critical to look at food scientifically, and break away from popular wisdom and simplistic analogies. There is not one single thing called fat but many different types of fat.

In the context of our nutrient-rich diet, we need to consume plenty of fats. Fat is of the highest importance to our metabolism:

- Fats play a broad role, both in the structure and function of all the cells across our body: membranes, ligaments, tendons; you name it.

- Fat is necessary for neural transmission: the myelin sheath, responsible for the speed of nerve transmission, is mostly made of fat. Without myelin and fat, we don't have a functional neurological system.

- Many vitamins (A, D, E, K) are only soluble in fat, so consuming them without fat has about the same nutritional value as eating cardboard.

- Fat is a good source of energy.

- Fat makes most people feel full more efficiently than sugar and carbohydrates. And contrary to conventional wisdom, eating fat doesn't make you fat[*]: unlike sugar, fat doesn't trigger the hormonal responses that lock body fat in.

- As surprising as it may sound, the relationship between dietary cholesterol[*] and heart disease in the general population has been disproved; it is now well established that sugar causes the production of hormones responsible for cardiovascular disease.

The next few pages expand and justify these surprising assertions.

Saturated vs. Unsaturated Fats

The backbone of fatty acids (the building blocks for all fat molecules) is a chain of carbon whose structure defines whether the fatty acid is saturated or unsaturated:

- If the carbon chain contains no double bonds, the molecule is *saturated*. Pictured below is butyric acid, a saturated fat found in dairy. (Note that there is a double bond between the final C and O, but we are looking only at the bonds between C atoms.)

$$H-\overset{\overset{\displaystyle H}{|}}{\underset{\underset{\displaystyle H}{|}}{C}}-\overset{\overset{\displaystyle H}{|}}{\underset{\underset{\displaystyle H}{|}}{C}}-\overset{\overset{\displaystyle H}{|}}{\underset{\underset{\displaystyle H}{|}}{C}}-C\overset{\displaystyle O}{\underset{\displaystyle O-H}{}}$$

- Otherwise, the molecule is unsaturated, *mono* or *polyunsaturated* depending on the number of double bonds in the carbon chain. In the classical 2-D representation, double bonds are shown as a double line. Pictured below is a polyunsaturated fat molecule containing 2 double bonds in its carbon chain.

$$H-\overset{\overset{\displaystyle H}{|}}{\underset{\underset{\displaystyle H}{|}}{C}}-\overset{\overset{\displaystyle H}{|}}{\underset{\underset{\displaystyle H}{|}}{C}}-\overset{\overset{\displaystyle H}{|}}{C}=\overset{\overset{\displaystyle H}{|}}{C}-\overset{\overset{\displaystyle H}{|}}{C}-C\overset{\displaystyle O}{\underset{\displaystyle O-H}{}}$$

 All foods contain a mix of saturated and unsaturated fat. However, animals tend to have a larger proportion of saturated fat than fruits and vegetables.

An unsaturated molecule can be made saturated by breaking all its double bonds and attaching more hydrogen atoms. And vice versa, a saturated molecule can be unsaturated easily by our body: enzymes can remove atoms and create double bonds between two adjacent carbons.

Fat has a shape

Molecules are not flat or linear. They have a 3-dimensional structure from which they get physical and chemical properties. While saturated fats are relatively straight, the double bonds create "kinks" in unsaturated molecules, as depicted below.

saturated fat   unsaturated fat

Fatty acids must have a specific length and shape in order to perform their tasks. Our body has a whole array of mechanisms to convert available fat molecules to fill the job: by saturating or desaturating them, it can turn them very precisely into the required unit. One of these mechanisms is through the enzyme *desaturase*, which, its name says it, transforms saturated fat into unsaturated fat by creating double bonds.

Another effect of unsaturation is that the molecule is thinner at the location of the double bond. This "notch" is important: for example, it allows a fat molecule to insert itself properly in the cell walls. The position of the notch matters also: for the molecule to be functional, the notch needs to be exactly in the right place.

For this type of functionality, the body cannot use random polyunsaturated fat molecules, because the position of their double bonds will not necessarily fit the need. It is easier for us to desaturate[*] a saturated fat instead.

Our body is very good at doing this, when and where a specific fat molecule is required. This process works better than relying on artificially desaturated fats from our diet. (Natural unsaturated fats found in wild animal meat are fine because they are the ones our body can use "as is.")

In conclusion, saturated fats are more versatile than unsaturated fats: they can be viewed as the universal donor from which various structurally different fats can be built.

However, this marvelous mechanism has a limitation: the enzyme desaturase can desaturate bonds in all positions, except for the ones closest to the molecule's extremity, hence the essential omega-3 and omega-6 fats that we cannot produce in sufficient quantities.

Essential fatty acids, omega-3, omega-6

Our body needs a vast array of fatty acids, but it can fabricate most of them. There are, strictly speaking, only 2 fatty acids that we cannot synthesize:

- **Alpha-linolenic acid (ALA)** is an 18-carbon chain member of the omega-3 family. It is a poly-unsaturated fat, with the first double bound located at the 3rd carbon from the omega end.

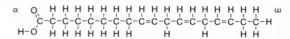

Our body uses ALA to synthesize **EPA** (20-carbon) and **DHA** (22-carbon), longer chain omega-3 molecules that are vital to our metabolism: they are the building blocks for some hormones that control immune function, blood clotting and cell growth, as well as components of cell membranes.

ALA is found in plants such as flax, hemp, pumpkin seeds and walnuts.

- **Linoleic acid (LA)** is the shortest member of the omega-6 family, also 18 carbons long. It is also an unsaturated fat, with its first double bond in the 6th position.

Our body uses it to synthesize prostaglandins, an important group of hormones involved in, among other things, inflammation.

LA is present in abundance in vegetable oils.

As an additional complication, conversion from ALA to EPA and DHA is inefficient. In fact, some people just cannot synthesize EPA and DHA. For these reasons and others, longer chain fatty acids such as DHA and EPA may be an important factor in our diet. These come mostly from fish and meat; they are not found outside of animal sources (except for some recently engineered algae-based DHA).

Note that the essential fats are not essential in terms of energy production. For fuel, the body will use any type of fat indifferently.

As a general rule, it is good to consume fatty acids of different lengths: we can transform them into the whole spectrum that we need, more easily than if we only ate the shorter ones.

The conversion from one fatty acid to another requires other nutrients: nutrient deficiency will impair that process. This is yet another reason to eat plenty of micronutrients.

Is fat really the villain?

Just about anybody will assure you that eating fat, especially saturated fat, causes heart disease. This is, most of the time, an unquestioned belief. Where does this conviction come from?

- The initial bad rap for fat was based on early analysis of arterial plaque: the inadequate imaging of the time led researchers to think that atheromas were solely made of fat.

When more detailed imaging became available, it was established that plaques are also full of other things (white cells, bacteria, etc.), but the initial notion that "plaque equals fat" has stuck.

Plaque is a repair mechanism for the lesions, like a scab is a healing response to a cut, not the cause of the cut. The lesions themselves are the real danger. Their causes include shear forces, damage to lining cells (due to insulin), inflammatory signaling (which insulin is part of) and infection.

- Various studies, most notably Ancel Keys's[*], have linked saturated fat, cholesterol and heart disease.

Although these studies are presented to the public as definitive medical certainties, the reality is that the scientific community has always been divided about their validity. After almost a century of investigating, no mechanism for how fat clogs the arteries has been proven. In other words, the negative effects of fat, saturated or unsaturated, are unsubstantiated. This refers to natural fats; man-made fats[trans fat] are another story.

Modern analysis of these past studies reveals that they are flawed. After re-examining them with rigorous mathematical analysis, no correlation was found between saturated[*] fats and cardiovascular disease.

We now know that eating saturated fat increases HDL level (the "good cholesterol") and LDL particle size (making "bad cholesterol" less harmful).

The finger points to sugar and insulin.

While no study has proven the negative effect of fat on cardiovascular health, many studies have linked insulin[*] with cardiovascular disease.

Insulin is secreted by the pancreas when the level of blood glucose rises; it allows our body to remove excess glucose from our blood.

"Overshooting" is a common occurrence, where excessive insulin production causes the blood sugar level to drop below its initial value. This means that eating sugar can, paradoxically, lead to hypoglycemia and the craving for more sugar, a situation many people have experienced. Satisfying the craving generates more insulin and starts a vicious cycle of sugar addiction.

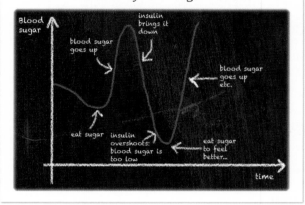

Fat is good!

• **Fat can readily produce energy**. Many of our cells can use either glucose or fatty acids for energy production: in fact, the heart and skeletal muscles favor fatty acids. Contrary to popular belief, the brain can also use some fatty acids as a source of fuel[gluconeogenesis].

Fat is a cleaner source of energy in the sense that it doesn't trigger the insulin vicious cycle like sugar does.

• **Fat makes most people feel full** more effectively than sugar. Fat is straightforward: when you eat fat, that's it. You don't crave more. Eating fat also gives you a larger window to use the energy before it turns into body fat.

• **Fat calories are better than sugar calories.** Yes, fat packs more calories than sugar or proteins, but calories have different biological impacts on your body: fat revs up your metabolism, glucose slows it down. Calories[*] are not interchangeable.

It is healthy to eat a larger portion of our diet as fats, including saturated fats, instead of starches and sugar.

So how did the *hypothesis* that "fat causes heart disease" acquire *fact* status?

A number of recent books explain this situation as the unappealing product of a mixture of incomplete science, politics and business interests[*]. Other reasons include the incentive for scientists to publish only positive results, failure by policy makers to recognize the limitations of scientific studies, misunderstanding of study results, pressure to conform...

An early scientific mistake was the cause that for decades, all potential explanations of heart disease had to coexist with the erroneous belief that dietary fat was the primary cause of coronary heart disease. Although insulin and sugar offered a simpler, better explanation that matched the observations, a whole assortment of theories have sprung forward in an effort to reconcile evidence and dogma.

Or, in the end, is it that the notion adheres so well to the image of fat and cholesterol sluicing down our arteries and clogging them? A seemingly logical, simplistic yet powerful, picture congealed in our collective mind.

Greater detail is beyond the scope of this book. Those interested will find further reading in the *Appendix*.

It is only a matter of time until doctors advise us to eat saturated fats. But the years it takes for public recommendations to reflect advances in science will take even more years off your life.

The journey to understand fats, and nutrition in general, is a long, winding one, but for your health's sake it is definitely worth the effort. Dare to challenge the establishment and take charge of your own health instead of trusting it to industry "experts."

We cannot predict exactly what you'll find at the end of your journey because any diet must take into account individual responses. But one thing is certain: along the road you'll find that common beliefs are shattered. And, if nothing else, frustration will make you fully appreciate the limitations of past studies.

Trans fats

For a given chemical formula, molecules can take different shapes; "trans" and "cis" refer to the position of the C atoms on each side of a double bond (therefore the notion applies only to unsaturated molecules): in the trans configuration, the molecule is fairly straight, whereas in the cis configuration, it is bent. A "trans fat" is an unsaturated fat molecule with at least one double bond in the trans configuration.

The slight variation in shape results in vastly different physical and chemical properties.

Oleic acid (cis)   *Elaidic acid (trans)*

At room temperature, oleic acid is liquid, elaidic acid is solid. They share the formula $C_{18}H_{34}O_2$.

Although uncommon, trans fats do exist in nature. Trans fats in man-made ingredients are the by-products of partial hydrogenation, a process used to harden vegetable oils. These hydrogenated vegetable shortenings were developed by the food industry for practical reasons and marketed very successfully to replace butter and traditional animal fats such as lard.

Our body is generally well adapted to the consumption of natural fats, whether trans or cis:

- Trans[*] fats from properly sourced dairy and meat have beneficial metabolic effect.

- Humans have coevolved and adapted their metabolism to the natural fats.

In nature, fats exist mostly in the cis configuration (with some notable exceptions, like beef and dairy), and most of our structural requirements are for cis forms. **Consuming man-made trans[*] fats, which our body isn't equipped to deal with, leads to serious problems.**

One of many examples: the altered shape of artificial trans fat molecules will cause structural defects in our membranes[*], of which fats constitute important building blocks.

Omega-3 and Omega-6

Omega-3 and omega-6 are two important classes of polyunsaturated fatty acids (PUFA).

The fatty acid molecule is a linear chain of carbon, with a carboxyl group (COOH) at one end and a methyl group (CH_3) at the other. The carboxyl end is labeled alpha; the methyl end is labeled omega.

The "3" in omega-3, or "6" in omega-6, refer to which carbon has the first double bond, counting from the omega end.

Pictured above, a PUFA with its first double bond at position 6, therefore an omega-6 fatty acid. Below, a simplified representation of the same fatty acid omits the C and H atoms, showing only the position of the bonds.

- **Omega-3:** this is not a single molecule but a whole class of fatty acids with different lengths. The shortest is ALA (*alpha-linolenic acid*) with an 18-carbon chain. EPA (20-carbon) and DHA (22-carbon) are other important omega-3 fatty acids.

ALA

EPA

DHA

- **Omega-6:** similarly, omega-6 molecules can be of different lengths, and they are equally important to our metabolism. The shortest chain omega-6 is LA (*linoleic acid*, 18-carbon).

LA

Our body uses omega-6 fatty acids to build hormones that generally counter-balance the effects of those built with omega-3.

The omega-3 / omega-6 debate

Many think that there is an optimal omega-6 to omega-3 ratio in our diet. It was once believed that a 1 to 1 ratio was closer to our ancestors' diet. This ratio is important to the school believing that all oxidation and inflammation is bad, since it is correctly noted that the longer omega-6 goes straight into the inflammatory pathway.

The fact is that, in modern western diets, there are few sources of omega-3, whereas omega-6 is plentiful: one cause is the almost exclusive usage of vegetal oils, all extremely rich in omega-6, which have displaced the traditional animal fats.

Our position

Ratio becomes less relevant when you realize that our body can build almost everything from anything and discard what is not needed: excess ω-3 or ω-6 will be eliminated, unless the imbalance is completely overwhelming.

We can deal with a reasonable excess in ω-3 and ω-6 fats, but we can't cope with deficiency: since our body cannot make them, it's important for us to consume enough of all the essential fats.

The assumption that inflammation is 100 % negative is misguided: good health is not all about anti-inflammation and anti-oxidation. We want to create a balanced environment where the body can kill cells when needed: very excessive ω-3 is associated with stroke and cancer, a result of suppressing the initial inflammatory response necessary to fight disease.

In the current state of nutritional science, an optimal ω-3 to ω-6 ratio cannot be defined. But a sure fact is that ω-3 supplementation has never shown benefits and has been linked to some forms of harm: for example, high ω-3 levels in the prostate are linked with cancer.

Conversely, while ω-6 is not necessarily evil in itself, excessive amounts are definitely a symptom of bad sourcing of food: unhealthy animals produce a lot of ω-6 in response to chronic inflammation.

Omega-3 to omega-6 ratio is not the main issue: more importantly, seek healthy sources of fat and proteins. The contribution of our food to inflammation due to general reasons is probably more significant than its omega-3/omega-6 ratio.

Beware of deficiency in either omega-3 or omega-6: get enough of each. We are more at risk for omega-3 deficiency due to our modern eating habits and the way our food is produced.

Use common sense and don't overwhelm your body's regulation capability with a huge excess of one or the other: omega-3 supplementation can lead to health problems. If you follow a nutrient-rich, soundly sourced, real food diet, with a wide array of fats and proteins, there won't be excess.

Given the current knowledge (or lack thereof), here is our best bet concerning fats:

- Eat the fats we coevolved with, including natural trans fats and saturated fats, as found in meat and dairy.

- Don't eat man-made trans fats.

- Eat fats that provide the essential omega-3 and omega-6 fatty acids. Use common sense and don't overwhelm your body with either one.

- Eat a large variety of fats, with a variety of molecule lengths: long-chain fatty acids are desirable as the most common length used for structural purposes in our body; short-chain ones are beneficial because they can cross the blood-brain barrier.

Oils - Check the heat tolerance of the oil before using it at high temperatures. Most importantly, vary your oils!

Nuts and seeds - They are one of the most efficient ways to get ALA and LA, as well as a source of nice uncomplicated saturated fats.

Eggs - (From healthy hens eating a healthy diet.) Omega-3 supplemented eggs are probably useless: chickens can make omega-3 themselves, and anyway, should chickens really live on flax seeds? For high quality eggs, pasture-raised hens make more sense.

Dairy fats - Cream or butter from grass-fed cows; whole milk yogurt and cheese. They contain a class of saturated fats with unique health properties. Make sure your dairy comes from healthy cows.

Avocados and other oil-rich plants (olives, coconuts...)

Animal fat - Meat always comes with fat. When properly sourced (grass-fed beef, free range chicken, lamb, duck, wild animals), meat is rich in long-chain omega-3 and omega-6, as well as good saturated fat.

Cold-water oily fish - Salmon, herring, mackerel, anchovies, sardines... All contain a lot of omega-3, in particular long-chain EPA and DHA. Check sources, especially for salmon.

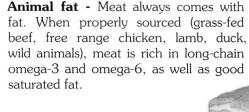

Macronutrients and Energy

This might not be suitable table talk, but a minimal understanding of our digestive system is required in order to see how nutrition affects us, in particular concerning energy production, and to dispel dangerous yet well-established myths.

The purpose of food, in addition to its social function and the pleasure it provides, is to supply energy and raw material for building and repairing our body.

This happens through digestion: at various points between the mouth and the intestine, food is mechanically and chemically broken down; the proteins, fats and carbohydrates that we ate are disassembled respectively into amino acids, fatty acids and sugars (glucose mostly). This operation involves many of our organs communicating through an exceedingly complex web of hormonal and electrical messages. The whole process is regulated mostly by our liver.

The resulting nutrients are absorbed through the lining of the small intestine into our bloodstream and transported to the liver to be detoxified and broken down further. Proteins and transport molecules are also synthesized in the liver.

The blood is then circulated to our entire body. All our cells grab nutrients on this "conveyor belt" as needed, and use them for a million purposes, including energy production.

From food to energy

Energy is generated through *cellular respiration*, a complex series of chemical reactions that take place in small organelles present in our cells, the *mitochondria*. It is an *aerobic process*, requiring the presence of oxygen.

Two other mechanisms can quickly generate short bursts of energy in response to particular needs: the *Anaerobic* system and the *Creatine-Phosphate* system.

However, we'll focus on the aerobic process, since it generates the bulk of our energy.

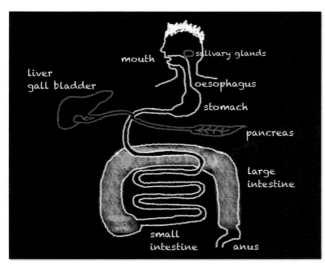

Cellular respiration generates ATP molecules, the energy currency that is used everywhere in our body. It consists of:

- the *Tricarboxylic Acid cycle* (*TCA cycle*, also known as the *Citric Acid cycle,* or *Krebs cycle*) and

- the *Electron Transport Chain (ETC)*.

It is important to note that the three types of macronutrients, carbohydrates, fats and proteins, can serve as fuel.

All three are processed in similar ways, delivering CO_2 (that we breathe out) and ATP molecules (the energy).

Historically, the TCA cycle was described with a sugar molecule as its "fuel" or "input", thus creating the enduring belief that sugar equals energy. It has nevertheless been known for a while that, in fact, fat or protein will work as well.

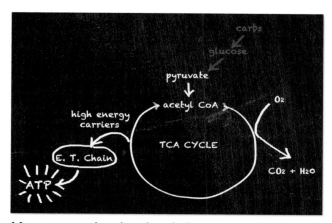

Memorizing the details of the chemical reactions and molecule names is not required, but a general understanding of the process is necessary in order to realize that nutrients don't provide energy by magic, but only through a complex sequence of chemical reactions.

Carbohydrates and energy

Carbohydrates are traditionally classified as sugars or starches.

- *Sugars* are small molecules. Our metabolism uses several sugars but the most common simple sugar in our body is glucose.

- *Starches* are long chains of sugar, up to tens of thousands of units. Pictured below is the structure of a relatively short starch, amylopectin:

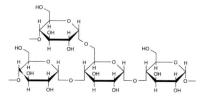

Carbohydrates must undergo several transformations before they become energy:

1. They are broken down into their basic building blocks: for example, glucose molecules.

2. The glucose molecule is split into two pyruvate molecules.

3. The pyruvates are oxidized to produce Acetyl CoA.

4. Acetyl CoA enters the TCA cycle. The TCA cycle generates high energy electron carriers.

5. The electron transport chain uses the high energy electron carriers to produce the bulk of the ATPs.

One molecule of glucose will produce, under ideal circumstances, 38 ATP molecules.

Glucose is special among sugars in our body because it can readily be cleaved into 2 pyruvates. This is not the case for fructose.

Fats and energy

In our body, fats are present in the form of triglycerides, phospholipids or free fatty acids.

- *Fatty acids* are linear chains of carbon.

- *Triglycerides* are made of 3 fatty acids attached to a glycerol backbone, as pictured below.

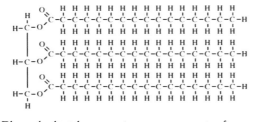

- *Phospholipids*, a major component of our cell membranes, have a slightly different structure with 2 fatty acids per molecule.

Fatty acids are therefore the building blocks common to all our fats. We also have free-floating fatty acids that are unattached to other molecules.

Triglycerides can be thought of as storage and transport units. The fats involved in energy production are mainly the fatty acids, either resulting from the break down of triglycerides in our fat tissue or the transient free fatty acids in our blood.

Fat produces energy through cellular respiration, very much like sugar does:

1. Triglycerides are broken down into glycerol and fatty acids.

2. Glycerol goes into the cycle as pyruvate, with only minimal change.

3. Fatty acids are cleaved into shorter molecules and enter the cycle as pyruvate; they also have a path to enter at the acetyl CoA stage.

It should be noted that less chemical energy is required to generate pyruvate from fat than from sugar. In this sense, fat is the shorter, straight line to energy, as opposed to the traditional representation of sugar as the natural energy source.

Each fat molecule yields large amounts of ATP. This explains why fat stores a lot of energy: 9 Calories[*] per gram, against 4 for sugar.

Proteins

Proteins consist of long chains of amino acids, folded into complex 3D structures. They fulfill countless functions in our body as building material, antibodies, hormones, enzymes...

Pictured here is an amino acid where R (different for each type) is the group of atoms that gives the amino acid its personality.

Amino acids resulting from the breaking of proteins (either from our diet or through recycling of other proteins in our body) also appear in energy production.

The path from protein to energy is less direct than for the other two macronutrients, but in spite of the extra processing (represented by the green blob in the picture) and additional complexity, the energy output of protein is similar to that of sugar, about 4 Calories per gram.

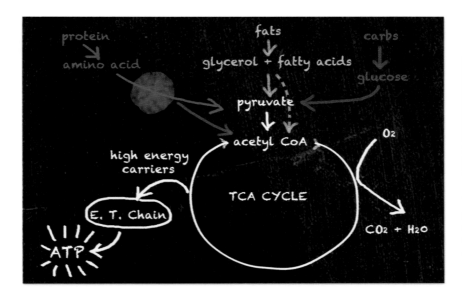

TCA / Krebs Cycle

All three types of macronutrients (carbohydrates, fats, proteins) behave in a similar fashion.

This is a simplified diagram! Not shown are other carbon inputs to the TCA, which also offer an easier path to the carbons that are derived from fat.

Most cells can shift between energy sources, or *pathways*. How do they chose which path to use?

The selection between fat, sugar or protein is driven by the presence or absence of the many *hormones* and *enzymes* that are necessary to enable the chemical reactions[energy].

The different cell types in our body have their preferences, due to the local enzyme distribution:

- Heart and skeletal muscle cells prefer to run on fat: the enzyme *lypase* liberates the fatty acid contained in the triglycerides present next to these cells.

- Contrary to the old belief, the brain also works well with fatty acids. The blood-brain barrier (separating blood flow from brain cells) only allows short and medium-chain free fatty acids through: butyric acid, a short-chain fat in butter, is good for your brain!

The body is a beautifully adaptable machine:

• **If blood glucose is high, the enzymes that favor sugar for energy will be induced, and the body's energy preference will be tilted towards burning sugar.**

• **When blood glucose is lower, the body will produce the enzymes that make it possible to burn fat for energy.**

For a person who is very dependent on sugar, switching to fats may take time: the process is a matter of weeks, maybe months in especially difficult cases.

People modifying their diet to eat fewer carbs and more fats might crave starches in the beginning. They might lack energy because their body is not yet equipped to use fat for fuel. Yet the final result is well worth the effort, in exactly the same way that quitting smoking is worth the initial pain.

This "carbohydrate withdrawal" condition will subside after the new energy pathway has been established (contrary to the hunger caused by calorie restricting diets.)

The average person burns a mix of sugar and fats for energy. Proportions vary from individual to individual, but a person with high blood sugar will be more dependent on sugar to generate energy.

This mechanism is not fixed rigidly. If there is a dominance of a given macronutrient, the body will induce (that is, create or increase) the corresponding pathway for generating energy.

By switching to a diet that is richer in fats and poorer in carbs, we can train our body to predominantly use fats for energy.

Note 1: Being able to burn fat to produce energy through the TCA cycle is different from *ketosis*[*] where the body is running exclusively on fat. Here we are still running on a mix of fat and sugar.

Note 2: Sugar is addictive for many reasons. In particular, sugar dependency[*] can be a symptom of malnutrition. (You can be *malnourished*, meaning you don't get the right nutrients, even if you are not *undernourished*).

This kind of sugar addiction is a different problem than sugar dependency for energy. It might take longer to clear, since the malnutrition issue has to be solved first.

Fat is a good, clean, versatile energy source

Switching our energy dependency from sugar to fat, aside from avoiding the negative effects of sugar, has beneficial results of its own:

- Eating fat doesn't trigger hormonal cycles like sugar does.
- Fat in the diet supplies essential fatty acids you might be deficient in otherwise.
- The presence of fat facilitates the absorption of the other nutrients.
- We have a nearly infinite amount of fat, compared to the limited amounts of glycogen.
- By accessing our fat cells for energy, we renew and rejuvenate our cells.

DO YOU KNOW THAT...

Our metabolism needs sugar, but our liver can produce it entirely from virtually any source, including fat and protein. So, even for those cells that favor glucose, it needn't come from our diet.

Elevated blood sugar impairs our ability to use fat for energy.

The sugar pathway for energy is more fragile than the fat pathway: while we have a large supply of fatty acids, the sugar supply needs replenishing, leading to the sugar/insulin cycles and the associated problems.

The current popular thinking regarding sugar is mostly a historical legacy:

- It was thought, falsely, that the only sugar available to our metabolism came from our food (dietary sugar). In fact our body can manufacture the sugar it needs.

- The belief was that the brain is dependent on the rest of the body for glucose management. The brain can in fact produce its own glucose and insulin, and regulate its sugar level[gluconeogenesis].

- It was assumed that the long starch molecules are slower to break down, hence the myth of slow carbs. This concept was also proved to be false.

- Contrary to popular wisdom, athletic activity is generally not dependent on glucose.

Sugar is a risky energy source

Excess sugar in the blood has many damaging effects in the long and short term.

- Hormonal: sugar stimulates higher than necessary insulin (toxic in several ways) and triggers a vicious hormonal circle leading to more blood sugar.
- Glycation: the presence of sugar on "construction sites" causes the production of defective molecules.
- Cancer: the preferred metabolic pathway of all cancers is glucose dependent, i.e. cancer feeds on glucose.
- Diseases: sugar is linked with diabetes, cardiovascular disease, dementia[*], tooth decay, etc.
- Fat: excess sugar stored as body fat cannot be used for energy since the excessive level of sugar in the blood impairs the fat energy pathway.

Try it!

*You'll be surprised to find
that you can avoid starches
and yet not feel hungry,
while having plenty of energy.*

*It might be hard at first to break
the sugar habit, but the result
is well worth the effort.*

Weight Loss - Body Fat

Even though weight loss is not the purpose of this book, it is necessary to touch on the subject because it is seldom absent from people's minds.

The temptation is great to modify the diet advocated here, maybe cutting down on fats, or changing a few other elements, in order to adapt it to some weight loss belief. But in fact, we are confident that respecting the principles offered in these pages is the surest path to a pleasant body image.

As a society, we need to get away from the thought that "thin" equals "healthy" and think in terms of nutritional quality instead. Weight loss is not desirable per se: if you lose tendon, bones, ligaments and muscle, you become less healthy. If you choose to become thinner, make sure that the loss is restricted to body fat.

Most of the discussion here is directed to people that really need to lose weight for health reasons, not to those who would like to shed a few pounds for cosmetic purposes (those will achieve their goal effortlessly on our diet).

Low-calorie diets don't work

The current popular dieting wisdom sees our body as a bag that inflates if we put more calories in (by eating) than we take out (by exercising) and vice versa.

This simplistic view has been proven wrong: all the controlled experiments to make people lose weight by restricting their caloric intake have failed; not only were the subjects very disturbed physically and mentally, but they regained all the weight and then some once they went off the diet.

Most of the time, failing to lose weight is not due to lack of will. How many people exercise for hours, walk, jog, run, work out, starve themselves to death, without any result? They don't lose any significant weight; they feel hungry and lifeless...

(Note that exercise is highly desirable, but for other reasons. The pursuit of weight[*] loss often results in ill health: most people are metabolically weaker, and their VO_2max goes down after they lost weight.)

Fat regulation

How much fat is stored in our cells is a complex, tightly regulated system, with the body trying very hard to stabilize the amount of fat around a set value. Even when we pack more fat than we'd like, usually we gain weight until some kind of equilibrium is reached. Those who gain weight indefinitely are few.

(This leads people to think that they can diet to lose the undesired pounds, and then go back to their old ways. Indeed, since they were stable, albeit a little heavy, wasn't it that what they ate balanced exactly what they expended? The fact that people gain all the weight back once they go off the diet is another proof that the view of the body as a bag is wrong.)

The set value for body fat is a function of our genetics, as well as our long term nutritional behavior, environment and medical history; with age our body is less resilient, our machinery doesn't work so well anymore, and coping with excesses becomes more difficult.

It is true that weight gain can be associated with more calories in than calories out. But what is the cause, and what is the effect? Is eating causing weight gain, or is gaining weight causing the eating? This question seems pretty stupid, but think about it: a child going through a growth spurt eats a lot. Is he growing because he's eating, or is he eating because he is growing (as noted by several authors)?

If, for any reason, a person's metabolism wants to store calories as fat, this person has to eat more in order to maintain a proper level of disposable energy.

Pre-requisites to fat loss

The built-in regulation explains why willpower has so much trouble dealing with the problem. It is very difficult to change the regulation set point, and it takes time.

But, in spite of all the shattered beliefs, some things remain certain. If we want to lose fat, we need to:

1. Either burn the fat in the fat cells, or get it out of the cells for burning elsewhere.
2. Be able to burn fat, that is, use fat for energy in the Krebs cycle, which also takes place at the cellular level.
3. Accumulate fat at a slower rate than we burn it.

Conversely, people don't lose fat because:

- Their fat is locked in the fat cells.
- They lack the enzymes that would allow them to burn fat for energy.
- They accumulate fat faster than they can burn it.

Believe it or not, most of the time (we're not talking about special pathologies) all these causes are related to one and only one fact: the excessive presence of glucose in the blood.

1. *Elevated blood glucose induces the enzymes that favor using sugar for energy.*

   The body is a marvelously adaptable machine that can work with whatever it has. If there is a lot of glucose in the blood, the body will induce the enzymes to burn glucose for energy. If the body sees less glucose, it will induce the pathway that uses fat.

   In addition, the insulin production that inevitably accompanies high blood sugar (except for type I diabetics) inactivates the enzymes needed for fat burning and impairs the action of hormones[HSL] that release fat from fat cells.

2. *Elevated blood glucose next to fat cells locks the fat inside the cells.*

   Fat is travelling in the blood or stored in cells under the form of triglycerides. However, triglycerides cannot cross the cell walls: to go in and out of the cell, triglycerides are disassembled into free fatty acids and glycerol (which can cross) and reassembled into triglycerides on the other side of the wall.

   Contrary to common sense, the fat molecules in the fat tissue are in perpetual motion, constantly crossing the cell walls into the blood stream and back into the cell, being disassembled and reassembled.

   Surprisingly, this process is also regulated by the levels of insulin and blood sugar: insulin causes fat cells to take in glucose and burn it for fuel; this produces a glycerol-phosphate molecule, which in turn provides the glycerol molecule that binds with free fatty acids to create triglycerides.

   Thus, burning glucose in the fat cells reduces the number of free fatty acids that can escape the cell and increases the proportion of free fatty acids locked as triglycerides *inside* the cell.

3. *Elevated insulin, a consequence of high glucose, puts the body in fat storage mode.*

   The action of insulin is to put our body in fat storage mode. High insulin signals that glucose (i.e. immediate energy) is available; fat is therefore not needed and should be stored for later use. Insulin activates the enzymes that enable fat storage[LPL].

   The lower the glucose level in our blood, the lower the insulin level, causing the cells to release fat.

   This seems obvious now, but the fact has eluded weight loss researchers for a century. Instead, the notion that eating fat makes you fat still prevails.

There are several more mechanisms that cause fat to be stored, all involving sugar. Some were mentioned in *The Hormonal Effects of Food*, earlier in this book.

Body fat is not an inert bag. It must be viewed as an organ, with its complex regulation mechanism involving various processes and hormones: insulin, in particular, plays a key role in fat metabolism.

There are people who eat too much, and for those, the diet proposed in this book will automatically fix the problem.

For the majority though, fat gain is an issue of excessive sugar and starch consumption. It is a progressive long term process that matures over decades. The solution is to take away the insulin stimulus, but there is no quick fix: getting back takes years. However, the diet advocated here addresses all the points from which unhealthy body fat gets into the picture.

Dried fruits are delicious! They are also very rich in sugar.

Soups, Salads
and Appetizers

Beware of food dogmatism

There is not one diet that will work for everybody: each of us must pay attention to his or her individual response.

However, some principles need to be re-established because our modern diet has strayed so much from a healthy way of eating. Natural foods have been forgotten, and misconceptions have piled up one upon another during the last century.

The first step is to eat real food, as opposed to the heavily processed products that are the norm today.

Once there, there are gradations of excellence: as long as you eat real food, a little sugar is not that serious. Once you've made the decision of eating whole real food, you've stepped into a new world!

Eat a little bit of everything?

Popular wisdom has it that we should eat a balanced diet, that is, "a little bit of everything." And indeed, the notion is at the very heart of this book's philosophy. But what does that mean in practice?

In the grocery store, quantity and variety make bread, pasta and frozen pizza appear as food groups!

The sheer volume of the offering can lead you to think that ice cream and cookies should be an important part of our diet.

But in reality, just because supermarkets devote whole aisles to breakfast cereals doesn't mean that cereal is a basic food group.

The basic macronutrients are *carbohydrates*, *fats* and *proteins*. By eating a nutrient-dense, real food diet, we get a variety of each.

It is true that food should remain a pleasure and that thinking too much has the potential of turning meals into a chore.

However, some understanding of nutrition is necessary if we want to make informed choices. Without guidance, nobody can resist food marketing and the food industry[*].

Your food choices are the result of many considerations: practical, cultural, personal taste... But, in any case:

Choose what you eat. Don't let the food industry decide for you!

Supermarkets want to give the impression that they offer a large choice. But in fact, a huge effort goes into making you buy certain items. If you enter the store without a buying strategy, you're doomed!

Micronutrients

Those expecting to find a detailed list of nutrients here will be disappointed: the number of nutrients is so large and their interaction in our body so complex that any list can only be reductive and misleading.

Beware of supplements!

Carotenoids are a family of pigments present in orange vegetables. There are hundreds of carotenoids in nature, of which 3 are known for their vitamin A activity in humans, an important feature.

However, vitamin A is only the tip of the carotenoid iceberg. By focusing on vitamin A, we risk losing all the other benefits of carotenoids: antioxidant, protection against chronic diseases or cancer, just to name a few.

By taking vitamin A supplements instead of eating plain carrots, we deprive ourselves of the benefits of lycopene and lutein.

And if we ate only carrots instead of a range of orange vegetables, we would miss hundreds of other carotenoids.

Based on current knowledge, our best bet is to eat the greatest diversity possible of foods.

Consume the widest variety of:
- Micronutrients
- Minerals (a.k.a. elements)
- Essential amino acids
- Essential fatty acids

In order to provide some guidance, nutrients will be addressed, but only in terms of the large families known to be important in our body.

- Vitamins don't get special treatment: vitamins don't share a common chemical structure, and they are included in the other families of nutrients.

- Flavonoids, an important family of nutrients, are also colorful: another argument for eating a spectrum of colors without looking at individual nutrients.

MICRONUTRIENTS BY COLOR

Micronutrients, with a few important exceptions, are colorful and can be easily classified by color.

We deliberately won't enumerate subclasses (carotenoids include alpha-carotene, beta-carotene, lycopene, etc.) because this could appear like an exhaustive list of nutrients. At this point, science is very far from being able to provide one: just consume the widest possible range of carotenoids and don't single out any particular one!

Eating by color is a guarantee that you'll get many forms of nutrients.

BLUE - PURPLE - RED

Anthocyanidins, anthocyanins and other similarly named substances constitute a large family of purple-blue pigments. The nomenclature of bluish chemicals is very complex and could obscure their nutrient value. Don't get a headache, forget about names, just eat blue stuff! We'll call them "cyans" for the sake of simplicity.

"Cyans" are found in many berries (grapes, blackberry, blueberry, cranberry, cherry), in the skin of other fruits (pear, apple, plum), red cabbage, red onion and everything that's dark red to blue.

Among other effects, they enable our immune system to respond to injuries and infection; they are associated with fighting cancer.

"Cyans" are mostly advertised as antioxidants, but don't focus on that property: we don't want to eat antioxidants only. Food works in the context of the whole nutrient symphony. Taking antioxidant supplements, apart from being inefficient, can make you miss the many other properties, known or yet to be discovered, of "cyans."

RED - ORANGE - YELLOW

This is the color signature of *carotenoids,* the red of a ripe tomato, the orange of a carrot.

While carotenoids are famous for their vitamin A activity, they have many other benefits. For example, lycopene, a carotenoid with no vitamin A activity, has cancer fighting properties. Other carotenoids help with macular degeneration.

A diet rich in a large array of carotenoids has beneficial effects on prostate cancer. On the other hand, lycopene supplements don't seem to help: another example that the healing properties of food depend on a large number of parameters.

See the big picture, eat all types of red, orange and yellow food and don't rely on supplements!

GREEN

Chloroplasts are organelles in plant cells that use the famously green chlorophyll to perform photosynthesis, transforming light into chemical energy.

Chloroplasts are densely packed with enzymes (proteins) and coenzymes (usually minerals) that are necessary for digestion.

Chloroplasts also contain carotenoids and some "cyans." Although the color of the carotenoids in the chloroplasts is concealed by the green, the presence of chlorophyll can be taken as an indicator of carotenoids and "cyans."

Chloroplasts are present in the young stems (eat the stems of your veggies too), but their richest source is in the leaves.

EXCEPTIONS

Sulforaphanes (in cabbages and dark leafy greens) are not very colorful, but extremely important nonetheless. The same can be said for the allium family (garlic, onion, etc.).

Note that the green in the dark leafy vegetables is due to chlorophyll.

Of course, most foods contain a mix of micronutrients. You can pretty much figure out what's in your vegetables just by looking at their color. By training your eye to register subtle hue variations, you'll learn to distinguish the bluish red of "cyans" from the yellowish red of carotenoids: red cabbage is more orange than radicchio, and indeed, it contains more carotene.

Mostly "Cyans"

"Cyans" & Carotenoids

Mostly Carotenoids

Carotenoids & Chlorophyll

Chlorophyll & Sulforaphanes

Allium family

Fennel, green pepper

Fresh herbs

etc.

Asparagus & Leek Soup

This soup is an opportunity to enjoy the first of the young spring asparagus. Choose medium-sized asparagus (neither pencil sized nor too large) and look for tips that are tight and free from flowering.

Although you can serve the soup "as is," the cream garnish brings valuable dairy fats.

Asparagus, in addition to being a good source of fiber, has one of the most complete spectrums among vegetables both for amino acids and elements.

Asparagine, a fairly common amino acid with a distinctive smell, is rarely found in such abundance as in the asparagus. It is a good thing to have because it is used by our body to make a variety of other amino acids.

For these reasons, asparagus should be a staple in our diet instead of an exotic food.

Efficiency, Completeness, Spectrum, Quality

All these words refer to the same notion: how many key nutrients are present in a given food? This is an important question: if you compare[*] whole wheat to asparagus for example, you will find that the asparagus is much richer in micronutrients and protein.

- **Protein -** A "complete" or "efficient" protein source contains all 9 essential amino acids, in proportions suitable for our body: excess in any particular amino acid results in imbalance. Although our body can adjust within a certain range, it cannot deal with overwhelming imbalance[*]. By eating a variety of proteins, we avoid stressing our body's regulation capability.

- **Fat -** Fat quality is determined by the quality of its source: fat is not an isolated molecule, it comes within a whole matrix[*] of other ingredients, and those must be healthy too. Healthy fats come from healthy animals and healthy plants.

- **Micronutrients and elements** that have a physiological function in our body are too many to count. If you eat a restricted diet, you will forgo many healthy nutrients.

Serves 6 ~ ⧗ ⧗

- 2 medium leeks (white to light-green part only)
- 2 lb medium-sized asparagus
- 2 tablespoons unsalted butter
- 4 cups chicken stock

Citrus cream:

- 1 tablespoon minced flat-leaf parsley
- ½ cup crème fraîche
- Zest and juice of one lemon

⚠ Over-emphasizing "completeness" may lead to problems, though. Restricting your choice of proteins to the "efficient" ones narrows your options and impoverishes your diet.

Eating a large variety of proteins is a better way to take care of efficiency!

1. Clean the leek and mince them into ¼-inch thick slices.

2. Trim the asparagus and cut diagonally into 1-inch long pieces, reserving the tips (1 inch).

3. In a heavy-bottomed stock pot, melt the butter over medium heat. Add the minced leek and sauté, without browning, until soft and translucent, about 10 minutes.

4. Add the asparagus pieces and chicken broth. Bring to a boil over high heat, then reduce heat and simmer until the asparagus are cooked, about 10 minutes.

5. Meanwhile, mince the asparagus tips very thinly.

6. **Citrus Cream:** prepare the cream by mixing the crème fraîche with the zest and juice of the lemon. Add the minced parsley.

7. Purée the soup until smooth. Return to the pot, add the minced asparagus tips and warm over medium heat for an additional 5 minutes. Make sure the tips stay crunchy, though.

Leeks, *although in the same allium family as onions and garlic, don't go through the same flavor change when they are cooked; they retain their distinctive taste.*

Being sulphur donors, like all the members of the allium family, they are good for the immune system, joints and cartilage. They have a very broad spectrum of essential amino acids (which is rare for vegetables), extremely low glycemic load and glycemic index, and some anti-inflammatory properties.

Season with salt and freshly ground black pepper. Adjust consistency with additional broth if necessary.

Serve the soup in bowls with a dollop of citrus cream.

For a simpler everyday meal, you can skip the citrus cream. The soup is delicious "as is."

Acorn Squash Soup with Greens

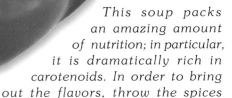

Serves 4 ~ ⏳⏳⏳

- 1 medium acorn squash
- 1 teaspoon ground cinnamon
- 1 teaspoon freshly ground nutmeg
- 3 scallions
- 3 cups chard (or other green of choice, spinach, kale, etc.)
- ¾ cup roasted pumpkin seeds (¼ cup reserved for garnish)
- 2 tablespoons oil, divided
- 2 tablespoons butter, divided
- 2 teaspoons garlic powder
- 1 carrot
- ½ onion
- 2 stalks celery
- 2 bay leaves
- 4 cups chicken broth
- 2 cups cooked wild rice (optional)

This soup packs an amazing amount of nutrition; in particular, it is dramatically rich in carotenoids. In order to bring out the flavors, throw the spices in the oil, rather than in the broth. You can substitute your favorite squash for the acorn squash.

Fall and winter squashes

When winter approaches, everything concentrates, nutrients as well as sugar: like all fall fruits, fall squashes (the pumpkin types) contain more sugar than summer squashes.

In spite of their sugar content, fall squashes are acceptable because of their nutrient concentration: in that respect, all fall squashes are similar.

The amount of sugar they contain varies, though: spaghetti squash and sugar pumpkin have three times less sugar than acorn squash; butternut squash is somewhere in between. As a general rule, the deeper the color, the richer the fruit, both in nutrients and sugar.

But don't become a food accountant! If you focus on eating whole real food, a little sugar in the occasional squash is not too serious.

Delicata

Hubbard

Acorn

Butternut

Spaghetti

Turban

Sugar pumpkin

- 64 -

1. Preheat the oven to 375 °F. Split the squash, remove the seeds. Brush the halves with oil and sprinkle with cinnamon, nutmeg, salt and black pepper. Bake, cut side up, until soft (about 30 minutes). Allow the squash to cool, then scoop out the flesh (yields about 2 cups of purée).

2. Mince the scallions (both white and green parts); coarsely chop the chard and the pumpkin seeds.

3. In a medium skillet, heat half the oil and butter over medium heat. Add the scallions and garlic powder. Sauté until soft, about 2 minutes. Add the chopped greens and fold together until just wilted, 1 or 2 minutes more. Remove from heat; fold in the chopped seeds, season with salt and pepper. Optionally, combine with the cooked rice. Set aside.

4. Peel the carrot and onion. Dice the carrot, onion and celery into ¼-inch pieces.

5. In a medium-sized saucepan, heat the remaining oil and butter over medium-high heat. Add the onions, carrots, celery and bay leaves. Sauté, stirring frequently, until the onions are tender, 5 to 7 minutes. Add the squash purée and enough stock to cover. Bring soup to a boil, reduce to simmer and cook until the carrots are soft, 10 to 15 minutes.

⚠ *Wild Rice & Whole Grains*

Many health benefits are attributed to whole grains because they are less refined than regular cereals. However, with wild rice, usually the husk (containing the bulk of the fiber) has been removed, and wild rice is still mostly starch.

In the end, whole grain is not so different from refined: it is grain with a coat that possesses not much nutritional value.

Whole grain is a wolf in sheep's clothing; although it contains a little more fiber, it is not a nutrient-rich fiber source.

The recipe on this page is already very rich in sugar. Only add wild rice as a special treat, or if you need the extra calories.

6. REMOVE THE BAY LEAVES. In a blender, purée the soup until very smooth. Return to the pot and bring to a simmer. Adjust the consistency with the remaining stock (soup should be of medium thickness, not too thin). Season to taste with salt and pepper.

Ladle soup into serving bowls. Place about ½ cup of the green mixture in the center of the soup, top with remaining seeds and serve immediately.

Carrot, Ginger & Coconut Soup

Turmeric and cinnamon play an important part in many traditional medicines, in particular Ayurvedic. Western medicine also acknowledges specific health benefits for turmeric, notably regarding its impact on insulin resistance.

Carrots are related to parsnip, fennel, parsley, anise, caraway, cumin and dill.

Serves 4 to 6 ~ ⏳ ⏳

- 1 piece of fresh ginger, about 2 inches
- 5 large carrots
- 1 medium onion
- 3 cloves garlic
- 2 tablespoons oil or butter
- 2 teaspoons turmeric
- 2 cups vegetable broth
- 8-oz can coconut milk
- Coconut chips and minced chives for garnish

⚠ As everyone knows, carrots contain **carotenoids**, which confer them the orange tint: beta-carotene is very widely publicized these days, but in fact, it is not necessarily better or more important than the other hundreds of carotenoids.

Rather than focusing on buzzwords such as alpha-carotene, beta-carotene, etc., seek all sorts of orange foods that will supply a variety of carotenoids.

While we usually associate carrots with the color orange, they can actually be found in a host of other colors. In fact, purple, yellow and red carrots were the only color varieties of carrots to be cultivated before the 15th century.

Carrots that reflect the colors of the rainbow are not only beautiful; their pigments hide a treasure trove of nutrients.

- Red carrots are rich in lycopene (another carotene), the same pigment found in tomatoes.
- Yellow ones are rich in xanthophylls and lutein.
- Purple ones have extra "cyans."

Their core, usually colored differently, contributes additional value.

Many of the carotenoids are very heat tolerant: tomato sauce can be cooked for hours and still retain its nutrients.

⚠ Eating carrots alone doesn't take care of your carotenoids: you need to consume all the shades of carotenoids found in beets, tomatoes, squash, peppers and all the other orange-red vegetables.

1. Peel and mince the ginger: first make slices then cut crosswise.

2. Peel and dice the carrots and the onion into ¾-inch pieces. Mince the garlic.

3. In a medium saucepan, heat the oil (or butter) over medium heat. Add the onions, ginger, garlic and turmeric and sauté until the onions are soft, about 3 to 4 minutes.

4. Add the carrots and broth and stir to combine. Bring to a boil and reduce to simmer. Cook for 8 to 10 minutes.

5. Add coconut milk to taste and continue to cook until the carrots are soft.

6. Blend the soup. Season to taste with salt and freshly ground black pepper. Adjust the consistency by adding broth as needed.

To serve, ladle soup into serving bowls and garnish with coconut chips and minced chives.

NOTES

You can also garnish with a dollop of the creamy top of the coconut extract.

Don't pour in too much broth at the beginning. It's always easier to add some later than to remove it!

Chestnut Soup

This simple, hearty soup makes a good fall or winter starter. Chestnuts used to be standard fare in the French countryside, most of the time cooked in milk for supper.

❧

The soup is extremely easy to prepare with peeled, pre-cooked chestnuts. It is quite an ordeal to make it with whole raw chestnuts, though!

Serves 6 ~ ⧗

- 1 onion
- 3 oz bacon
- 1 tablespoon oil
- 1 tablespoon Brandy
- 1 lb peeled, pre-cooked chestnuts
- 1 qt broth
- Crème fraîche or sour cream

Chestnuts belong to the "nut and seed" family, but contrary to most edible nuts, they contain almost no fat. This, by the way, is not a virtue: our body needs fats of all kinds in order to be healthy.

For a given weight, they are no starchier than other nuts but you tend to eat more of them. They are gluten free. But beware if you treat them as a vegetable: their starch content is similar to that of starchy foods like potato, sweet potato or plantain.

Their nutritional profile is not great but they make a nice treat on a cold winter day, especially if you're planning on going out to chop wood.

1. Mince the onion; cut the bacon into matchsticks.

2. Heat up the oil in a heavy pan. Cook the onions and bacon over medium heat until the onions become translucent (about 10 minutes).

3. Add the Brandy.

4. Add the chestnuts.

5. Pour in the broth. Season with salt and pepper. Simmer for 20 minutes.

Serve hot with a dollop of cream on top of each bowl.

6. Blend the soup (the plunger blender is the most convenient tool for that purpose), optionally adding water so that the soup is not too thick, nor too liquid. Adjust seasoning with salt and pepper.

Bacon

Don't be afraid of bacon (when it comes from a healthy source)! Bacon is wonderfully tasty and provides good saturated fat, which our body can desaturate[*] as needed.

Select bacon that is as plain as possible. By definition, bacon is cured pork, but "curing" can mean many things: adding salt or chemicals, smoking... Curing always causes a transformation in the meat that modifies its nutritional value.

Bacon is healthier when it has fewer added chemicals such as nitrates. Naturally, choose bacon with no added sugary ingredients.

Is frying bacon carcinogenic? The AMES[*] test that established a link with cancer was flawed.

⚠ *Current science has demonstrated that dietary saturated[*] fat and cholesterol[*] don't contribute to heart disease.*

Have bacon, but not for every breakfast! Eat a variety of fats and proteins.

And, as always, select bacon that comes from a healthy animal: dangerous fat soluble chemicals resulting from bad farming practices can accumulate in the animal's fat tissues. (This is also true for humans.)

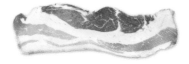

Gazpacho with Avocado Relish

This pleasantly cold summertime dish hails from the southern Spanish region of Andalusia. The uncooked soup is usually made from a mixture of tomatoes, sweet bell peppers, onions and cucumbers. This version adds herbs for a burst of freshness and is finished with a cool relish of crisp cucumbers and mellow avocado.

Avocados, dairy and eggs are rich in medium short-chain fatty acids, which can cross the blood-brain barrier: they provide the good fats necessary for brain health.

Serves 6 ~

Soup:

- 2 English cucumbers, peeled
- 6 medium, ripe tomatoes, peeled
- 1 red pepper, seeded
- 1 tablespoon fresh lemon or lime juice
- 1 tablespoon avocado oil
- 2 tablespoons extra-virgin olive oil
- 2 cloves garlic, minced
- 3 tablespoons coarsely chopped fresh cilantro

Avocado Relish:

- 1 firm but ripe avocado, diced into ¼-inch pieces
- ½ cucumber diced into ¼-inch pieces
- 1 large, firm but ripe tomato, peeled and seeded, diced
- ¼ cup diced red onion
- ⅓ cup chopped fresh cilantro
- 1 tablespoon olive oil
- Avocado oil

Soup

1. To peel the tomatoes, place them for 1 minute in a pot of boiling water, then transfer to a bowl of cold water. The peel should then come off easily.

2. Coarsely chop the cucumbers, tomatoes and bell pepper. Combine with the lemon juice, oils and minced garlic. Purée in batches in a blender or food processor until just blended but still slightly chunky.

3. Pour into a non-reactive bowl. Stir in the chopped cilantro, season with salt and freshly ground black pepper to taste. Cover and refrigerate for at least 1 hour or up to 8 hours.

Avocado Relish

4. Combine all the ingredients for the relish in a non-reactive bowl. Season with salt and freshly ground black pepper and finish with some avocado oil. Fold gently to combine.

To serve, ladle the chilled soup into bowls. Garnish with a generous portion of the relish and a pinch of chopped cilantro.

*In addition to its wonderfully fresh fragrance, **cilantro**, also known as **coriander**, stands out among the herbs thanks to a particular property of its oil: cilantro oil has the ability to bind to toxic metals in our tissues, loosening them and thus acting as a cleanser.*

(When we think of herbs, we don't generally think of oil, but in fact, the herbs' aroma is due to chemical compounds and oils that transport it.)

⚠ *Raw vs. Cooked*

Raw food is perfectly fine as a way to add variety to our eating; however, eating most of our food raw is not particularly beneficial.

*Cooking has the valuable effect of making nutrients more **bioavailable**, so a larger proportion of the nutrients contained in the food is usable by our body.*

There is reliable anthropological evidence that cooking has been around long enough to be incorporated in our genetic response. Some argue that cooking is what allowed early humans to extract more nutrition from their food, definitely an advantage in times of scarcity.

Curried Broccoli Soup

Serves 4 ~ ⧗ ⧗

- 1 lb broccoli
- ½ onion, diced into ½-inch pieces
- 1 tablespoon good oil
- 2 tablespoons almond meal
- 1 tablespoon yellow curry powder
- 1 teaspoon ground ginger
- 3 cups chicken stock
- ½ cup whole milk or almond milk
- 2 cups baby spinach
  or other greens of choice, chopped

Garnish:

- ¼ cup crème fraîche (optional)
- ¼ cup slivered almonds,
  toasted and coarsely chopped
- Fresh greens of choice
  (spinach, arugula, etc.)

Puréed broccoli soup often has a strong herbaceous flavor, a result of the broccoli being cooked a long time in order to obtain a smooth consistency. This recipe subdues the flavors by including a variety of spices.

੭

The finish with fresh greens also neutralizes flavors, adds nutrition and restores a bright green color, which might have been lost after extended cooking.

Curries *are complex compounds of many herbs and spices. While you can buy them over-the-counter, here is a great opportunity to experiment with your own mix. The same goes for chili powder. Play with your spices and keep in mind that they bring rich nutritional value to your diet.*

Spices can be introduced at different points in the cooking, affecting how they blend together and adding variety to the eating experience.

1. Peel the broccoli stems and dice them into ½-inch pieces. Chop the broccoli florets coarsely. Dice the onion.

2. Heat the oil in a large stock pot over medium-high heat. Add the onion and cook until translucent, about 3 minutes.

3. Throw in the chopped broccoli, almond meal, curry powder and ground ginger. Mix well.

4. Pour in the chicken stock. Bring to a boil, reduce heat, cover and simmer for 10 minutes or until the broccoli is tender.

5. Add the milk and fold in the greens until they are wilted, 2 or 3 minutes more.

6. Remove the pot from heat and purée the mixture. Season to taste with salt, freshly ground black pepper and additional curry powder, if desired.

   Serve in a bowl with a dollop of crème fraîche, toasted almonds and fresh greens on top.

Dinner *- Soups make perfect light single course dinners. Just add protein: cheese, nuts and seeds, hardboiled or poached egg, bacon... (Meat broth contains some protein, but not enough to constitute the protein part of a meal.)*

Homemade broth *is dynamite as far as micronutrients are concerned! It is much richer than store-bought broth since it is not so heavily processed or cooked at high temperature.*

Almond meal *is a great substitute for flour or bread crumbs in many cases, and we consider it real food.*

⚠ ***Almond milk,*** *on the other hand, is not a whole food since a fair amount of processing is required to manufacture it. It is a good choice for those who are lactose intolerant or allergic, but otherwise cow's milk is preferable.*

Seasonal Vegetable Chowder

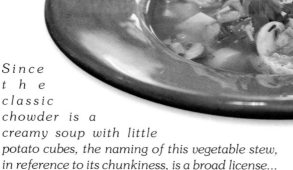

Since the classic chowder is a creamy soup with little potato cubes, the naming of this vegetable stew, in reference to its chunkiness, is a broad license...

In spite of its long list of ingredients, this is not a complicated recipe: the vegetables can be varied to use whatever produce is in season or conveniently available. (View this as an opportunity to get rid of items that have stayed a little too long in your refrigerator.) Not appearing in this variation, but suggested, are: cauliflower, asparagus, sugar snap peas, Brussels sprouts, broccoli rabe, sweet potatoes, green beans, arugula, spinach and assorted leafy greens. Whatever you select, just remember to cut everything the same size for cooking time and aesthetics.

Serves 4 ~ ⏳ ⏳

- 2 tablespoons oil
- 1 medium onion, diced
- 1 carrot, diced
- 1 rib celery, diced
- 3 cloves garlic, minced
- 2 teaspoons thyme
- 1 red bell pepper, diced
- 1 medium zucchini, diced
- 1 yellow zucchini (crookneck), diced
- 4 crimini mushrooms, diced
- 4 cups chicken or vegetable stock
- ¼ Savoy cabbage, core removed and shredded
- 2 leaves kale, ribs removed and shredded
- 2 cups broccoli florets, chopped
- 1 large, firm ripe tomato, diced
- 1 cup grated Parmesan or other hard grating cheese

Frozen vs. Canned

Use **fresh** vegetables whenever possible, but in the dead of winter, don't be afraid to resort to frozen produce as the next best thing.

Frozen foods are a practical way to keep a handy, varied stock.

⚠ **Canned** food is a whole different matter and, except for a few special items, should be avoided. Canned food usually begins with lower quality ingredients, which are processed in a way that impairs their nutritional value in order to prolong their shelf life. In spite of that, chemical degradation still occurs in the can. In addition, many foods are affected by being maintained in a liquid environment.

Freezing is better at holding the food in a biological inert state, and the ingredients are generally of better quality to start with: you can readily find organic frozen vegetables. Freezing is better at preserving the nutrient value.

Wash and trim all the vegetables.

Mince the garlic. Shred the cabbage and the kale (and any other leafy vegetable).

Cut the other vegetables into pieces of roughly equal size (about ¾-inch cubes).

The chowder is cooked in three stages: first the ingredients that bring aroma; then the vegetables that take long to cook; finally, the faster cooking ones.

1. Bring out the fragrance

In a medium saucepan, heat the oil over medium-high heat. Add the onion, carrot and celery and sauté until they begin to soften, 2 to 3 minutes. Add the garlic and thyme, and cook 30 seconds longer.

2. Slower cooking vegetables

Add the bell pepper, zucchini and mushroom. Sauté, stirring frequently, until the vegetables have softened and lightly browned, approximately 3 minutes. Pour in the broth: if the vegetables are not covered with liquid, add a bit of water. Bring to a boil, reduce to a simmer and cook over medium heat for 8 to 10 minutes (or until the vegetables are done to your liking).

3. Fast cooking vegetables

Add the cabbage, kale, broccoli florets and tomato. Cook for 5 minutes longer.

Season to taste with salt and freshly ground black pepper. Ladle into bowls and top with grated cheese.

Chickpea & Lentil Soup
Harira

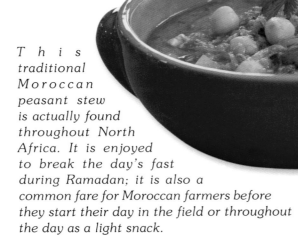

T h i s traditional Moroccan peasant stew is actually found throughout North Africa. It is enjoyed to break the day's fast during Ramadan; it is also a common fare for Moroccan farmers before they start their day in the field or throughout the day as a light snack.

This recipe can be modified to use any herbs or dried beans of choice (but select your beans wisely!). It is usually served with hardboiled eggs and garnished with ground cumin, dates and other dried fruits.

Serves 8 ~ 🍽 🍽 🍽

- 2 tablespoons olive oil
- 2 onions
- 1 large can (28 oz) stewed tomatoes
- 1 teaspoon ground ginger
- 1 teaspoon ground cinnamon
- 1 teaspoon ground turmeric
- 20 sprigs fresh cilantro
- 10 sprigs fresh flat-leaf parsley
- 1 cup lentils, rinsed
- 6 cups water
- 1 can (15 oz) garbanzo beans (chickpeas) with their liquid
- 1 egg
- Lemon wedges for garnish

Vegetarian soups - *All the soups presented in this section can easily be adapted for vegetarians' needs and become a perfect single course meal: use vegetable broth and add protein in the form of cheese, nuts and seeds, egg, etc.*

Watch out for lectins!

Lectins[*] are linked to health issues, in particular they can impair the absorption of some nutrients, thus causing deficiencies.

They are especially abundant in grains and legumes, another reason to consume legumes sparingly.

Wonder why we soak dry beans? It's not to soften them; after all, they have a lot of time to soften while cooking. It is because, and on that one popular wisdom is right, soaking, fermenting and cooking help reduce the negative impact of lectins.

⚠ **Legumes** *are very rich in carbohydrates, compared to other vegetables; Another reason to consume them sparingly.*

1. Thinly slice the onions. In a soup pot, heat the oil and cook the onions over medium heat, stirring occasionally, until tender, 6 to 8 minutes.

2. In a blender or food processor, combine the tomatoes, ginger, cinnamon, turmeric, cilantro, parsley. Season with salt and pepper. Purée the mixture, in batches if necessary, until fairly smooth.

3. Combine the tomato purée and the cooked onions, and bring to a boil.

4. Add the lentils and the water. Cover tightly and reduce heat to low. Simmer the soup until the lentils are tender, 30 to 35 minutes.

5. Add the garbanzo beans and their liquid. Bring soup back to a low boil.

6. Beat the egg, pour it in the soup and stir so it forms strands.

Ladle the soup into bowls and serve with lemon wedges.

Being a Vegetarian
(is not easy)

There are many reasons why a person would want to be a vegetarian; we will only comment on the health aspect of vegetarianism.

The China Study is considered the founding book, proving that vegetarians are healthier and live longer than the rest. On this highly touchy topic, enough reliable sources have pointed to serious deficiencies in *The China Study*[*]. Vegetarians are urgently advised to go and look for themselves at the conflicting evidence, rather than trusting their health to flawed research and special interest.

Not eating meat is often an ethical choice, and this honorable concern should be respected, but don't think you're doing your body a favor:

- Studies say protein[*] of animal source is protective in many ways.

- Using *The China Study* data itself, which is available to the public, it can be shown that meat consumption is associated with a longer life.

- Our dentition and gastrointestinal tract are definitely those of omnivores. Several studies on the evil effects of red meat were performed on rabbits, notorious herbivores!

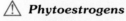

⚠ Phytoestrogens

Soybeans and **mung beans** *must be soaked before using, or cured in brine, or fermented, in order to reduce the negative effects of the lectins and phytoestrogens they are rich in.*

Eating a lot of soy means taking phytoestrogens at pharmacological level. Since they are female hormones, abnormally high levels of phytoestrogens are understandably bad for men, but could they be beneficial for women?

When a food has such a specific effect, it is affecting the balance in the person: at this point the long term effects of this imbalance are unknown (hormone replacement is potentially harmful).

Although once in a while is OK, soy should not be a dominant part of our diet. Don't splash soy sauce on everything!

Not surprisingly, vegetarians need to pay particular attention to the protein they eat. Higher protein[*] diets raise HDL cholesterol, which is protective against cancer of all kinds, stroke, heart attack and all cardiovascular diseases.

Eat, by order of importance:

1. Fatty proteins that help absorption of the fat soluble vitamins (A, D, E, K). The most protective proteins in that respect are dairy and eggs, and both happen to provide a relatively fatty environment: cheese, butter, ghee, yogurt, kefir, farmer's cheese... Egg yolks are the only source of B12 for vegetarians.

   (This is addressed to the ovo-lacto vegetarians, as there is, unfortunately, not a lot of advice for the vegans[*], people consuming no animal products at all).

2. Nuts and seeds, while healthy, come in second because they don't provide the animal fats and animal proteins our body needs.

3. Other fatty fruits and vegetables: avocados, hearts of palm, coconuts.

4. Vegetables other than grains: dark leafy greens, cruciferous vegetables, colorful root vegetables.

5. Legumes that are not high in antinutrient activity.

Beware of antinutrients

Foods rich in lectin, such as rice, beans and soy beans, can impair the absorption of protein and other nutrients.

Grains and legumes are complementary in their amino acid content: grains are poor in *lysine* and rich in *methionine,* and vice versa for legumes. Hence the widespread idea of associating grains and legumes to provide a wider range of nutrients. ⚠ *The danger is that many legumes actually bind to the protein in the grain and inactivate its nutritional value.*

The better legumes include: chickpeas, lentils, peas. To be avoided because of their high lectin concentration are: kidney beans, navy bean, red beans.

Avoid phytoestrogens

Mung bean, alfalfa beans and sprouts are in the same family as soybeans: high in phytoestrogens, they pose a danger for women at risk of breast disease (not for the general population); for men they are objectionable because they raise estrogens to abnormal levels.

⚠ Lectins = antinutrients

Lectins[*] are a family of "sticky" molecules that can attach themselves to carbohydrates and cell walls.

Some lectins might have beneficial effects, but they also impair the absorption of nutrients: in that respect they qualify as "antinutrients," as their excessive consumption may lead to nutritional deficiencies. They might also cause other serious health problems, in particular by harming the lining of the intestines.

Lectins are particularly abundant in **grains**, **legumes** (especially **dry beans** and **soy beans**) and to a lesser extent in seeds, nuts and nightshade vegetables such as potatoes.

Lectins are pretty much everywhere, but some are more dangerous than others:

- Lectin in beans (kidney, navy, pinto, fava) is highly concentrated, thorough cooking helps inactivate them.

- Green beans are fine: since we consume the whole pod, they don't count as a legume; a serving doesn't contain much lectin.

- The lectin in garbanzo beans (chick peas), lentils and peas is less concentrated.

⚠ Phytic acid = antinutrient

Phytic acid can prevent the absorption of important minerals by binding to them.

This lowers the bioavailability of these minerals, that is, the proportion of minerals that can be used by our body: a demonstration that the nutrient content of a given food doesn't tell the whole story about its value to humans.

Grains and seeds are rich in phytic acid: therefore vegetarians relying on these foods for their diet are particularly at risk for deficiencies.

In addition, the binding of phytic acid to minerals produces phytates, which are salts that can irritate our mucus membranes, the lining of our stomach and intestines.

Chopped Winter Salad

Salad greens bring freshness and variety to our meals. However, don't get addicted to salad and don't make salad the "vegetable" portion of your meal too often: unless you eat a huge quantity of salad leaves, you will not get much nutritional value since salad leaves are made mostly of water. Its nutrient spectrum might be good in terms of variety, but there is not much of anything in a salad leaf!

On the other hand, the salad featured here, unlike most typical restaurant salads, is replete with nutrients:

- Fat soluble vitamins from the dark greens
- Sulforaphanes from the dark greens
- Nutrients from the allium family
- Minerals from the seeds
- Amino acids and a large spectrum of minerals from the celery.

Serves 4 to 6 ~ ⏳ ⏳

Salad:

- 1 head romaine lettuce, chopped, washed and dried

- 2 cups wild or baby arugula, chopped

- 2 cups chopped Lacinato, Dino or Tuscan kale

- ½ small red onion, diced into ¼-inch pieces

- 2 ribs of celery, diced into ¼-inch pieces

- ½ English cucumber, unpeeled, diced into ¼-inch pieces

- 1 Granny Smith apple, diced into ½-inch pieces

- 1 Crimson pear, diced into ½-inch pieces

- ½ cup dried fruit of choice (dates, apricots, cherries, figs) chopped, if necessary

- ¼ cup toasted pumpkin seeds

Dressing:

- ½ cup Vinaigrette Dressing*

Although cucumber is mostly water, it is a source of some less common minerals. The problem (burping to be specific) that some people experience with cucumber resides in its peel: by peeling, we eliminate the issue, but we lose the minerals. Tough choice...

⚠ **Dried fruits** should be used sparingly as they are a very dense sugar source. Don't live on them!

Drying is otherwise a good way to preserve the nutrients in fruit.

Combine all the salad components in a large bowl.

Ladle about 2 large spoonfuls of Vinaigrette on the salad and toss until coated. Taste, adjust seasoning with salt and pepper, or add more Vinaigrette. Be careful not to over-dress.

That's it!

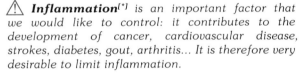

Allium

Allium (Latin for garlic) is the generic name of a large family of bulbous plants widely used for cooking. It includes garlic, onions, shallots, leeks, scallions, chives...

Their roots are deeper than those of squashes, but not as deep as those of fruit bushes.

Within the allium family, there are differences: for example leeks possess more nutritional value than onions as far as amino acids are concerned; on the other hand, onions have excellent anti-inflammatory properties.

*"Alliums" are strong sulphur donors. **Sulphur** is necessary for joint, cartilage and skin health. Although it is present in many foods, it is not always bioavailable (accessible to our body). Alliums are special because their sulphur is readily accessible to our metabolism.*

*"Alliums" also contain **lecithin** (do not confuse with lectin), which confers them a particular texture and mouth feel, a slight sliminess... Lecithin also contributes to cartilage and brain health.*

⚠ ***Inflammation**[*] is an important factor that we would like to control: it contributes to the development of cancer, cardiovascular disease, strokes, diabetes, gout, arthritis... It is therefore very desirable to limit inflammation.*

However, we also need to keep in mind that inflammation is an appropriate response of our body when fighting disease and that our nutrition should not be all about anti-inflammatory properties.

*The same applies to the much feared free radicals, resulting from **oxidation**: under some conditions, our body uses them to kill infectious invaders. Our nutrition should not be all about antioxidants[*].*

Fried Radicchio with Garlic Cream

Radicchio is an Italian chicory available year-round, with a peak season from mid-winter to early spring. Choose firm heads that have crisp, full-colored leaves with no brown spots. Radicchio is often used as a salad "green," but, as in this dish, it also lends itself to frying, grilling, sautéing or baking. Be careful not to confuse it with purple cabbage!

Serves 8 ~ ⧗ ⧗ ⧗

Radicchio:

- 2 medium heads radicchio
- 3 eggs
- 1 cup almond meal
- ½ cup grated Parmesan cheese
- 1 teaspoon salt
- ⅓ teaspoon ground white pepper
- Oil for frying

Garnish:

- 2 cups baby greens
- 1 bunch chives
- ½ cup capers, fried

Garlic cream:

- 1 hardboiled egg
- 1 tablespoon roasted garlic
- 2 tablespoons lemon juice
- ¾ cup olive oil
- 1 tablespoon drained capers, rinsed

Its color says it all: radicchio is rich in "cyans" and carotenoids. Chicories are also famous for their flavonoid content.

More unexpected is the fact that radicchio belongs to the "leafy greens" and as such is rich in the nutrients characteristic of the family (vitamin K and sulforaphanes in particular).

Radicchio is also a good source of minerals.

This recipe allows you to fry it, while retaining its nutritional value since the "breading" acts as a shield against excessive heat.

Besides, frying at high temperature is not necessary: the crust turns golden and crunchy with medium heat and not a huge quantity of oil.

Radicchio

1. Split the radicchio in 8, being careful to slice exactly through the stem at its base so the leaves don't fall apart.

2. Beat the eggs with 1 tablespoon of water. On another plate, combine the almond meal, cheese, salt and pepper.

3. Coat the radicchio pieces thoroughly in the egg mixture, then lightly in the almond meal mixture. The "breading" might not cover the radicchio perfectly, unlike a fritter, but don't worry about it.

   Chill, uncovered, for at least 30 minutes to ensure the coating adheres well.

Although chicories are cruciforms, they are more lettuce-like with regard to their leaf clustering.

4. In a sauté pan, pour the oil to a depth of ¼ inch and heat up. Add the radicchio and evenly brown over moderate heat. Wait until breading forms a crunchy crust before turning over. Transfer to paper towels to drain. Watch that the egg batter that sneaks in between the leaves is cooked, though.

Garlic Cream

5. **Roasted garlic:** cut ¼ inch off the top of the garlic head to expose the cloves. Drizzle with a little oil, season with salt and pepper. Place in a 350 °F oven for 30 minutes.

6. Mash the hardboiled egg with 1 tablespoon of roasted garlic and the lemon juice. Blend, slowly adding the oil until the mixture thickens. The sauce should be thick but still pourable.

   Add the capers and season with salt and pepper.

To serve, arrange the baby greens on a dish, place fried radicchio atop. Drizzle with garlic cream and top with snipped chives and fried capers.

Asparagus & Collard Greens Slaw

Serves 8 ~ ⏳ ⏳

- 1 small bunch collard greens
- 1 lb medium asparagus
- 2 carrots
- 1 red bell pepper
- 1 clove garlic, peeled and minced
- ½ small Savoy cabbage
- ½ small purple cabbage

Paprika Vinaigrette:

- ½ cup champagne vinegar
- ¼ cup extra-virgin oil
- 1 tablespoon dry mustard
- 1 tablespoon celery seeds
- 1 tablespoon sweet Spanish smoked paprika

Collard greens and cabbages are among the mildest tasting vegetables of the family, making this a perfect beginner's dish. When selecting collard greens, avoid those that are too large, have yellow, flabby, pitted leaves or thick, fibrous stems.

❧

Dark leafy greens are rich in carotenoids although their color doesn't show (the orange of the carotene is hidden behind the green chlorophyll).

The color spectrum of the various types of cabbage (Savoy, Napa, purple...) reflects the presence of different nutrients and flavonoids.

Purple cabbage   Napa cabbage

Green cabbage   Savoy cabbage

⚠ **Malnutrition**[*] *(not getting the right kind of nutrients) should not be confused with* **undernutrition** *(not getting enough calories).*

Paradoxically, overeating may be a consequence of malnutrition, the body seeking in vain to correct for missing nutrients.

This is another incentive to focus on the quality of our food: a well nourished (in terms of quality) body is less prone to overeating.

1. Rinse the collard greens. Remove and discard the ribs. Halve the leaves lengthwise, and then thinly slice crosswise in ¼-inch wide strips.

4. **Paprika Vinaigrette:** whisk together the vinegar, oil, dry mustard, celery seeds and paprika. Season to taste with salt and freshly ground black pepper.

⚠ *It's not only what you eat that matters, but also **what you don't eat**: by consuming a lot of any given food, you rob yourself of the opportunity to add different nutrients in your diet.*

Bacon is good, but if you have bacon every morning, you're not having all the other foods that are available.

2. Wash and trim the asparagus by snapping the spears at the natural breaking point. Remove the tips and reserve. Slice the asparagus spears diagonally into ⅛-inch thin slices. Slice the tips in half lengthwise.

3. Cut the green and purple cabbages in half lengthwise, lay them flat side down, remove the cores and thinly slice crosswise, ¼-inch thick. Julienne cut the carrots and the red bell pepper.

5. In a large mixing bowl, combine all the ingredients. Pour the dressing over and toss to coat. Season generously with salt and freshly ground black pepper. Refrigerate until the collard greens are softened, tossing occasionally, for at least 30 minutes.

Whole Real Food

Whole real foods are fresh foods that received as little processing as possible. As a general rule, these foods are located in the periphery of the grocery store, since they have a shorter shelf life and need to be refrigerated.

Real foods are those that don't require a nutrition label. They should be as close as possible to how they appear in nature.

These cannot be considered whole real food:

- Grains, whole or not, and their derivatives (flour, bread, pasta, cereal, cookies, crackers, chips): visualize how grains appear in nature and imagine the amount of processing involved in bringing them to the store. Grains are naturally enclosed in a fiber jacket and grow on stalks. They are not whole food, unless you also eat the hulls and stalks; and even then, this would be very starchy food, not nutrient-dense.

- Power bars, even those with "healthy" ingredients, always contain a lot of carbohydrates and are more like a nutritional experiment than food.

- Supplements are the exact opposite of whole real food, of course. Isolated from the rest of the plant or animal, they don't work, and the extracting processes are nasty.

- Artificial sweeteners (obviously).

- Soy, almond or any industrial vegetable milk, because of the amount of processing involved in producing it.

- Yogurt sold with fruit, sugar or jam in it.

- Low-fat dairy because it has natural components removed and unnatural ones added.

Whole real foods include:

- Fresh, colorful, nutrient-dense, non-starchy vegetables. Even then, there are some gradations of excellence. Take carrots: carrots are OK; to make them "wholer," wash them, but keep the skin with its bacteria, digestive enzymes and nutrients. If the producer is reliable, there is no danger in ingesting a little soil[*].

- Dairy from healthy animals. The less processed, the better. (Yogurt is processed milk; however, fermentation is a naturally occurring process; adding sugar or jam is not; so get plain whole milk yogurt.)

- Meat, eggs and seafood, consuming as much as possible of the animal. Make sure the animal was fed the healthy food that it was meant to eat.

- Nuts, seeds and nut "butter" ground from whole nuts, without additives.

- Herbs and spices.

- Dried fruit (beware of the sugar content though.)

Some convenient ingredients always have to go through a little manufacturing: oils, dairy, nuts and seeds, spices. Look for those with the least processing: roast the nuts yourself, buy mechanically extracted oil.

This is what whole grain looks like.

Poached Chicken

Pan-searing the chicken before poaching it guarantees a flavorful meat. You can prepare chicken legs or breasts in the same manner.

To get technical, pan-searing causes a Maillard reaction, a chemical reaction named after a French chemist. All we need to know is that this reaction is responsible for creating hundreds of flavorful compounds.

Some dishes may seem complicated at first. But you'll find that, after you made a dish once, you do it again and again, in simplified form using whatever is available in your refrigerator, or in your own more elaborate version.

Once you have poached chicken, you can use it for Harvest Chicken Salad* as presented in the next pages, or just enjoy this great technique and make simple everyday meals by tossing in whatever vegetables are available.

⚠ Note, however, that this way of consuming chicken deprives you of all the nutrients from the discarded bone, skin and fat.

Ingredients ~ ⏳

- Boneless, skinless chicken breast
- Chicken broth
- Oil

---

1. Season the presentation side of the chicken breast with salt and freshly ground pepper.

2. In a non-stick skillet, heat the oil until almost smoking. Place the chicken, seasoned side down, and sear until golden brown, about 2 minutes. Season again and turn, searing the other side for 30 seconds.

3. Pour in some broth to half the height of the meat. Reduce heat to a simmer, cover and cook until the meat is cooked, about 12 to 15 minutes.

Remove to a plate and let it rest for 5 minutes before carving.

Harvest Chicken Salad

This recipe illustrates the poaching technique for cooking chicken breast, but actually, it could use chicken meat cooked in any other way.

✍

Note that the fruits used in this dish are all seasonal northern fruits.

Serves 4 ~ ☗ ☗

- 2 boneless Poached Chicken* breasts

Salad:

- 1 Fuyu persimmon
- 1 Fuji apple
- 1 Crimson pear
- ½ small red onion
- 2 stalks celery
- ¼ cup roasted pumpkin seeds

Mayonnaise Vinaigrette Dressing:

- ½ cup Homemade Mayonnaise*
- 2 tablespoons extra-virgin oil
- 1 tablespoon Dijon mustard
- 2 tablespoons white wine vinegar
- 2 teaspoons dried thyme
- 1 teaspoon garlic powder

Garnish:

- Salad leaves (Romaine, spring mix)

Celery, a nice fibrous vegetable, lends its wonderful and unique flavor to this composition, once more making the point that nutrition and taste are closely linked.

Celery is nutritionally rich, with a good mineral and protein spectrum (for a vegetable). Thanks to its fibrous structure, it is very heat stable, therefore good for cooking without loss of much nutrient value.

Look for light green celery stalks that are crisp and firm.

> ⚠ **Mayonnaise** - Store-bought mayonnaise contains a lot of ingredients and involves a good amount of processing.
>
> If you consume a lot of mayonnaise, it's easy to make your own, using a variety of oils to increase the diversity of fatty acids in your diet.

You could replace the mayonnaise with yogurt, but why would you?

Mayonnaise is good for you! (Remember, we are not afraid of fat.) Prepare it yourself, varying the oils in order to broaden your nutrients; since it is not heated, any good oil can be used, regardless of its smoking point: for a change, try walnut or coconut oil.

✍

However, if you choose yogurt, make it whole milk: the fat in yogurt is good fat, removing it involves undesirable processing, and the fat removed is often replaced by sugar for taste and texture.

1. Prepare the Homemade Mayonnaise* and the Poached Chicken* breasts.

2. Cut the chicken breasts into ½-inch cubes.

3. Cut all the fruits, onion and celery into cubes (peel the onion only.) Celery and onion are diced into ¼-inch cubes, the rest into ½-inch cubes.

4. In a large bowl, whisk together the mayonnaise (or yogurt), oil, mustard, vinegar, thyme and garlic powder. Season to taste with salt and freshly ground pepper.

5. Add the cubed chicken, onion, celery, fruit and pumpkin seeds, and stir gently to combine. Cover and refrigerate for 30 minutes before serving.

Serve over chopped romaine and spring mix.

Seasonal northern fruits *are fall fruits growing in northern temperate climates, where there is a risk of frost.*

Due to their growth cycle, they go through a phase of hyper-concentration in nutrients and sugar just before they are ripe.

We prefer them to tropical fruit because of their much higher nutrient to sugar ratio.

These include:

- *Fall northern berries (blueberries, blackberries, raspberries)*
- *Apples, pears*
- *Apricots, peaches, nectarines*
- *Cherries are sweet, but so loaded with good things that they get an exemption.*
- *Figs and persimmons are nutritious. Use them for variety, but sparingly as they contain a lot of sugar.*

Pan-Seared, Oven-Finished Chicken

This very convenient technique can also be used for fish.

❧

Pan-searing and flash-cooking just prior to serving is one of the most useful cooking techniques that you will use over and over everyday. It ensures the meat is properly done and moist, and the dish is hot when served.

You can sear the meat in advance and keep it refrigerated for a few days. When you need it, just plop it in the preheated oven.

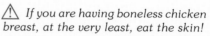

Ingredients ~ ⏳

- Boneless Chicken breast
- Salt and pepper
- 2 tablespoons oil

⚠ *If you are having boneless chicken breast, at the very least, eat the skin!*

Without being the magic bullet advertised by some, the skin is nutritionally rich: it brings fats and other useful substances into your diet.

1. Season the presentation side (skin side) of the chicken breast with salt and freshly ground pepper.

2. In a non-stick skillet, heat the oil until almost smoking. Place chicken, seasoned side down, and sear until golden brown, about 2 minutes. Season with salt and pepper then turn, searing the other side for 2 minutes more. Transfer to a baking dish. Set aside.

3. Just before serving, place seared chicken breasts in preheated 450 °F oven until done (12 to 20 minutes, depending on thickness). Remove from oven. Let rest 5 minutes before cutting.

"Doneness" is tested by pressing the thick part of the meat with a finger. When the meat is done, its consistency should feel quite firm.

Mediterranean Chicken Salad

This recipe builds on the Pan-Seared, Oven-Finished Chicken*. You can also simply buy a roasted chicken at the market and shred the meat.

This is a simple, tasty salad, which can be used as a snack or an entrée. To serve, fold in wild arugula or place over a bed of your favorite salad greens.

❧

And obviously, don't fret if you are missing some of the ingredients, as long as you have variety!

Serves 4 ~ ⧗ ⧗

- 2 Pan-Seared, Oven-Finished Chicken* boneless breasts
- ½ red bell pepper, cut into ¼-inch strips
- ½ yellow bell pepper, cut into ¼-inch strips
- ½ orange bell pepper, cut into ¼-inch strips
- ½ red onion, thinly sliced
- ½ cup pitted olives, chopped
- ½ cup roasted pumpkin seeds
- ¼ cup minced flat-leaf parsley
- 2 tablespoons extra-virgin oil
- 2 tablespoons red wine vinegar
- ½ cup crumbled feta cheese
- 2 cups salad greens or arugula

⚠ Roast the nuts and seeds yourself if you can. Otherwise you might end up with such crazy things as pumpkin seeds or peanuts roasted in Canola[*] oil!

1. Cook the chicken breasts using the Pan-Seared, Oven-Finished Chicken* technique.

   Shred the chicken meat.

2. In a large bowl, combine shredded chicken, peppers, onion, olives, pumpkin seeds and parsley. Add the oil and vinegar and fold to combine.

3. Fold in the crumbled feta cheese. Taste and adjust the amount of dressing and seasonings.

4. Chill for 30 minutes prior to serving. Fold in wild arugula or serve over salad greens of your choice.

Cooking Oils

Vary your oils! Different oils have different nutritional properties: oils are not a single substance but a mixture of omega-3 / omega-6, saturated / unsaturated fatty acids. Take into consideration the balance of all these components.

Avocado oil - The highest smoke point of all, but relatively expensive.

Peanut oil - High smoke point. Its neutral taste works well for most cuisines (in particular Asian, where olive oil tastes very foreign).

Olive oil - "Pure" is adequate for cooking at moderate temperatures; extra-virgin has a lower smoke point and is not recommended for general sautéing, but rather as seasoning. Its strong flavor can overpower some dishes.

Palm oil - Good natural saturated fat (palmitic acid is a pretty common part of most saturated fats).

Coconut oil - A wonderful oil, full of good saturated fats that don't oxidize or go rancid easily.

Corn oil - Reasonable enough, but it has a large ω-3/ω-6 imbalance (as does soybean oil). Even though our body can cope with some amount of imbalance, it cannot deal with overwhelming imbalance, so corn oil shouldn't be used exclusively.

Sunflower oil - Made from pressed sunflower seeds. Overall a good oil, it also has a very large ω-3/ω-6 imbalance so it shouldn't be the only oil you use,

Safflower oil - Made from safflower seeds (related to sunflower). High smoke point, neutral flavor, but also with a very large ω-3/ω-6 imbalance.

It is important to consume less usual oils in order to increase the variety of fatty acids present in our diet:

Nut oils (walnut, hazelnut, pistachio, almond...) - Nut oils usually have a high smoke point, but they are more expensive and usually considered as specialty, flavoring oils.

Seed oils (pumpkin seed for example) - Seed oils, with the exception of grape seed, which has a high smoke point, should be refrigerated and used for seasoning only.

Sesame oil - A nice seasoning oil with a very strong, characteristic Asian taste. Store in the refrigerator.

⚠ *AVOID*

Soybean oil is not recommended for the same reasons that soy is not recommended in general: its strong estrogen effects have the potential to create hormonal imbalance in our body.

Canola oil is not recommended. It is a totally unnatural oil made from genetically modified rapeseed. Ironically, it is being touted as healthy because it is the poorest in saturated fats.

Man-made trans fats must be avoided at all costs.

Flaxseed (linseed) oil - Its claim to fame is that it is rich in omega-3. It goes well in a trail mix to balance the sunflower and pumpkin seeds. The drawback is that it is a delicate oil (too delicate for cooking), which becomes rancid easily; it sometimes contains particulates (like lignans) that can affect our hormonal balance in unpredictable ways.

On the other hand, you need not fear **natural saturated fat:** every well conducted large scale medical trial has shown no risk associated with saturated fat.

Saturated fat has been wrongly demonized in the nutrition literature.

Curried Chicken Salad

Another illustration of the Pan-Seared, Oven-Finished Chicken* technique.

❧

Remember: there is no reason to remove the skin from the chicken breast! It brings valuable nutrients.

⚠ *The presence of other nutrients, that is, what you ate over the past days or even weeks, affects the amount of nutrition that you can extract from the food you eat today.*

Serves 4 ~ ⧗

- 2 boneless Pan-Seared, Oven-Finished Chicken* breasts
- ¼ cup Homemade Mayonnaise*
- 2 tablespoons extra-virgin oil
- 1 tablespoon Dijon mustard
- 2 teaspoons yellow curry powder
- 1 teaspoon ground turmeric
- 2 tablespoons fresh lime juice
- ½ small red onion, finely diced
- 2 stalks celery, cut into ¼-inch dice
- 1 cup halved red grapes
- 4 tablespoons toasted pumpkin seeds
- 2 cups wild arugula

1. Cook the chicken breasts using the Pan-Seared, Oven-Finished Chicken* technique.

   Dice into ½-inch cubes.

2. In a large bowl, whisk together the mayonnaise, oil, Dijon mustard, curry powder, turmeric and lime juice.

3. Add the cubed chicken, onion, celery, grapes and pumpkin seeds, and stir gently to combine. Season with salt and pepper and adjust flavorings with curry and lime juice. Cover and refrigerate for at least an hour to allow the flavors to meld.

4. Before serving, taste and adjust seasonings. Serve on a bed of wild arugula.

Cheese Soufflé

Here is a dish featuring a variety of dairy products: milk, butter, cheese, eggs.

It is spectacular and not so hard to make, but you have to sit at the dining table as soon as it is ready: it will deflate if you wait too long.

A nice treat to prepare when you want to surprise the family, this fancy dish uses simple ingredients that are almost always in stock in the kitchen.

Serves 6 ~ ⧗ ⧗ ⧗

- 3 oz butter
- 4 tablespoons flour
- 2 cups milk
- 1 pinch nutmeg
- 6 eggs
- 5 oz aged Swiss cheese

DAIRY

The overall goodness of this dairy-dense delicacy definitely excuses the modest amount of flour present. The benefits of dairy cannot be overemphasized:

- **Good fats**

  Dairy contains the short and medium length fatty acids that are necessary for brain health. Some of the dairy fats have also been shown to increase insulin sensitivity, another desirable property.

- **Good source of proteins**

  Whey protein is very efficient in terms of amino acids. It is a clean protein with very little adverse neurohormonal effects (which is not true of all proteins).

- **Great source of calcium[*] and minerals**

  Thanks to the simultaneous presence of minerals, vitamins and fats, dairy calcium is more readily usable than calcium in other foods (for example, calcium in spinach can be poorly absorbed).

Milk and Evolution

Many nutritionists point out rightfully that cow's milk is better designed for calves than for humans. While it is true that animal milk poses problems for some (allergies, intolerance, even serious diseases), for most people the benefits of milk[*] outweigh its inconveniences.

The problems of a few should not be extrapolated to the whole population. We did in fact evolve a capability to use cow's milk: that is **lactase,** an enzyme that specifically breaks up dairy. Although in some populations lactase disappears in adults, lactase can be induced[*]: if they consume milk, adults will start producing lactase again.

Choose organic, grass-fed, full fat dairy! Concerning raw dairy, there are sound arguments for and against it.

1. Preheat oven to 300 °F.

2. In a saucepan, melt the butter, then add in the flour, mix and cook for 3 minutes. Pour in the milk progressively, stirring all the while. Grate some nutmeg, add salt and pepper to taste. Cook until you obtain a thick sauce, stirring continuously.

3. Separate the egg yolks from the whites. Incorporate the yolks in the saucepan.

4. Grate the cheese and add it to the mix.

5. Beat the egg whites with a pinch of salt to hard peaks. Incorporate delicately in the Béchamel, lifting the preparation from the bottom to the top, without stirring too hard.

6. Butter the soufflé mold. Pour in the preparation, leaving some room on top for it to expand.

7. Right after putting in the oven at low temperature (300 °F), set the oven to let the temperature rise to 355 °F. Cook 30 to 40 minutes (check "doneness" by sticking a thin blade in, as for a cake).

Serve immediately!

NOTE

If the oven is very hot right from the start, the crust hardens too quickly, and the soufflé has trouble puffing up.

⚠ *For vegetarians, concentrating on the protein part of the diet is the most important. Dairy and eggs are their best sources of fatty proteins.*

Cauliflower Crust Pizza

This is probably not the best way to eat cauliflower: by squeezing the water out, we end up with a lot of starches, and nutrients will escape with the water. True, but this is still better than regular flour for nutrients and fiber.

Although a far cry from the real Neapolitan thing, this method yields a reasonably crunchy crust if you resist the temptation to pile the topping on too thick.

The preparation can serve as a crust substitute in many savory pies. In fact, it does such a good job that it's hard to remember the dish is 100 % low-starch.

For a 10" pizza, serves 4 ~ ⧗ ⧗ ⧗

Crust:

- 4 cups grated cauliflower florets (1 medium head)
- 1 large egg
- 2 oz shredded Swiss cheese
- 1 tablespoon oil

Pizza topping example:

- Fresh tomato slices
- Tomato paste
- Mozzarella
- Olives
- Anchovies

Preheat the oven to 400 °F.

1. Break the cauliflower into large florets. Grate the florets using the large holes of a box grater: start with the sides of the florets, so you don't end up with small broken pieces that are difficult to deal with. You can also use a food processor and pulse until the florets are reduced to a rice-like texture.

2. Measure the required quantity of shredded cauliflower and place in a steamer basket. (The left over can be used for cauliflower polenta in Eggs Benedict with "Polenta"*). Bring a small quantity of water to a boil in a pot. Place the steamer basket on top. Cover and steam for 5 minutes. Remove from the heat. Let cool.

3. Transfer the steamed cauliflower into a clean dish towel and turn, squeezing out as much water as possible.

4. In a large bowl, mix the strained cauliflower with all the other ingredients for the crust. Season to taste with salt and pepper.

5. Line a baking sheet with parchment. Pat the mixture in a circle about ½-inch thick, with slightly raised edges. Lightly drizzle with oil. Bake for 40 minutes in the preheated oven. The crust is ready when it is golden.

6. Top with the ingredients of your liking, but don't add too much or the crust will be soggy.

Pizza:
Tomato paste is preferable to tomato sauce because it provides a lighter, drier topping.

Flamenkuchen:
- 4 oz onion, minced
- 3 oz bacon, cut into matchsticks
- 4 tablespoons sour cream

In a skillet over low heat, let the bacon sweat for a few minutes; add the onions and cook until they are translucent.

Spread the sour cream on the crust. Top with the onion and bacon mixture. Note that this makes an "ideal plate" by itself, with vegetables, proteins and fats.

In both cases, season to taste with salt and pepper. Bake for another 10 to 15 minutes. Serve very hot.

Note: you can replace the steamed cauliflower with baked Spaghetti Squash*. After scooping the squash threads out of the shell, squeeze them to extract as much water as possible, then use them in the same way as the steamed cauliflower.

The flamenkuchen topping

Vegetables

This is a whole system!

For the advice to make sense, it must be in the context of a *diversified real food diet*. Don't combine it with another type of diet. Don't pick elements that you like from various diets.

- Select vegetables with a high nutrient to sugar ratio.

- Don't be afraid of fat: low-fat diets are unhealthy.

- Eat protein: they are your body's building blocks.

- Eliminate or, at a minimum, limit sugar and starch consumption (including whole grains and cereals).

If you eat a real food, micronutrient-rich diet, you don't need to add sugar and starches. You will get all the carbohydrates you need from your micronutrient-rich vegetables.

Don't think in terms of calories: think in terms of diversity and richness of your food.

Vegetable Families

To get the broadest value out of your food, think in terms of nutrient families instead of single nutrients.

In the same vein, think of vegetables as families and make sure you get the widest variety within each group: while families have general characteristics, each individual in the family possesses its own personality.

Cruciferous vegetables / Dark leafy greens

Their signature is an abundance of sulforaphanes, a chemical with huge health benefits.

Sulforaphanes are colorless, and the distinctive green color of these vegetables is due to chlorophyll: in addition to being a useful nutrient, chlorophyll can also be a promise of carotenoids, as the two pigments are often found together (both are involved in harvesting energy from light).

Some members of this family are more colorful, showing a stronger presence of other nutrients. As a bonus, cruciferous vegetables and dark leafy greens are good for intestinal transit, thanks to their high fiber content.

Septate fruits / Mediterranean vegetables

These are, technically speaking, all fruits. They include: squash, tomatoes, eggplants, peppers, cucumbers, watermelons...

The members of this family owe their unique nutrient density to their seeds, the germs of life. They are mostly rich in carotenoids, but some also contain a fair amount of "cyans."

Root vegetables

Carrots, potatoes, turnips, beets, radishes, yams...

Starchy, but nutrient-dense, their strong suit tends to be the carotenoids, as evidenced by their yellow or orange tint. Thanks to their deep roots, they have a nice tap into mineral sources different from those of most vegetables.

Their contribution to the intestinal flora is essential for vegetarians; in particular, their skin harbors a whole biome of useful bacteria: eat the skin whenever possible; don't peel carrots!

Allium

Leek, shallot, onion, green onion, garlic...

Their uncommon chemistry is rich in flavonoids, and they are unique in sulforaphane concentration. Another of their strengths is the capability to donate sulphur, which contributes to cartilage and joint health.

Fruits
(Other than septates)

Fruits are not created equal: the farther North and winterward you go, the more nutrient-dense the fruits. (Possibly so hibernating animals can load up.)

Use fruits sparingly because of their high sugar content. The good news is that their skin is the single richest source of "cyans" (short for the bluish nutrients, cyanidins, anthocyanidins, anthocyanins...).

Nuts and seeds

These are great sources of minerals that are relatively rare in other foods (zinc, magnesium, manganese). They constitute a healthy source of essential omega-3 and omega-6 fatty acids, as well as short and medium-chain saturated fats. They are also a source protein with a fairly broad spectrum. Vary the nuts and seeds you consume, as they complement one another.

Legumes

Legumes are plants that carry their seeds in pods. Usually only the seeds are consumed: legumes are rich in starches, and more importantly in antinutrients such as lectins and phytates; therefore, they should be used with caution.

Green beans are in a separate category since we eat both seeds and pods.

And all the others!

The list of vegetables is endless. Many important vegetables don't belong to any of the families above: fennel, asparagus, celery, artichoke, herbs and spices, just to name a few.

Eat the widest possible variety of vegetables!

Broiled Vegetables

This cooking method is very valuable when you are in a hurry. You can mix and match vegetables, but cooking times vary, so it's safer to broil them separately.

❧

Although you can use virtually any vegetable, it helps to select those that are fairly substantial and meaty; however, salad-like radicchio works well too.

Occasionally, use winter root vegetables. A medley is nice, since they are on the heavy side compared to the other vegetables. Consider turnips, rutabaga, carrots, golden beets, celery root...

Use the lowest broiler temperature that will provide a satisfactory result.

For fibrous vegetables such as asparagus, the slight burning caused by broiling is not a problem: the nutrients are protected by the fibers. But better still, the top and bottom half could be cooked separately, since the bottom is harder and takes longer to cook.

Vegetables, select:

- Asparagus
- Broccoli
- Brussels sprouts
- Bell pepper
- Cauliflower
- Eggplant
- Fennel
- Radicchio
- Zucchini
- Summer squash
- Root vegetables
- etc.

Seasonings:

- Various oils
- Salt and pepper
- Lemon juice
- Almond meal
- Grated Parmesan cheese
- Homemade Mayonnaise* or Aioli*

Paradoxically enough, "pure" and "extra-virgin" olive oils have opposite virtues.

- ***Pure oil*** *means that it has been filtered and proteins have been removed.*

- ***Extra-virgin oil*** *has protein contaminants, which give flavor but lower the smoke point.*

⚠ ***For cooking at higher temperatures select pure oil.***

Some vegetables are better blanched first: fennel, Brussels sprouts...

Others don't need to be: asparagus, cauliflower, eggplant, zucchini, radicchio...

1. Wash and cut vegetables if needed.
   - Asparagus, Brussels sprouts: leave whole.
   - Eggplants, zucchini: slice crosswise or lengthwise, in ⅛-inch thick slices.
   - Broccoli, cauliflower: bite-sized florets.
   - Fennel: slice lengthwise in ¼-inch thick slices.
   - Radicchio: quarter in 8 pieces.
   - Bell pepper: quarter.

2. If vegetables, such as Brussels sprouts, don't cook well just by broiling, blanch them for about 3 minutes in boiling water. Very fibrous vegetables like fennel can be blanched longer. Most others don't need blanching.

3. Spread evenly on a broiler safe dish. Sprinkle with salt and pepper. Drizzle with oil.

   For an appetizing golden "gratin" look, sprinkle the dish with almond meal and a little bit of oil. Sprinkling with Parmesan cheese works very well too.

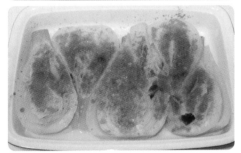

4. Broil until golden.

Finish seasoning with: oil, lemon juice, etc.

Fennel - Olive oil and Parmesan cheese.

Cauliflower

Root vegetables - Serve with aioli.

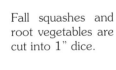
Fall squashes and root vegetables are cut into 1" dice.

Radicchio goes well with walnut oil and a splash of lemon.

Asparagus seasoned with oil and lemon.

Lemon juice will offset the bitterness of the strongest vegetables such as radicchio. It works well with asparagus too.

Spring Ratatouille

This is a great spring dish to accompany grilled or sautéed fish and poultry.

Your favorite vegetables may be substituted for those listed here. It is important that the vegetables be served "al dente" and not overdone. "Baby" vegetables are a popular addition to the combination.

The variety of vegetables included here guarantees an abundance and diversity of nutrients.

Serves 8 ~ ⧗

- 2 tablespoons oil

- 1 medium eggplant, diced into ½-inch pieces

- 3 lb summer squash (zucchini, etc.), cut into wedges

- 1 lb medium asparagus, cut diagonally into 1-inch pieces

- 1 red bell pepper, diced into ½-inch pieces

- 3 fresh tomatoes, diced or a 15-oz can of diced tomatoes

- 4 cloves garlic, minced

- ½ cup basil leaves, cut into thin strips

Nightshades

The nightshades are a large and diverse family including seemingly unrelated plants such as tomatoes, bell peppers, chili peppers, eggplants and potatoes, as well as tobacco, mandrake and belladonna.

In the family, the **septates** are exceptionally healthful. (Of all the commonly consumed nightshades, only the potato is not a septate.)

There is a great deal of unfounded mythology about the nightshades, although some of them such as the belladonna, also known as "deadly nightshade," are actually very toxic.

⚠ Controversial substances in nightshades are the **alkaloids**, some healthy, some with toxic effects. Alkaloids may cause health problems for a few people who are particularly sensitive to them. Cooking, by reducing the alkaloid contents, helps.

1. In a medium sauté pan, heat the oil over medium-high heat. Add the eggplant and sauté, stirring occasionally for 3 or 4 minutes. Add the squash and sauté until slightly softened, another 4 to 5 minutes. Add the asparagus, red bell pepper and diced tomatoes (optionally you can peel and seed the fresh tomatoes before dicing them).

2. Remove the vegetables from the heat and add the minced garlic. Mix thoroughly.

3. Season with salt and freshly ground black pepper.

Just before serving, add the basil strips.

Tomatoes are rich in lycopene, a non-vitamin A carotenoid with many health benefits.

⚠ Note that the cancer protection property has only been observed with cooked tomatoes[*].

Septate vegetables

These "vegetables" are in fact a family of fruits growing on vines. Their particularity is that their flesh is divided by walls into chambers containing seeds. They have in common a strong nutrient density.

They are mostly rich in carotenoids; some, like eggplants, are also rich in "cyans."

Seek septate fruits that are high in nutrition relative to their starch load.

The most common are:

- Bell peppers
- Hot peppers
- Squashes
- Tomatoes
- Eggplants
- Cucumbers
- Watermelons

Green Beans

With this recipe, even the most reluctant kids (or adults) will eat green beans, guaranteed!

Garlic, parsley and almond meal add color, flavor, nutrition, visual appeal and mouth feel.

Herbs, leaves and roots – parsley, cilantro, bay leaf, basil, tea (!), horseradish, etc. – are all rich in flavonoids and vitamins. They are a great source of digestive enzymes that aid absorbing the other nutrients.

Serves 4 ~ ⏳

- 10 oz green beans
- 1 clove garlic
- 2 tablespoons oil
- 1 tablespoon almond meal
- A few sprigs of parsley

Green beans vs. Peas

Do not confuse green beans and peas. Peas are a legume. Although in the same plant family as peas, green beans are not considered a legume because the whole pod is consumed, and therefore the proportion of starch is much smaller.

Green beans are very high in chloroplasts (they give the green color) and carotenoids (whose color is hidden by the green). They are also very rich in fiber.

Green beans are better without any question: they contain less sugar for the nutrient value and more fiber. When you have a choice between two related ingredients with the same nutrients, pick the one with the least sugar.

⚠ **Legumes** are often recommended as the healthy choice, but in fact, their protein contents pales in comparison with meat, fish and eggs. Their fiber and nutrient density is not as good as the other vegetables' either.

Learn how your garden grows!

Depending on the length of their roots, plants extract nutrients from the soil at different depths:

- Butterleaf or iceberg salads are very shallow; so is spinach.
- Radicchio goes a little deeper.
- Chard and kale go deeper still.

The plants with deeper roots also have the ability to extract more minerals.

Consume vegetables that extract nutrients from different depths for a broader spectrum of minerals and nutrients.

Sustainability

The same principle applies to the grass that cows eat: if cows are kept in the same area all the time, eventually the grass gets depleted. The pastures must be rotated in order to keep the soil rich.

1. Wash the green beans and, if necessary, trim the hard ends. Bring a large pot of water to a boil and drop the beans in, one handful at a time, waiting for the water to boil again between handfuls: this way the beans will stay a brighter green. Do not cover. Cook for 3 minutes. Drain.

2. Peel and mince the garlic as thinly as you can.

3. Wash and finely chop the parsley.

4. Heat the oil in a large pan, sauté the garlic until it is golden (but not burnt!). Add the almond meal. When it is golden, add the parsley, stirring all the while to avoid burning.

5. Toss in the green beans, mix well, season with salt and pepper.

Serve hot!

Spaghetti Squash

This fall squash deserves a special mention as a great resource for those with nostalgia for pasta. Its wonderful texture and versatility make it an easy solution for the everyday meal or for entertaining.

Young squashes work better as their flesh is firmer and yields nice firm strands.

Although boiling is an option, baking is the preferred method here, due in part to the technical difficulties in finding a large enough pot.

Baking face-down allows the squash to cook in its own steam. Moreover, after baking, the outside takes a bright shiny aspect, making this natural container the most perfectly elegant serving platter.

Serves 4 ~ ⏳

- 1 medium spaghetti squash

To serve as a savory dish:

- Oil, salt, pepper
- Italian Meat Loaf*

To serve as a dessert:

- Butter, cinnamon, nutmeg...

⚠️ A good metabolism?

It's true that some people can eat all the starches they want without getting fat. However, obesity is not the only metabolic consequence of eating starches and sugar.

Appearance is not the main concern. By consuming large amounts of starches, people deprive themselves of the other nutrients they could have eaten instead.

In addition, digesting starch requires a lot of fluid and can have a wash out effect that depletes the body of minerals[gelatinization].

Like all fall squashes, spaghetti squash is rich in nutrients of all sorts, sugar included. However, compared to other squashes (sugar pie, butternut, acorn...) their sugar content is much lower: their glycemic load is at most half that of most other fall squashes.

Color perception is strongly linked with nutrient density and taste: as a general rule, a paler squash contains less sugar and also less nutrition. There must be reasons why we evolved to see colors...

1. Preheat oven to 375 °F.

2. Cut the squash in half. Discard the fibers and seeds in the middle, clipping the stringy fibers with scissors if necessary.

3. Sprinkle salt and drizzle oil onto each half.

4. Bake squash, cut face down, for 30 to 60 minutes, depending on size.

5. Using a fork, gently scrape the flesh of the squash: you will get strings that are reminiscent of spaghetti strands.

Spoon meat sauce on top of the "spaghetti." Sprinkle with Parmesan cheese and enjoy!

For a dessert, replace the oil with butter when cooking, and sprinkle with cinnamon and nutmeg before serving.

Glycemic Index vs. Glycemic Load

- *The **glycemic index (GI)** of a given ingredient indicates how quickly the sugar it contains passes into the blood.*

- *The **glycemic load (GL)** additionally takes into account how much sugar is present in the ingredient. It is a better number for assessing the effect of a food on your blood sugar level.*

Here is an illustration:

- *Carrots have a rather high glycemic index: their sugar goes rapidly into your blood, but their glycemic load is low, because they don't contain much sugar.*

  Carrots will not raise your blood sugar level as much as other foods with high sugar content, such as mashed potatoes, and should absolutely not be placed in the same category. This is unfortunately often the case when only glycemic index is taken into consideration.

  In addition, carrots are so loaded with nutrients that they are worth eating in spite of the sugar!

- *Beets on the other hand have a relatively high GI and heavy GL. They should not be used as freely as carrots, but since they have a lot of nutritional value, they can be part of our vegetable choices, although not too often.*

⚠ *When picking food, look at the big picture, instead of focusing on any single property.*

Take the example of al dente pasta versus potato :

- *A potato is a complete nutrition matrix rich in vitamin K, minerals and unusual enzymes.*

- *Pasta has a lower glycemic index, but a much lower nutritional value.*

When evaluating an ingredient, take into account its glycemic index, glycemic load and nutritional value.

Root Vegetable Ratatouille

Here is a wonderful fall or winter medley of root vegetables and tubers. This method of cooking brings out their flavor and sweetness. Other combinations of root vegetables may be used.

Serve it as a side dish or as a bed for roasted chicken, pork or grilled fish.

Serves 4 to 6 ~ ⧖ ⧖

- 1 medium turnip
- 1 small rutabaga
- 1 carrot
- 1 small sweet potato
- 1 medium golden beet
- 1 tablespoon oil
- 3 tablespoons butter, divided
- 1 tablespoon finely minced sage

Yes, a recipe with starches!

No food is forbidden, just don't eat starches every day, but only once in a while. Select the nutrient-dense ones and eat them for what they are: a nice load of sugar!

Root vegetables are an opportunity to vary and enrich our diet with nutrient-dense foods. However, their use must be limited due to their starchy nature. As always, select the deeply colored ones: prefer a colored turnip over a white one, pick a purple potato over a plain white one!

❧

Train your palate to make each bite memorable: perceive the sugar in the potato and enjoy it for what it is!

Our palate is a good (although not infallible) guide. Train it to distinguish the various tastes, and it will help you choose food wisely: you'll be able to tell that, by its bitterness, turnip is less sugar laden than other roots and therefore preferable; you will, on the other hand, learn to discern the high sugar content in the sweet potato.

Root vegetables

Since they are fairly rich in starch, they should constitute only a small fraction of our quest for brightly colored foods.

Root vegetables are probably not the optimal way to get many of the nutrients that can be obtained from less starchy foods, but they are perfectly sound, if they come from a reliable source.

Sourcing *is particularly important for roots and, more generally, fast growing seasonal vegetables: this make them effective extractors from the environment for both desirable nutrients and toxic agents.*

1. Peel and cut all the root vegetables (turnip, rutabaga, carrot, sweet potato, beet) into ¼-inch cubes.

2. Heat the oil and ⅓ of the butter in a large skillet over high heat until it's just about to smoke.

3. Add the cut vegetables and toss to coat with the oil and butter. Allow the vegetables to rest and develop a slight browning. Toss and let the vegetables rest again.

4. Once the vegetables are thoroughly browned, about 5 minutes total time (depending on your stove), reduce the heat to medium-low and continue to cook until the vegetables are tender-crisp. Remove them from the skillet and set aside.

5. Place the remaining butter in the skillet over medium heat. Swirl the butter until the solids begin to brown slightly. Add the sage and continue to heat until the mixture is tan in color.

6. Immediately add the previously cooked vegetables and toss to coat. Season with salt and freshly ground black pepper. Serve immediately.

⚠ **Browning the butter** brings bitterness and contributes to the flavor of the dish. However, smoking the butter may not be the best practice: as a general rule, don't heat the fat to smoking point because this changes its chemical structure, which impairs its nutritional properties.

Note however, that previous studies attributing carcinogenic effects to cooked butter[*] may have been flawed.

Rancidity is the result of changes in the chemical structure of the fat molecules, a process that occurs in particular when fats are heated to smoking point. This alters their nutritional properties.

For example, an important component of dairy fat is trans-palmitoleic acid, known to improve insulin sensitivity and blood pressure, and to reduce long term risk of diabetes and coronary-arterial diseases: all these beneficial properties are impaired when butter is overheated.

Deconstructed Ratatouille

This dish, known in southern France as "Tian de Légumes," is actually a ratatouille in elegant disguise.

❧

The rainbow of colors, from yellow-red to purple is already a promise of nutrients. This recipe uses a variety of common septate fruits: zucchini, eggplants, bell peppers, tomatoes.

- Summer squashes are rich in fiber, chlorophyll and carotenoids.
- Peppers are dense in carotenoids and sometimes "cyans," depending on their color.
- Eggplants, as can be guessed by their color, are rich in "cyans."
- Tomatoes are the greatest ever source of lycopene (a carotenoid) ever, and one of the greatest source of lutein (together with eggs).

Serves 4 ~ 🍷🍷🍷

- ½ onion
- ½ eggplant
- ½ bell pepper
- 1 clove garlic
- 2 zucchini
- 4 Roma tomatoes
- Herbs to taste (thyme, etc.)
- Grated Parmesan cheese or almond flour (optional)
- Oil

Bioavailability

Unfortunately, not all the nutrients we consume can be used by our body.

Cooking tomatoes increases the "bioavailbility" of their lycopene: this means that a greater percentage of the lycopene (from the tomato we ate) reaches the places in our body where it can be absorbed and used.

Since lycopene is fat soluble, adding oil also improves its assimilation by our digestive tract.

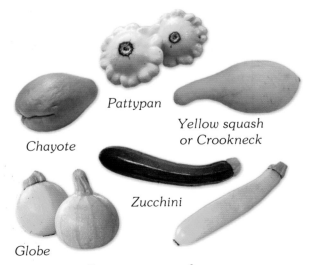

Pattypan

Yellow squash or Crookneck

Chayote

Zucchini

Globe

Summer squashes

1. Peel and mince the onion; thinly slice the eggplant; cut the bell pepper into strips; peel and crush the garlic.

2. Heat 2 tablespoons of oil in a non-stick pan and cook the onion, bell pepper, eggplant and garlic over low heat until they are soft and take a bit of color (the eggplants will absorb most of the oil).

3. Spread the cooked vegetables on the bottom of a baking dish. Preheat the oven to 360 °F.

4. Wash and thinly slice the zucchini and tomatoes. Arrange in the baking dish, alternating neat, regular rows of tomatoes and zucchini.

5. Sprinkle with herbs, salt and pepper. Drizzle some oil over the top. Bake for about 45 minutes, until the vegetables are soft.

6. About 15 minutes before the end, you can optionally sprinkle the top of the dish with almond meal or Parmesan cheese. This will give you a golden crunchy finish.

Raw vs. Cooked

- On the one hand, cooking vegetables breaks down the fibers and frees up the nutrients. Therefore most foods are more nutrient-rich when cooked (gently) than when raw.

- On the other hand, "raw foodists" claim that cooking creates complex molecules that don't exist in nature, thus modifying the foods that mankind has evolved with and adapted to. Natural enzymes present in food are impaired if their structure is altered.

The answer is in the balance of two conflicting effects: enzymes are proteins whose shape is indeed essential for effectiveness. Is the shape affected by cooking? In most cases, the balance is in favor of some gentle cooking, such as blanching.

Concurrently, and although there is no proof at this time, it seems reasonable to think that eating some amount of raw food can create beneficial enzymatic activity in our metabolism.

Eating mostly raw food might work if, like chimpanzees, we had time to chew food for hours. Since we don't have that leisure, cooking helps us extract nutrition.

⚠ **Microwaving** is a different story: the heat is focused on the water molecules in the food, causing intense hot spots that definitely destroy the nutrients next to them. On average, the food might not be so hot, but at the microscopic level, the effect is destructive.

If you use the microwave, run it in short bursts so that the heat has time to distribute.

Cruciferous Vegetables

The cruciferous family is an important group of vegetables, with amazing nutritional properties. Its name comes from the shape of its flowers, four petals arranged as a cross. In the plant, the branches and leaves tend to intricately cross each other.

This class of vegetables is more tightly linked to cancer prevention than any other.

Romanesco, the spectacular fractal vegetable

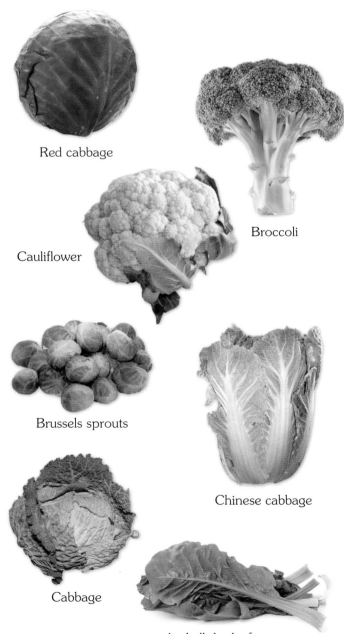

Red cabbage

Broccoli

Cauliflower

Brussels sprouts

Chinese cabbage

Cabbage

And all the leafy greens...

The cabbage and cauliflower types are all members of the cruciferous family:

- Cabbage
- Brussels sprouts
- Chinese cabbage
- Cauliflower
- Romanesco
- Broccoli
- Broccoli rabe

So are the dark leafy greens. (They are so important that they have their own page.)

All cruciferous vegetables contain sulforaphanes, to different extents. They are also rich in other "cyans."

Although most micronutrients are richly colored, sulforaphanes are an exception to the rule. The green tint of most cruciferous vegetables is due to chlorophyll, which has beneficial properties of its own, such as digestion enzymes and chloroplasts associated with carotenoids.

Most people are familiar with broccoli and cauliflower, but it's important to eat the others also because they bring a different spectrum of nutrients.

Steamed Broccoli & Cauliflower

Broccoli and its cousin, the cauliflower, are relatives of the cabbage and Brussels sprouts from the cruciferous family. They lend themselves to a variety of cooking methods including blanching, baking, steaming and sautéing, or they can be simply eaten raw.

As for everything else, select nice fresh broccoli with firm stems.

Cooking techniques - Preserving nutrients

When cooking with water, serve the cooking "broth" too: it contains valuable nutrients. You can do a reduction if you don't want to much liquid in your dish.

- **Steaming:** put as little water as possible in the bottom of the steamer, so the nutrients don't leach out.

- **Blanching:** this procedure should be quick so the nutrients don't all escape in the water.

- **Boiling** is the same as blanching except longer. Be careful not to lose the water soluble vitamins, do not discard the broth.

- **Sautéing** is fine for most everything.

- **Stir-frying:** make sure your oil can withstand high temperatures.

- **Deep-frying** is generally too hot for good nutrition.

- **Baking:** 300 °F and below will preserve the nutritional value of most vegetables.

- **Broiling:** do it briefly, otherwise the high temperatures involved will cause nutritional loss.

Serves 6 to 8 ~ ⧗

- 1 medium bunch broccoli (1 ½ lb)
- ½ cauliflower
- 2 tablespoons chopped parsley

Lime Dressing:

- 1 teaspoon lime zest
- 1 tablespoon lime juice
- ½ teaspoon ground cumin
- Tabasco or other hot sauce
- 1 teaspoon salt
- 3 tablespoons oil
- 2 shallots, finely minced

⚠ Even when steaming, the nutrients can escape in the cooking water. In fact, you can do without the steamer: put very little water in the saucepan together with your vegetables, bring to a boil and cover: this creates enough steam to cook the food.

The color of the water after cooking these purple carrots demonstrates that nutrients do escape.

1. **Lime Dressing:** in a small bowl, combine the lime zest, lime juice, ground cumin, salt, hot sauce and oil. Mix until well blended. Stir in the minced shallot. Set the dressing aside.

2. Wash the broccoli. Trim the florets. Peel the stems and cut into 1-inch long pieces. Cut the cauliflower into bite-sized pieces.

3. Fit a saucepan with a steamer basket and pour just enough water to cook the vegetables. Bring the water to a boil and add the broccoli and cauliflower to the basket. Cover and steam until the vegetables are tender, about 5 minutes.

4. Remove broccoli and cauliflower from the basket and place in a bowl.

Toss with the prepared dressing, transfer to a serving platter and top with chopped parsley. Serve warm or at room temperature.

Broccoli stems vs. florets

Don't discard the stems of the broccoli: they possess as much nutritional value as the florets.

The stems contain more chloroplasts and the associated chlorophyll and carotenoids, they also have more fiber.

The maturation of nutrients in the stem and in the floret are different and complement each other.

Cauliflower doesn't need to be plain white anymore. Nowadays, you can find several colorful varieties: they are not only pretty, their color reflects real nutritional value in addition to the sulforaphanes:

- *Purple: "cyans"*
- *Orange: carotenoids*
- *Green: chlorophyll and carotenoids*
- *White: still loaded with sulforaphanes!*

Mashed Cauliflower with Leeks

Mashed cauliflower is a great substitute for mashed potatoes, similar in taste without the high sugar contents.

The salt moistens and softens the kale: generally speaking, salt is a great means to enhance and bring out the sweetness of ingredients without resorting to sugar.

Leave the cauliflower on the chunky side as its texture adds to the complexity of the dish, and don't overcook, or it will disintegrate. You may also steam it.

Serves 4 to 6 ~ ⧖ ⧖

- 1 medium head of cauliflower
- 1 leek
- 4 cloves garlic
- 1 bunch Tuscan (dino) kale
- 1 cup cherry tomatoes
- 2 tablespoons unsalted butter
- 2 tablespoons extra-virgin oil

Listen to your body!

A variety of vegetables such as kale, spinach, chard and the stronger leafy greens, feel astringent: this is due to the presence of phytic acid. For some people, it gives a sense of rawness on the tongue. (This may happen with kiwi too.)

Phytic acid *can bind with minerals to produce salts that can be irritant. Watch out for such reaction, the effect on your tongue might reflect what happens to your gastrointestinal mucosa, in which case you may want to avoid these ingredients.*

You are special! *Not everybody reacts in the same way to a given ingredient, so pay attention to your body's response and adjust your diet accordingly.*

But if you avoid every ingredient that is a problem for some part of the population, you'll end up with nothing in your plate!

This is as close as it gets to the magic bullet!

- *For starters, all the cruciferous vegetables (cauliflower, Brussels sprouts, broccoli) possess a number of important qualities, not the least being cancer protection.*

- *Kale is one of the richest sources of vitamin K, which is the most commonly missing nutrient that is needed for the body manage calcium.*

- *Tomatoes are amongst the most lycopene-rich foods known, protecting against vascular disease. Even though it is a fruit, its sugar content is trivial in light of its nutrient richness (potassium and a broad range of carotenoids).*

- *With leeks and garlic, the allium family is also well represented in this recipe.*

1. Preparation:
   - Discard the cauliflower stems and cut the florets into bite-sized pieces.
   - Clean, trim and mince the leek.
   - Mince the garlic.
   - Discard the stems of the kale and coarsely chop the leaves.
   - Half the tomatoes through the stem.

2. Place the cauliflower in a pot and cover with water. Place over medium-high heat; bring to a boil, reduce to a simmer and cook for 10 - 15 minutes or until the florets are soft. Drain the cauliflower, return to the pot and mash coarsely with a fork or potato masher.

3. Heat the oil and butter in a large skillet over medium-high heat. Add the leeks and garlic and sauté until soft, without browning, about 3 minutes. Add the chopped kale, tomatoes and a pinch of salt, and sauté on medium-low heat until tender, about 5 – 7 minutes.

4. Add the sautéed leeks, kale and tomatoes to the mashed cauliflower and gently fold to combine. Season to taste with kosher salt and freshly ground black pepper.

Curried Cauliflower with Walnuts

Serves 4 ~ ⧖

- 1 medium head of cauliflower
- 2 onions
- 3 cloves garlic
- ½ cup toasted walnuts
- 2 tablespoons flat-leaf parsley
- 2 tablespoons unsalted butter
- 1 tablespoon turmeric
- 1 tablespoon ground cumin
- 1 pinch of red pepper flakes
- 1 pinch of salt
- ¼ cup chicken broth

The flavors in the dish (turmeric, cumin and crushed red pepper) can be adjusted to suit individual tastes. These spices add not only interest to the dish, but also nutritional value.

Somewhat similar in looks, pecans and walnuts are distinct nuts with different properties. Pecans are a little sweeter than walnuts; walnuts are slightly more bitter.

pecans

walnuts

Sulforaphanes

The nutritional property common to all cruciferous vegetables is that they contain sulforaphanes, which have many beneficial properties: in particular, they protect against UV radiation, contribute to joint health and help the immune system fight cancer.

Cauliflower is one of the many members of the cruciferous family. It is an example of non-colorful, but nevertheless nutrient-rich vegetable. Although it is in the same family as the blue-red "cyans," its sulforaphane is colorless.

In alternative medicine, cauliflower is believed to be goitrogenic, but so far there is no strong substantiation to the claim.

1. Cut the cauliflower florets into bite-sized pieces (discard the stem). Steam the florets for 3 minutes.

2. Peel and cut the onions into ½-inch dice. Peel and mince the garlic. Coarsely chop the walnuts. Finely mince the parsley.

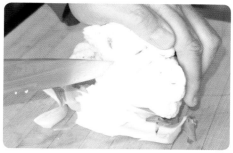

3. Heat the butter in a large skillet over medium heat until frothy. Add the onion and garlic and sauté until just tender, about 2 minutes.

4. Sprinkle in the turmeric, cumin, pepper flakes and salt. Stir to coat the onions and brown them slightly. Add the chicken broth to form a sauce, stirring until all the ingredients are incorporated. Cover and cook on low heat for 10 minutes.

5. Add the florets to the sauce and stir to coat. Cover and cook for 5 minutes or until the cauliflower is soft.

6. Uncover, raise the heat to high and cook for another few minutes to reduce and thicken the sauce. Add the walnuts and parsley.

Adjust seasoning and serve immediately.

Brussels Sprouts with Pecans

Serves 4 to 6 ~ ⏳

- 2 lb Brussels sprouts
- 2 tablespoons oil
- 4 shallots, thinly sliced
- 2 cloves garlic, minced
- 6 sprigs fresh thyme
- ½ cup dry white wine
- Juice and zest of 1 lemon
- ½ cup pecan halves, toasted

Brussels sprouts are mini cabbages available from September through March, but they are best in the early winter after the first frost. When choosing Brussels sprouts, look for very small, bright green, compact heads. Buy the sprouts fresh and use them within a few days, or they will develop a strong, unpleasant flavor.

⚠ Supplements

Focusing on individual nutrients leads to the temptation of using supplements, generally speaking a bad idea. An example:

Lycopene: *It was observed that men who eat a lot of tomato sauce are less prone to prostate cancer. Since tomatoes are rich in lycopene, the idea emerged that lycopene prevents prostate cancer. But in fact, a well executed study found that taking lycopene[*] supplements increased the frequency and severity of the disease.*

Supplementing with an isolated nutrient resulted in a worsening of the disease.

Whole real food is protective!

At this point, it is known that some foods protect against diseases, but why and how is still a mystery.

*The **Brussels sprouts**' bitterness is caused by the sulphur compounds common to the Brassica family, the most notable being sulforaphane.*

It is speculated that plants use these strong chemicals to repeal predators. (Note that salt helps counteract the bitterness.)

The fresher Brussels sprouts tend to be milder and consequently contain fewer sulforaphanes! You decide...

Although Brussels sprouts are high in vitamin A and C, and a good source of iron, don't focus on the individual vitamin and mineral contents of each food, as great as they may be, because this detracts from the fact that nutrients work together. Food comes with matrices of nutrients, and they need each other to be useful.

1. Wash the Brussels sprouts, discard the outer leaves if necessary, trim and quarter the sprouts.

2. In a medium sauté pan, heat the oil over medium heat. Add the sliced shallots and minced garlic. Sauté until softened, about 3 minutes.

3. Add the Brussels sprouts and thyme. Stir to combine. Add the white wine, cover, reduce the heat and simmer for 15 minutes, or until the sprouts are tender, but still have a bite (most of the liquid should have evaporated).

4. Season with salt and freshly ground black pepper. Add the lemon zest and fresh lemon juice to taste. Allow to cool slightly.

5. Add the toasted pecans, toss well and serve.

NOTE

For those who find the smell of Brussels sprouts offensive, it helps to blanch the sprouts by plunging them in boiling water for 3 minutes before sautéing.

Shallots are members of the allium family. Use them to add variety to your diet: their nutrients, in particular flavonoids, are different from those in other members of the family such as onions.

Drying onions in Dogon country, Mali.

Get to Know Your Leafy Greens

Leafy greens are grown mostly for their edible leaves, although the stems are often good too. Apart from salad leaves, leafy greens are all cruciferous plants. (Salad greens are not in the same family and not in the same league for nutrient density.)

Preparing leafy greens

To enjoy your leafy green as much as they deserve, vary the components, combinations and techniques.

Here are some keys to cooking them with confidence:

1. Use a variety of moist-heat cooking methods:

   Blanch - Plunge briefly into boiling water then drain; a good indicator is when the colors have brightened up).

   Steam - This helps to retain the water-soluble nutrients by not diluting them. Use very little water.

   Sauté - This gives flavor, especially if adding other flavorful ingredients such as onion, garlic, etc.

   Braise - Sauté in fat, then simmer in a small amount of liquid. Serve the liquid too, it contains the nutrients.

2. Include a full spectrum of greens. Start out with the more neutral, mild-tasting ones. They will balance the stronger flavors of the others.

3. Use base flavoring to add dimension or mute strong flavors: extra-virgin oils, butter, garlic, shallots and onions. Use seasonings to create depth and full flavors, experiment with various salts. Use acidity to mute the bitterness: citrus juice, zest, vinegar, tomato, wine. Add spices for a pleasant finish: black pepper, red pepper flakes, dried chiles, cayenne pepper, curry, hot smoked paprika.

   Check *Dark Green Threads** for a basic greens recipe and see how oil, garlic, shallot, lemon, salt and pepper are combined.

4. Use mushrooms to provide umami or earthy flavors: crimini, shiitake, chanterelle, oyster and other wild varieties.

   See *Wilted Greens with Mushrooms** recipe.

5. Incorporate toasted nuts and seeds for added nutritional value and texture: almonds, whole or slivered, walnuts, pumpkin seeds, sunflower seeds, pistachio.

   See *Curried Broccoli Soup**.

6. Incorporate hard cheeses: Parmesan, asiago, dry jack, manchego for finish and mouth feel.

   For example *Creamed Bitter Greens**.

7. Incorporate greens in egg dishes: into omelettes and scrambles, or as a bed for poached eggs.

   See *Frittata**.

8. Incorporate greens into soups, stews, casseroles, vegetable side dishes or classic dishes:

   *Acorn Squash Soup with Greens**, *Shepherd's Pie with Cauliflower**, *Roasted Chicken with Herbs**.

Invent your own recipe!

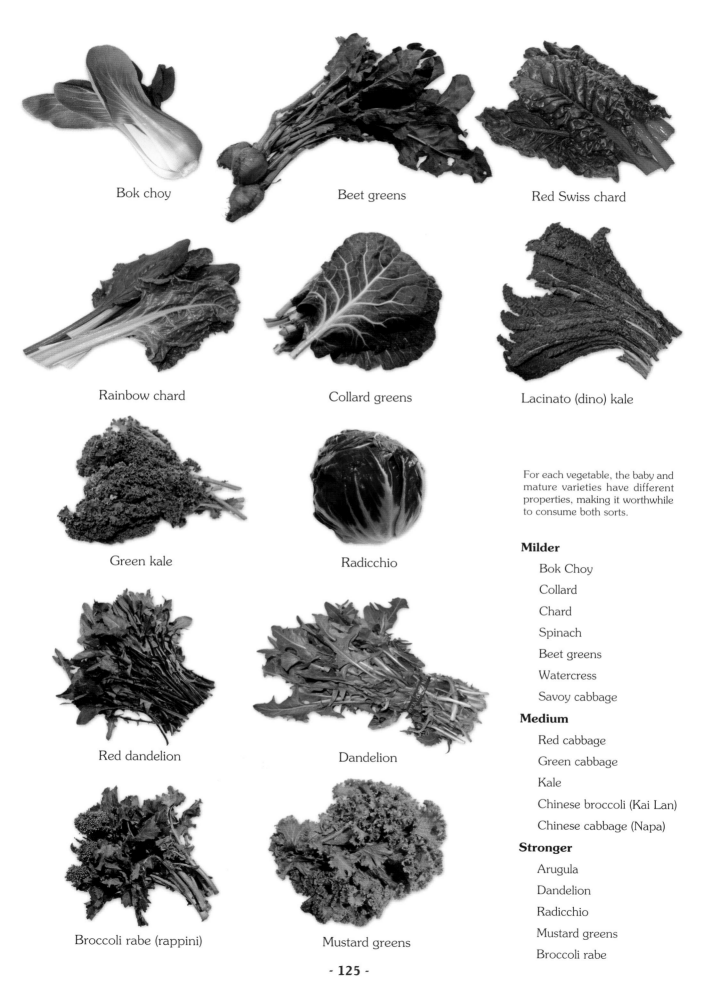

Bok choy

Beet greens

Red Swiss chard

Rainbow chard

Collard greens

Lacinato (dino) kale

Green kale

Radicchio

For each vegetable, the baby and mature varieties have different properties, making it worthwhile to consume both sorts.

Milder

Bok Choy

Collard

Chard

Spinach

Beet greens

Watercress

Savoy cabbage

Medium

Red cabbage

Green cabbage

Kale

Chinese broccoli (Kai Lan)

Chinese cabbage (Napa)

Stronger

Arugula

Dandelion

Radicchio

Mustard greens

Broccoli rabe

Red dandelion

Dandelion

Broccoli rabe (rappini)

Mustard greens

Kale Chips

These crispy treats are not as crunchy as potato chips, but they are every bit as addictive and incomparably healthier, guaranteed!

A word of advice: these are in fact so addictive that you will be tempted to eat kale exclusively in this form. This would be a mistake, given the other numerous delicious ways to enjoy kale.

This recipe works with any type of kale: regular, lacinato, green...

Serves 4 ~ ⧖

- 1 bunch kale
- 2 tablespoons oil
- 1 tablespoon tahini (optional)

Easy to remember

Kale is a great source of **vitamin K**, one of best vitamins for helping the body deal with calcium.

In fact, for vitamin K, nothing is in the same league as Kale, not even close. The other dark leafy greens have ⅓ or at most ⅔ the amount. Collards come closest.

People with low vitamin K tend to have a lot of ectopic calcium, that is, deposition of calcium outside of the bones, where it doesn't belong, for example in the heart valves and the arteries.

⚠️ **Achieve your culinary goals with the lowest possible cooking temperature.**

Baking at 300 °F preserves the nutrients (vitamin K and "cyans") in kale.

Baking at 350 °F instead of 300 °F would decrease (but not destroy) the nutrient value of kale. The lower the temperature, the better: 300 °F works well for almost everything, 350 °F less so.

Below: green kale works well for chips too. It has very curly leaves and a hard, round stem.

Above: lacinato kale (also called dino kale) has dark bluish elongated leaves with a texture reminiscent of bubbles.

1. Preheat oven to 300 °F. Wash and carefully dry the kale.

2. Cut into chip-sized pieces. Optionally remove the hard central stem.

3. Toss with the oil and optionally the tahini, refraining from adding too much tahini: this would prevent the chips from becoming crispy.

4. Line two baking trays with parchment paper. Spread the kale chips.

5. Place in the oven. Bake for 25 minutes total or until crisp, switching upper and lower tray halfway through.

Sprinkle with salt and serve. To keep, store in an airtight container.

Getting Organized

Real food is more time consuming and costly than many of us would like.

To save some trouble with buying all these bulky vegetables, you could get them delivered from a local organic farm.

Remember that organic doesn't always equal nutritious: check the growers' credentials and verify that their agricultural practices are sound. Make sure you can select what's delivered to you.

Prepare in bulk - Fill the sink with water, wash the vegetables really well several times; dry them; cut them up and pack them in plastic bags so they are ready to use. (That will also save space in your refrigerator.)

You can quickly blanch cauliflower, green beans, broccoli, Brussels sprouts, etc. They keep better, and they will be ready for sautéing or any further preparation: cooking the next meal should only take minutes.

Wednesday's crop - Before...

... and after.

Dark Green Threads

This very basic preparation can be used with any leafy greens: chard of any color, kale of any type and collards are our favorite.

Once you start using it, you'll never stop! Dark leafy greens complement any meat or fish dish; they can accompany the eggs in your morning omelets 3 or 4 times a week; or just stand by themselves as a side dish.

The acidity of the lemon juice attenuates the bitterness of the threads.

You can even use salad leaves for this type of cooking: wilted salad, such as romaine, has a good mineral content. Compared to the heavier ones, the lighter leafy greens have much less protein efficiency, though. Their color content ("cyans," etc.) is also less.

Serves 4 ~ ⏳

- 2 bunches assorted leafy greens
- 2 tablespoons oil
- 2 cloves garlic, minced
- 2 shallots, minced
- 1 lemon

⚠ Organic vs. Nutrient-Rich

The more nutrient-rich and less contaminated the soils, the healthier the food produced on these soils.

The label "organic" doesn't mean "nutrient-rich": it just suggests "less contaminated."

For example, hydroponic vegetables, grown in water with nutrients added, are a very poor source of nutrients because of the unavoidable limitation of adding ingredients.

*This is another argument to **buy locally**: find out where and how your food is grown, possibly get to know the farmer!*

Crop and weed rotation, fallow and weed cycles help maintain the richness of the soil, since different plants draw nutrients at different depths.

1. Wash and dry the greens well. Separate the stalks from the leaves.

2. Roll the trimmed greens together and cut into ½-inch strips.

3. In a large saucepan, heat the oil over medium heat. Add the minced garlic and shallots and sauté until soft.

4. Add the green strips and toss continuously until softened. Season with salt and freshly ground pepper.

Serve with a squeeze of fresh lemon juice.

NOTE

Instead of discarding the stalks, especially when they are as gorgeously colored as in this rainbow chard, dice them and sauté with the garlic and shallots until soft, before adding the green threads.

Plants can be consumed in baby or mature form.

Both are useful and have different properties.

An important feature is the texture, crunchiness or mellowness: vegetables at various stages of maturity offer a different mouth feel experience.

This may seem minor, but this kind of variety influences the pleasure we derive from food.

Their nutrition value is also different: the younger forms are usually less fibrous and have better nutrient value for a given volume. More mature vegetables are more filling and contribute to satiety better.

Stem & leaf

In France, people tend to eat the stems of leafy greens such as chard and discard the leaves! In the U.S., it is the opposite.

In reality, stem and leaf both have nutritional value.

- *The leaves contain the sulforaphanes.*

- *The stems have unique nutrients that are not present in the leaf. Don't discard them: they are tasty and crunchy!*

Discard only the stems that are too tough, such as in some types of kale.

Creamed Bitter Greens

This recipe builds on the Dark Green Threads* preparation, the Béchamel sauce adding a layer of sophistication. You can use this technique with almost any vegetables: cauliflower, zucchini, broccoli...

This festive dish, suitable for all occasions, can be prepared in large amounts to be shared with family and friends! It has so much going for it:

- Calcium from the dairy and the leafy greens.
- Vitamin D (added in almost all milk supplied in the U.S.).
- Vitamin K from the greens.
- Dairy fat from the cheese, milk and butter.

Calcium

When it comes to nutrition, calcium[*] is at the top of people's concerns: the best known property of calcium is its long term effect on our bones and its role in fighting osteoporosis. But in fact, calcium is important for many other reasons: in the short term, it is necessary for muscle contraction, nerve function and more.

Sources of calcium include leafy greens and even meat. However calcium in the dairy is the most easily absorbed in our body, so dairy is an important source of calcium.

Vitamin D and K are needed for calcium to be used properly by our bodies.

⚠ The way nutrients are absorbed depends on which other nutrients are present in your body: for example, if you lack vitamin D, you can drink all the milk you want, you will not absorb calcium. (Hence the vitamin D fortified milk.)

Serves 4 ~ ⧖ ⧖

- 1 bunch leafy greens (kale, chard, mustard, collard)
- 1 tablespoon oil
- 1 clove garlic, minced
- 1 shallot, minced
- ¼ cup grated Parmesan Cheese or 3 oz shredded Swiss cheese

Béchamel Sauce:

- 1 oz unsalted butter
- 1 heaping tablespoon flour
- 2 cups whole milk

Béchamel is a pleasant way to inject some dairy into our diet. Whole milk is preferred over skim milk. What would be the point anyway, with all the butter and cheese in the recipe? Fats are good for you!

No food is forbidden!

If you need a tablespoon of flour to prepare a sauce that turns a plain preparation into a very special one, go ahead!

The benefits of a good tasting, healthful dish will prevail. Don't be afraid of any ingredient, but be aware of what you are feeding your family!

Greens

1. Preheat oven to 300 °F.

2. Wash the greens and dry well. Remove the stalks, roll the trimmed leaves together and cut into ½-inch strips, in the same way used for the Dark Green Threads*.

3. In a large saucepan, warm the oil over medium heat. Add the minced garlic and shallots and sauté until soft. Add the green strips and toss well. Cover and allow to steam until wilted and softened. Season with salt and pepper, remove from heat and set aside.

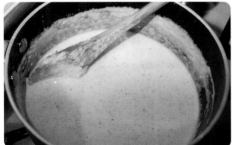

Béchamel Sauce

4. Melt the butter in a saucepan over medium-high heat. When the butter has become frothy, add the flour and quickly blend with the butter. Stirring constantly, allow the mixture to cook for two minutes or so.

5. Slowly begin adding the milk: the mixture will thicken at first, but will thin again as the remaining milk is poured in. Continue to stir until the mixture thickens, then turn off (as soon as a bubble is seen). Stir in half the cheese, season to taste, remove from the heat.

Finish

6. Mix the greens with the sauce until well combined and evenly distributed. Place in a baking dish. Top with the other half of the cheese.

7. Bake for 30 minutes or until bubbly. At the end, if necessary, turn on the broiler for a few minutes to give a golden brown finish to the top.

Serve very hot!

Mustard Greens

Bitterness is usually a defense mechanism, making the plant noxious to its predators (snails, birds and other animals): view it as nature providing protection to something valuable, the way thorns protect roses.

These substances, toxic in principle, are valuable to us because, by a similar mechanism, they protect us against our own predators[*].

The leaves of the mustard plant are popular in the American South, second only to collard greens. Mustard greens are members of the cruciferous dark leafy greens family.

Usually served as a side dish, they are best when accompanying roasted meats, particularly chicken and pork. When selecting greens, look for crisp young leaves with a rich green color.

Mustard greens, because of their initial bitterness, can be off putting until you appreciate that the bitterness blends so nicely with other ingredients, such as vinegar and nuts. Acidity, fat and other flavors help dampen the bitterness too.

Bitterness can be the promise of a special nutritional value. The art of the cook is to blend the strong flavors and make them pleasing to the palate.

Serves 4 ~ ⧗ ⧗

Greens:

- 1 bunch mustard greens
- ½ cup pistachio nuts, toasted
- 2 tablespoons extra-virgin oil
- 1 medium onion, peeled and diced into ½-inch pieces
- 3 cloves garlic, minced
- 1 teaspoon whole cumin seeds
- 1 pinch of red pepper flakes

Cumin Vinaigrette:

- 2 tablespoons extra-virgin oil
- 1 tablespoon balsamic vinegar
- 1 teaspoon Dijon mustard
- 1 teaspoon ground cumin

The brighter color of the cooked broccoli on the left is a reminder that cooking helps liberate the nutrients from the fibers.

1. Wash the mustard greens, discard the ribs; coarsely chop the leaves into bite-sized pieces.

   Coarsely chop the toasted pistachio nuts.

2. Heat the oil over medium heat in a skillet. Add the onions and sauté until soft, about 5 minutes. Add the garlic, cumin seeds and red pepper flakes. Sauté for another 2 minutes.

3. Fold in the greens in batches using a pair of tongs, until all are incorporated. Reduce the heat to medium-low, cover and cook, stirring occasionally, until the greens are very tender, about 15 minutes.

4. Meanwhile, mix all the ingredients for the vinaigrette. When the greens are done to your liking, incorporate the vinaigrette. Taste and adjust seasoning. Sprinkle with the pistachio nuts and serve warm.

⚠ *Enjoy the whole universe of nutrients that's out there, instead of twelve tablets of vitamins... Studies show that supplements[*] are useless at best, harmful a lot of the time.*

Serendipity

Vitamin K *decreases ectopic (outside of where it should be) calcium, one of the important factors in the hardening of the arteries.*

However, too much vitamin K creates a hypercoagulating state, one of the numerous reasons why you don't want to take supplements.

Fortunately, many foods that are rich in vitamin K also contain **vitamin A**, *whose anticoagulant property helps counterbalance the effect of vitamin K.*

Asian Cabbage Stir Fry

Although they are two distinct varieties, bok choy and Napa cabbage are both referred to as "Chinese cabbage." They are members of the dark leafy greens family and as such, rich in sulforaphanes.

One of the mildest leafy greens, Bok choy is under-used in Western cuisine. Also known as "Chinese white cabbage," it doesn't look like a cabbage at all, with its leaves attached in a cluster. It is a versatile vegetable, one of the milder tasting in the dark leafy green family. Choose bunches with firm, white stalks topped with dark green leaves.

Bok choy should be refrigerated and used within a day or two of purchase. It is available year-round in most supermarkets.

Napa cabbage is more similar to the traditional cabbage, but its shape is cylindrical instead of spherical.

Serves 4 to 6 ~ ⏳

- 2 cloves garlic
- Fresh ginger, about a 1-inch piece
- 2 medium heads of bok choy or 4 baby bok choy, coarsely chopped
- ½ head of Napa cabbage, shredded
- ¼ cup pure oil
- 1 teaspoon red pepper flakes
- 1 teaspoon soy sauce
- 1 tablespoon sesame seeds, toasted

Vitamins

Focusing on vitamins or any other specific list of nutrients is restrictive and fails to see the complexity of what's behind.

FDA and the National Academy of Sciences define "vitamins" as substances whose absence is associated with immediate disease. The list of vitamins hasn't been updated for decades.

Vitamins[*] are linked with short term disease and don't take into account nutrient deficiencies with long term consequences.

1. Peel and mince the garlic. Peel and cut the ginger into the thinnest possible threads.

2. Chop the bok choy, shred the cabbage.

3. Heat the oil in a wok over high heat. Add the red pepper flakes, garlic and ginger, and cook until fragrant, about 30 seconds.

4. Add the chopped bok choy and sauté until the stalks have softened, 3 to 4 minutes.

5. Add the shredded cabbage, sauté until softened and lightly browned, another 3 to 4 minutes.

6. Season with the soy sauce and cook for 1 minute more.

Remove to a serving platter, top with toasted sesame seeds and serve immediately.

Elements & Minerals

Chemical elements are substances made of a single type of atom. Dietary "minerals" such as iron, calcium, potassium, are in fact elements involved in our metabolism. In the context of nutrition, the terms "elements" and "minerals" are used indifferently.

Some elements play a key role in the chemical reactions that sustain our life: for example, hemoglobin requires iron; muscle contraction needs calcium and magnesium; potassium and sodium are essential for cell function; potassium is essential for cardiac conduction and sequencing.

The elements required are too many to list. The good news is that most of them are found in the nutrient-dense vegetables; nuts and seeds provide the rest, the rare ones.

***Nuts and seeds** are the most convenient and ubiquitous food. They can be anything, from the protein in the stir fry to a simple snack...*

They are a particularly good source of rarer minerals, essential fatty acids and shorter chain saturated fats, which can cross the blood-brain barrier and contribute to brain health.

Wilted Greens with Mushrooms

Serves 4 to 6 ~ ⧗ ⧗

- ½ lb shiitake mushrooms
- 1 small onion
- 3 cloves garlic
- ¼ cup toasted walnuts
- ¼ cup extra-virgin oil, divided
- 4 cups (about 2 bunches) leafy greens: Swiss chard, green, red or Tuscan kale, collard greens
- 2 cups baby or curly spinach
- 1 pinch of crushed red pepper flakes
- 2 tablespoons vinegar (Balsamic or sweet Muscat)

Salt comes either from the sea or from mines.

- *American table salt* is mined, then purified. Nowadays, iodine is added in an attempt to compensate for its deficiency in mined salt, thus the *iodized table salt*.

- *Sea salt* is probably better than mined salt in terms of mineral-richness. Paradoxically, if it is not reinforced, it might contain less iodine than iodized table salt.

- *Kosher salt* is sea salt that is harvested and processed according to kosher dietary laws. It is more neutral in flavor than sea salt and more broadly rich in minerals (except for iodine) than iodized table salt. It can be considered the middle way between the other two.

As with everything else, it is not a bad idea to vary your salts.

Mushrooms should be a regular part of your diet, not an exotic ingredient!

Almost all mushrooms offer a nice spectrum of uncommon minerals (manganese, selenium and potassium), so they are a nice opportunity to enrich your minerals without emphasizing the sodium. Potassium, in particular, is a very healthy element that is not present in much of our food.

1. Remove and discard the mushroom stems, cut the caps into ½-inch strips; peel and thinly slice the onion; peel and mince the garlic; coarsely chop the walnuts.

3. Wash and dry the greens well. Remove the ribs and stems and discard. Hand-tear or cut the greens into 1-inch wide pieces. Leave the spinach leaves whole.

4. In a large skillet or wok, heat the remaining oil over medium-high heat. Add the sliced onion and sauté until soft, one minute or so. Add the garlic and red pepper flakes and sauté until fragrant, about 30 seconds.

Remove greens to a serving dish, top with the roasted mushrooms and chopped walnuts. Serve immediately.

2. **Roast the mushrooms:** preheat oven to 350 °F; spread the sliced mushrooms evenly on a pan; using a pastry brush, lightly dab the mushrooms with oil and season lightly with salt and pepper. Roast in the oven for 10 – 12 minutes, or until mushrooms are browned and slightly crisp, but still tender. Remove from oven and set aside.

5. Add the cut greens. Using tongs, toss the greens with the onion and garlic, drawing them up from the bottom until lightly coated with the oil. Reduce the heat to medium and continue to turn the greens until soft, 2 to 3 minutes.

6. Fold in the spinach. Sprinkle the greens with the vinegar and season with salt and freshly ground black pepper.

Iodine

Kosher salt is not as rich in iodine as reinforced iodized table salt.

Iodine gets attention these days because of the epidemic of thyroid failure linked to iodine deficiency (although the deficiency might have other causes than dietary: fluoride could be a culprit by displacing the iodine).

Oddly, some sea salts are labeled as "not supplying iodine" since they don't meet the required pharmacological level for iodine.

Main Courses

Good Habits

Have your largest meals early in the day: eat *before* physical activity, *not after*.

Eat at regular intervals. Do not skip meals. Do not "graze" between meals.

Vary your food as much as possible to benefit from the widest range of nutrients.

The ideal plate consists of:

- ¼ proteins
- ¾ vegetables (proportions in weight)
- Enough fats for taste and satiety

Don't pick and choose from multiple diets: if you are going to eat fat, you must adhere to all the other principles presented in this book.

Sourcing

Organic Food

Our body is able to detoxify our food up to a certain extent: this is mainly the job of the liver. However, it cannot deal with overwhelming concentrations of toxins. In addition, there are contaminants that the liver cannot eliminate.

If you can avoid it, why take a chance and eat pesticides? If you cannot get everything organic, focus on the ingredients that have the highest potential for concentrated toxins:

- **Root vegetables** (carrots, beets, turnips, radishes) are efficient at extracting anything, nutrients and contaminants, from the soil. This is why they are so richly colored.
- **Berries** hyper concentrate anything present in the soil, including contaminants.
- **Dairy products**: cows are pretty good at filtering pesticides but not the other chemicals such as growth hormones and antibiotics; in fact, those are more concentrated in the milk than in the blood of the cow.
- **Some fruits** can be peeled, but you have to go quite deep to eliminate contaminants. Since a lot of the nutrients are in the peel, they are lost.

Looking at organic[*] food through the lens of old school nutrition, which doesn't pay much attention to micronutrients beyond a limited list of vitamins, one might conclude that "organic" is not worth the price difference. And this may well be true in some cases.

However, the fact is that most organic food tastes better than conventional food: taste reveals the richness in nutrients.

Beware that the definition of "organic agriculture" varies from place to place. The label "organic" is by no means an absolute guarantee.

Agricultural practices

Food grown with care is nutritionally richer and tastes better. Being organic is part of it, but it is not the whole story.

Other farming practices determine how rich the soil is, which in turn determines the quality and quantity of nutrients the plants can extract:

- Crop rotation (planting different crops in specific sequences on a given field) promotes soil fertility, nutrient richness and natural pest control.
- Companion planting (growing mutually beneficial crops close to one another) promotes biodiversity.
- Diversity (farms with a varied mix of crops) supports beneficial organisms that assist in pollination and pest management.
- Many common practices have undesirable effects. For example, fumigation and irradiation kill some of the biological activity of the food and bugs (we need them).

This is another argument for buying local ingredients, since it offers an opportunity to know your farmers and their growing practices.

GMOs

While consuming small amounts of GMOs doesn't present a biological danger to us, generalizing this agricultural practice carries serious implications:

- At our body's level, this means eating unnatural ingredients that change much faster than we can adapt.
- The technology involved in GMOs is such that the seeds come from a very limited number of sources. This impoverishes the variety of nutrients. GMOs accelerate a trend that started with agriculture, the on-going selection taking away vitality from the food.
- At the environmental level, the impacts are huge. Plants are selected for some kind of resistance. This affects the ecosystem with unforeseeable consequences.
- At a society level, GMOs affect local farming and local nutritional practices.

Proteins

If you work with the simplified model of nutrition that emphasizes macronutrients and calorie count, you ignore the thousands of useful micronutrients that are associated with proteins. The only way to access them is to eat the whole animal or vegetable at different stages of maturity.

Protein quality

The proteins we eat must bring us the essential amino acids that our body requires to function. But even more important is the context in which the protein exists: consider protein as a whole real food rather than individual amino acids.

In that respect, the modern American diet, by focusing on muscle as the meat of choice is missing out a lot:

- **Fats**
  A deboned, skinless chicken breast has very little fat and does not bring the much needed fatty acids.

- **Bones**
  Even if you don't chew on them, minerals from the bones leach into the food during the cooking. Bone marrow is a sulphur donor. (Sulphur is good for our ligaments, tendons, joints.)

- **Skin**
  The skin has great nutritional value. It is also a good sulphur donor: since sulphur is often present in a bound state that is not usable, foods that contain bioavailable sulphur are precious.

  Ceramides and collagens contribute to the plumpness and health of the animal's skin and ours.

- **Liver and organs**
  Kidney, gizzards, tripe, stomach, heart are all good.

  While it is the detoxifying site, liver is not the storage site for toxins: liver is healthy and nutritious since it is a distribution site for many micronutrients and minerals, including iron and B12.

Fat quality in meat

Protein almost always comes with fat: to be healthy, these fats must provide a wide range of essential fatty acids.

For that purpose, wild animals are superior: an active animal, employing its natural metabolism produces more essential fats.

The health of the animal is also crucial: healthy animals produce a well balanced combination of omega-3 and omega-6 fats, while sick animals overwhelmingly produce omega-6, as a response to inflammation.

Free living animals are always healthier due to their food source and activity level. The old American Indian view that "a healthy animal is healthy food" is definitely true!

Organ meat should be occasionally part of the diet, to provide some micronutrients that it contains in a uniquely dense way.

The exception is the lymphatic system, which is a garbage collector and should be avoided: cheap ground meat and some types of sausage might include it.

The main complaint about organs is their high density in purines. People suffering from gout have trouble clearing the uric acid resulting from the break down of purines.

However, the majority of people who have gout[*] are also insulin resistant. For these people, diminishing the insulogenic part of their diet reduces the gout symptoms.

Protein ideas

Our protein supply must be rich in healthy fats, fat soluble vitamins and a wide spectrum of minerals. This goes a long way to repletion.

- **Nuts and seeds:** think of them as protein too!

- **Dairy food:** all the cheeses, goat, cow and sheep; butter, cream, yogurt, farmer's cheese...

- **Eggs:** for vegetarians they are the unique natural source of vitamin B12, and for everybody they provide an incredibly efficient protein.

- **Beef, lamb, pork:** of all the traditional meats, lamb is the most likely to be grass-fed these days. Paradoxically, pork tends to be too lean nowadays.

- **Fish and seafood:** pay attention to where they come from!

- **Venison:** good because wild. Even though venison is often raised now and thus loses some of its benefits, raised venison is still "wilder" than traditional farmed meat because that kind of animal cannot be cooped up as much.

- **Fowl:** quail, pheasant, Cornish hen, pigeon... Wild fowl is in general healthier than chicken.

- **Exotic meats** such as ostrich, goat, bison, buffalo, for variety.

Cholesterol

We wholeheartedly adhere to the new U.S. Government health recommendation stating that dietary cholesterol[*] is harmless.

The cholesterol in our food is irrelevant: when choosing food, don't even consider its cholesterol contents.

The beef controversy

The main argument against beef is that raising cattle is wasteful: farming can produce a lot more food per acre of land than ranching, and, in theory, with less pollution.

While this might be true, keep in mind that nutrition is not all about calories: grass-fed beef[*] brings essential nutrients that you cannot get from vegetal sources, no matter how much grain you consume.

The way beef is raised in general is far from perfect, but when assessing the efficiency of land usage, we also must take into account the nutritional value of the food produced.

We need a better way to measure efficiency than just calories. This said, it wouldn't hurt, in most affluent countries, to reduce the per-capita consumption of beef: you don't need a large amount to get the benefits, and you should vary your proteins.

Grilled Steak with Sauces

This preparation is a classic: although grilling a steak may look like the simplest thing, doing so properly requires technique. The crosshatch markings bring texture and allow flavors to develop without overcooking or burning the meat. Tasty distinctive sauces complement the steaks and lend a professional finish to the dish.

Use the best steaks you can find, grass-fed if possible. Prepare the sauce while the steaks are grilling.

This method requires four turns and one to two minutes between each turn to evenly cook the steaks and create the proper crosshatch. Keep in mind that the thinner the steaks, the less time between turns. You might need to experiment until you find the cooking time that's perfect for your taste.

⚠ Don't trim too much

Trim to taste, but there is no reason to fear the fat! Grass-fed, grass-finished animals contain healthy fats with a high ratio of long-chain ω-3 and very few trans[*] fats.

Grass-fed meat is expensive, but you don't need large portions: 3 to 4 oz per person is adequate, accompanied with sauce and a lot of vegetables.

Since grass-fed meat tends to be leaner and drier, it is important not to overcook it. In addition, overcooking decreases the nutritional value of the ingredient by altering the molecules (fats, enzymes, proteins).

The danger of eating raw meat is overstated: not so long ago, it might have been a concern, but nowadays, in countries where food sourcing is closely monitored, there is not much risk.

Serves 4 ~ ⧖

- 4 grass-fed, grass-finished beef steaks
- 1 tablespoon oil or butter

Sauce:

- 4 tablespoons butter
- ¼ cup finely minced shallots
- 2 tablespoons minced parsley

   Blue Cheese Shallot Butter:
   - ½ cup crumbled blue cheese

   Or Red Wine Dijon Sauce:
   - 1 cup dry red wine
   - 1 tablespoon Dijon mustard

   Or Peppered Brandy Cream:
   - ¼ cup brandy or Cognac
   - 1 tablespoon Dijon mustard
   - ¼ cup heavy cream
   - 2 teaspoons drained green peppercorns
   - 1 teaspoon cracked black pepper

Heat a grill pan on high heat. Add the oil or butter. Season both sides of the steaks with salt and ground pepper.

1. Place steak at 10 o'clock diagonally across the grates of the pan; cook for 75 to 120 seconds.

2. Turn the steak over and place at 2 o'clock diagonally; cook for the same amount of time.

3. Turn over, placing at 2 o'clock again and cook for the same amount of time.

4. Do a final turn, place at 10 o'clock and cook for the same amount of time.

"Doneness" can be checked by reading the internal temperature with a meat thermometer:
140 °F for rare;   145 °F for medium rare;
150 °F for medium;   155 °F for medium-well.

Remove to a plate and cover loosely with foil. Allow to rest for at least 5 minutes before topping with a sauce and serving.

The sauces must be reduced and thickened to proper consistency, and each one has a different cooking time. In a skillet over medium heat, melt half the butter. Add the shallots and sauté until just soft, about two minutes. Then:

Blue Cheese Shallot Butter
Add the remaining butter, blue cheese, parsley and a pinch of salt and pepper. Combine and remove from heat immediately.

Red Wine Dijon Sauce
Pour in the wine, whisk in the mustard. Simmer for 5 minutes to reduce volume by half and thicken. Season with salt and pepper, add the parsley, whisk in the remaining butter. Remove from heat.

Peppered Brandy Cream Sauce
Add the brandy and ignite. Once the flames have died out, whisk in the mustard, heavy cream and peppercorns. Simmer for 5 minutes. Add a pinch of salt, the pepper and parsley. Whisk in the remaining butter. Reduce to a thickness that coats the back of a wooden spoon. Remove from heat.

Red meat - The bad reputation of red meat is mostly based on the outdated assumption that cholesterol and saturated fats are harmful. In fact, if sourced properly and eaten as part of a varied protein diet, red meat is completely safe. At time of writing, the studies linking red meat[*] to harm are all scientifically flawed, biased or with a hidden agenda.

Grilling meat - Eating only charred flesh is certainly not a good thing (for starters the fat is rancid, and the proteins are denatured). However, the only test[AMES] that established a link with cancer was flawed. If you rotate the preparation techniques as well as the proteins, grilling meat once in a while is not much of a concern.

Italian Meat Loaf

Polpettone

This Italian recipe comes from my friend Giacomo's mom, Annamaria.

You can vary the meats to your liking. For a change from red meat, turkey (thigh and breast) works well and is more delicate. Once in a while, add ground Italian sausage. And if you have overripe tomatoes, definitely use them!

This usually produces too much sauce but the left over sauce makes an excellent base for anything else.

You can also bake it like Dr. Mike does, in an open dish to allow the top to brown, for about 45 minutes.

Serves 6 ~ ⏳ ⏳

Meat Loaf:

- 1 lb ground beef, veal or turkey
- 1 lb ricotta
- ½ cup grated Parmesan cheese
- 1 egg
- ½ cup almond meal
- ¼ cup chopped flat parsley

Sauce:

- 2 lb canned crushed tomatoes
- 3 bay leaves
- 3 tablespoons olive oil

Did you know that...

Stearic acid, one of the dominant saturated fats in beef, is turned into oleic acid (the major component of olive oil) as soon as we digest it: eating stearic acid has the same effect as eating olive oil!

Grass-fed, grass-finished beef is higher in stearic acid than feedlot beef.

1. Mix all the ingredients for the meat loaf, first with a spoon then with your hands.

2. Pat the mixture into 2 loaves

3. In a non-stick pot, warm the oil on medium heat. Brown the meat loaves on all sides, 1 or 2 minutes per side.

4. Bring the crushed tomatoes to simmer, add the meat loaves and bay leaves, and simmer gently for about 1 hour, turning the loaves over once in a while (about 3 times total).

Adjust the seasoning with salt and pepper. Serve with green vegetables. Pour some sauce on top of the meat.

Frozen tomatoes are the best alternative to ripe, fresh ones, when not in season.

Canned tomatoes are easier to stock, but a concern:

- In the past, there was a significant risk of contamination, especially from lead and aluminium in the cans. This is less of a concern today since cans are made of biologically inert material, although this might not be the case with all imported cans.

- Another concern is BPA[*], a potentially toxic additive commonly used for lining the cans.

Keep in mind that canning involves heavy processing, thus destroying some nutrition. Tomatoes in **glass jars** or in **carton packaging** offer a safer alternative.

Roasted Chicken with Herbs

Eating the whole bird (skin, tendons, giblets, white and dark meat), is a tasty way to ensure a variety of nutrients.

If you can, why not take a "knife skills" class from a local chef? It is actually fun, believe it or not, and it will help turn a repeatedly frustrating fumbling experience into fun.

Serves 4 to 6 ~ ⧖

- 1 roasting chicken, about 4 lb
- ½ small onion, thinly sliced
- 4 cloves garlic, peeled
- ½ lemon, thinly sliced
- 6 sprigs fresh thyme
- 6 sprigs flat-leaf parsley
- Oil
- Trussing string

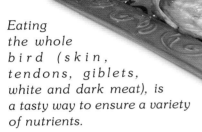

White vs. Dark Meat

The dark meat is fattier (this is a good thing) and richer in minerals. It contains more ligaments and tendons, more lecithin. It is nutritionally better than the white meat.

Absolutely eat the skin! It contains fats and collagen.

Some dedicated individuals even suck the marrow out of the bone! Bone marrow is a very nutrient-dense food, in particular for iron, magnesium, calcium and zinc.

The vegetables and aromatics used for the stuffing can be modified. For general sanitary reasons it is best to check the temperature of stuffing that was cooked in the bird if you are going to eat it. (Salmonella is not so common these days, but 150 °F kills it in any case.)

1. Preheat the oven to 375 °F. Remove the giblets from the cavity of the chicken, rinse the bird well inside and out, and pat dry with paper towels. Bruise the garlic by smashing it with the flat side of a chef's knife.

2. In a small bowl, combine the onion, garlic, lemon, thyme and parsley, and season with salt and freshly ground black pepper.

3. Press the mixture into the cavity of the chicken, fold the skin over to cover the opening, using a toothpick to secure.

4. Truss - Tuck the wings under the bird so that they don't burn in the oven.

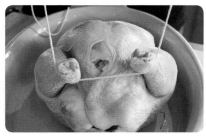

Loop the trussing string around the end of the drumsticks.

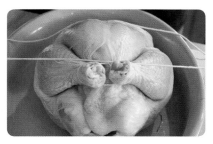

Pull the drumsticks close together.

Pull to the side and truss firmly, ensuring the legs and wings are tightly pressed against the body.

Pull under and tie at the opposite end of the chicken.

Rub the chicken lightly with oil and sprinkle with salt and freshly ground black pepper.

5. Roast - Place the chicken in a roasting pan, cover with foil and put into the preheated oven. The rack should be at lower third of oven. Roast for 45 minutes.

Remove the foil and roast for another 15 minutes or until the internal temperature taken at the thigh reads 160°F. Remove from the oven.

6. Carve - Cover with foil and let rest 15 minutes before carving. Place the chicken breast side up. Separate the whole legs by cutting straight through the joint where they attach to the body.

Find the joint that connects the thigh to the drumstick and cut straight down to make two pieces.

Separate the breasts, including the wing, using the breastbone as a guide.

Make 3 or 4 portions out of each breast by cutting at an angle.

Italian Meat Sauce

Ragù

This recipe illustrates the basic method for ground meat sauce:

- Sauté fragrant vegetables (onion, carrots, celery, garlic).
- Brown the ground meat (pork, beef, veal, lamb, turkey).
- Simmer in liquid (broth, wine, tomato in juice).

The famous "Ragù alla Bolognese" incorporates a ton of different meats: pork, veal, bacon, sausage... The recipe presented here is a simpler and lighter take on the Italian favorite, more adapted to modern times. Contrary to preconceived ideas, it doesn't include garlic.

Also contrary to established ideas, this is a delicate meat sauce with a light tomato flavoring, suitable for providing the meat portion of the meal, not just a little meat swimming in an ocean of sugary sauce.

Watch out: it takes an hour to cook, so don't get started at the last minute!

⚠ Ground meat

In spite of its versatility, it is preferable to not eat all your meat in ground form. Some nutrition literature suggest a decrease in nutritional value. In any case, it is certain that, since some components have been removed (in particular fat), the proportion of macronutrients in ground meat is artificial. Ground meat recruits less of the digestive system and is less of a whole food than a piece of steak (obviously).

Serves 4 to 6 ~ ⧖ ⧖

- 4 fresh tomatoes or 8-oz can stewed tomatoes
- 3 tablespoons olive oil, divided
- 1 small celery stalk
- 1 shallot or ½ onion
- 1 lb ground beef
- 1 carrot
- 1 bay leaf

1. Quarter and seed the tomatoes. Heat up ⅓ of the oil in a skillet, cook the tomatoes until the skin starts to come off. Peel them and chop them coarsely.

2. Finely dice the celery and shallot. Heat the remaining oil in a pot and sauté until translucent.

3. Add the meat, crumble it using the side of a wooden spoon. Let it brown for about 5 minutes (until you cannot see any pink). Add the tomatoes, grated carrot and bay leaf. Season with salt and pepper. Add water to cover.

4. Bring to the boil and simmer covered until the carrot and celery dissolve. (This might take up to 1 hour!) Take the lid off, adjust the seasoning and reduce the sauce to the desired consistency.

The result should be fairly thick, although you can keep it thinner if you intend to serve it with pasta. If you find it too dry, add a little oil.

Serve over any kind of vegetables, broiled, boiled or baked: summer squash, winter squash, cauliflower, etc.

It is especially nice as a "pasta" sauce for Spaghetti Squash*.

You can also layer it with eggplants for Moussaka*, or top it with mashed cauliflower as in the Shepherd's Pie with Cauliflower*.

Whenever possible, choose grass-fed, grass-finished meat.

- ***Grass-fed*** *beef is superior because it is a healthier animal. Cows were meant to eat grass, after all.*

- ***Grass-finishing*** *is equally important, to ensure that the animal was not ultimately fattened with grain.*

Moroccan Chicken Tagine

Serves 6 ~ ⏳ ⏳

- 2 lb chicken thighs
  or a whole chicken
- 1 large onion, minced
- 2 cloves garlic, minced
- ⅓ cup fresh cilantro, chopped
- ⅓ cup fresh flat-leaf parsley, chopped

Spices:

- 1 teaspoon ground ginger
- 1 teaspoon turmeric
- ¼ teaspoon saffron threads, crumbled
- ½ teaspoon ground black pepper
- ½ teaspoon salt

- ⅓ cup olive oil
- 1 cup green olives, pitted and halved
- 1 Preserved Lemon*
- 1 fresh lemon cut in 8

The word "tagine" designates a North African earthenware pot with a cone shaped lid, as well as the dishes that are cooked in it. The Moroccan tagine is a slow cooked stew, with several kinds of meats, vegetables, fruits and spices.

Chicken provides a whole range of amino acids and is a good protein in that respect. But if we look at overall meat quality, boneless, skinless chicken doesn't do so well, since it contains very little of the important fats and minerals.

Stealth Fat

Protein can be viewed as a "stealth fat delivery system," in the sense that it always comes with fat: since proteins naturally occur in a fatty environment, eating protein sneaks in fats at the same time.

To be considered of good quality, a meat must bring an abundance and variety of long-chain ω-3 and ω-6 essential fatty acids.

- 152 -

1. Cut the chicken meat into bite-sized pieces or larger, according to taste. Or use a whole chicken, cut into 8 or 12 larger pieces.

2. Combine the chicken, onion, garlic, cilantro, parsley and spices. Mix well. If time allows, marinate in the refrigerator for several hours or overnight.

3. Pour enough oil to coat the bottom of a tagine, Dutch oven or stockpot. Over medium-high heat, sauté the chicken and spice mixture until warmed through and fragrant, about 5 minutes.

4. Discard the flesh of the preserved lemon and mince the rind.

5. Add the olives, fresh lemon and preserved lemon rind. Drizzle the remaining oil all over. Pour in some water (almost to the level of the meat, but not so much that it would drown it), cover and bring to a boil over medium-high heat. Reduce to a low simmer and cook undisturbed for about an hour.

Once it's done, the tagine should yield a slightly thick sauce.

Optionally, put the flesh of the preserved lemon in the pot together with the minced rind.

Prefer the whole bird!

A whole chicken is slightly more trouble to deal with than boneless, skinless meat, but it is worth the effort. Eating only "nice," "clean" muscle meat restricts our access to nutrition. For instance:

- *A roasting chicken is a fatty bird. A deboned, skinless chicken breast is very lean and does not bring the much needed fatty acids.*

- *We benefit from the bone minerals that get into the cooking liquid.*

- *The skin of the chicken contains many beneficial compounds.*

Pan-Roasted Chicken with Greens

A good way to "roast" chicken, when you don't have a whole bird to cook.

You can accompany these chicken legs with just about anything.

Taste and Nutrition

The gamy taste (in the upper back part of the mouth, for those who possess that kind of sense) is in fact the taste of the healthy fats and nutrients in the animal.

Here is a simple illustration of this principle: sole is a mild tasting fish, salmon is tastier and better for you. The difference is in the amount of long-chain ω-3. To simplify, we can say that the healthy oils add the flavor. Along that line of thought, wild salmon is more flavorful and fatter than farmed salmon.

As a rule of thumb, if it's bland, it's useless. Unfortunately, as a culture we don't appreciate foods with strong flavors enough.

Serves 4 ~ ⏳

The Chicken:

- 4 whole skin-on chicken legs (drumsticks and thighs)
- 2 tablespoons oil
- 1 cup chicken stock

The Greens:

- 4 cups (2 bunches) leafy greens of your choice: Swiss chard, kale, collard greens...
- 2 tablespoons oil
- 1 small onion, cut into ¼-inch dice
- 3 cloves garlic, minced
- Pinch of crushed red pepper flakes
- 2 cups baby spinach

Rotate your proteins!

To ensure the widest range of nutrients, vary your sources of proteins as much as you can.

Pan-roasted chicken

1. Season the chicken legs with salt and freshly ground pepper.

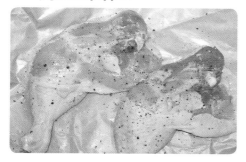

2. In a medium skillet with a tight-fitting lid, heat the oil over medium-high heat. Place the chicken legs skin-side down and sear 4 to 6 minutes, or until golden brown. Turn the meat over and sear the other side.

3. Pour the broth into the pan to a height of about ½ inch (do not cover the meat). Cover the pan, reduce the heat and simmer for 15 minutes or until the meat is cooked (it should be firm to the touch). Remove to a plate and cover to keep warm. Reserve any liquid remaining in the pan.

Greens

4. Wash the greens, discard the ribs. Cut the leaves into 2-inch wide pieces.

5. Heat the oil over medium-high heat. Add the onion, garlic and pepper flakes and sauté until soft, about 2 minutes.

6. Add the cut greens. Using tongs, toss the greens with the onion and garlic, drawing them up from the bottom until lightly coated with the oil. Reduce the heat to medium-low and continue to turn the greens until just wilted, about 2 minutes.

7. Fold in the spinach. Remove from heat and season to taste with salt and pepper.

To serve, place the greens on a platter or on individual plates, top with chicken legs and the reserved chicken broth.

Duck Cassoulet

Cassoulet started as a humble dish in the Languedoc region of Southern France. It has since evolved to become a quite elaborate casserole containing meat (pork, goose, duck or sometimes mutton) and white beans. Its authentic cooking vessel, the "cassole," is a round earthenware pot.

This variation is less complicated than the traditional one, which means that it can be enjoyed as an everyday meal and not necessarily as a celebratory dish.

Cannellini beans are among the better legumes in terms of nutrients and antinutrients.

⚠ The idea of mixing cereals and legumes to get a complete protein is an old one; however, many legumes actually bind to the protein, thus inactivating the nutritional value of the cereal.

Serves 4 to 6 ~ ⧗ ⧗ ⧗

- 4 whole duck legs (legs and thighs)
- 4 tablespoons oil, divided
- 1 yellow onion, diced into ½-inch pieces
- 2 bay leaves
- 2 tablespoons all-purpose flour
- ½ cup dry white wine
- 4 cups chicken stock, divided
- 2 carrots, peeled and cut into ½-inch pieces
- 2 ribs celery, cut into ½-inch pieces
- 15-oz can of cannellini beans, drained (or 1 ½ cups dry beans, soaked and prepared following package instructions)
- 2 tablespoons flat-leaf parsley, chopped
- **Slurry:** 2 tablespoons cornstarch mixed with 1 tablespoon water

1. Dry the duck legs with paper towels, rub with salt and pepper. In a braising pan or Dutch oven, heat half the oil over medium-high heat until nearly smoking. Place the legs skin-side down in a single layer. Reduce the heat to medium and sear for 3 minutes until well-browned. Turn the legs over and brown the other side, another 3 minutes. Turn over once more, cover, reduce the heat to medium-low and cook, turning a couple of times, until all the fat has been rendered and the meat is pulling away from the bones, about 20 minutes. Transfer the meat to a plate. Remove all but 3 tablespoons of the fat from the pan.

3. Return the duck legs to the pan and add half the broth. Cover, reduce heat to medium-low and simmer for 10 minutes.

5. Return the bones to the pan. Add the carrots, celery, remaining broth and stir. Cover and cook for 10 minutes, until the vegetables are tender.

Taste the broth, adjust the seasoning with salt and freshly ground pepper. Serve immediately.

2. Increase heat to medium-high. Add the onions and bay leaves and sauté for 2 minutes in the duck fat. Sprinkle the flour over and cook for 2 minutes, until lightly browned. Pour in the wine to deglaze, scraping all bits from the bottom of the pan.

4. Remove the meat from the pan, shred into bite-sized pieces.

6. Remove the bones and bay leaves. Add the duck pieces, beans and chopped parsley. Cover to warm, only 3 minutes. Check consistency and if necessary, whisk in the slurry to thicken the sauce.

Duck Confit

Duck confit is a staple of the cuisine of South-Western France. In the traditional recipe, duck legs are left to cure in coarse salt for a day or two. The meat is then covered with duck fat and cooked for several hours at very low temperature. This cooking method yields a meat that is incredibly tender and moist.

Confit, covered with the filtered cooking fat, keeps for a long time in an airtight container. Before serving, the extra fat is scraped off, and the meat is heated under the broiler: the skin turns golden and crunchy, a real treat, and you definitely don't want to discard it!

Saturated fat

It has been determined that saturated[*] fat is not a problem and that the ω-3 / ω-6 ratio[*] is fairly irrelevant, as long as there is no deficiency in any essential fatty acid.

Duck fat

There is a lot of myth surrounding duck and duck fat, but some benefits are quite real:

- Fat carries flavor and is an important building block of our body. Don't be afraid of saturated fat, it is now proven that its bad rap is unfounded.

- Eat the duck's skin! It is delicious and, not unlike the skin of an apple, harbors treasures of nutrition: in addition to the important fats, it contains long collagen, which is good for your own skin, bones, joints and ligaments.

Serves 8 ~ ⧗

- 8 duck legs, with thighs attached
- 4 tablespoons coarse salt
- Thyme or Herbes de Provence
- 1 lb rendered duck fat
- 4 bay leaves

1. Sprinkle the duck legs with coarse salt and herbs. Let them sit for about 24 hours, covered, in the refrigerator.

2. Remove all the salt, rinse the legs and pat them dry.

3. Place them in a heavy pot with the fat and the bay leaves. Cook for 3 hours at very low heat (the fat should be bubbling, but barely).

Green Bean Salad

Here is a typical way to present duck confit (although you can, of course, serve it with anything: a simple bed of cooked green leafy vegetables is perfectly suitable).

For an extra indulgence, add thinly sliced potatoes cooked in duck fat. Using a lot of water to cook the green beans and rinsing them afterwards helps preserve a bright green color. (However, this causes some nutrient loss.)

You can leave the duck legs whole or shred the meat, but in any case, be sure to serve the delicious, crispy skin.

Serves 4 ~ ⧗ ⧗

- 4 Duck Confit* legs
- ½ lb green beans
- 2 potatoes (optional), peeled and finely sliced
- 1 small crunchy salad
- 2 tomatoes, quartered
- 2 eggs, hardboiled and quartered

Hardboiled Egg Sauce:

- 1 egg yolk, hardboiled
- 1 teaspoon wine vinegar
- 1 tablespoon mustard
- 1 shallot, finely chopped
- ½ small bunch of chives, finely chopped

1. If the confit was preserved in fat, remove most of the grease (use it to cook the potatoes, or recycle it to prepare the next confit). Place the legs, skin-side up, on a single layer under the broiler until the skin is crisp, 10 to 15 minutes.

2. Trim the green beans. Bring a large pot of water to a vigorous boil, add salt and cook the beans for about 10 minutes, keeping them slightly firm. Rinse immediately in cold water and drain.

3. Optionally, sauté the potato slices in the duck fat until they turn golden.

4. **Hardboiled Egg Sauce:** mash the egg yolk, add all the sauce ingredients and mix well. Season to taste with salt and pepper.

On a serving platter, lay a bed of salad leaves; place the green beans, tomatoes, eggs and potatoes on top. Just before serving, pour the sauce on the salad and place the duck meat on top.

Fast "Duck Confit"

Duck confit is simple enough to prepare, but requires at least a day for the meat to cure in salt, plus several hours of slow cooking.

If you don't have the time or patience, here is a slightly faster substitute that will allow you to enjoy confit more frequently.

Serves 4 ~ ⏳

- 4 duck legs, with thighs attached
- 4 tablespoons oil (or duck fat)
- 2 bay leaves

1. Dry the duck legs with paper towels. Rub each leg with salt and pepper. Let rest for 15 minutes, then rinse off the excess salt and pat dry.

2. Over medium-high temperature, heat the oil in a heavy pot, just large enough the hold all the meat in a single layer. Place the legs, skin-side down. Reduce the heat to low and gently fry, turning each leg once, until most of the fat is rendered, and the pieces are browned evenly (15 minutes).

3. Optionally pour in the additional duck fat: the fat may not completely cover the meat, but the more, the better... Add the bay leaves, cover and simmer over very low heat, turning occasionally, for 1 ½ to 2 hours. When done, all the fat from the duck legs should be rendered, and the meat should be so tender that it is almost falling off the bone.

Use as you wish in salads, soups and main courses.

Tip - Collect the fat in a jar and freeze it to re-use next time you make confit. Don't recycle the fat perpetually, though. (Recycling once seems safe.)

Asparagus & Duck Salad

Serves 4 ~ ⧗

- 2 Fast Duck Confit* legs, with thighs attached

For the salad:

- 1 lb medium asparagus, trimmed
- 12 medium fresh shiitake mushrooms
- 4 cups baby arugula
- 3 tablespoons extra-virgin oil
- 1 tablespoon apple cider vinegar
- 2 oz shaved Pecorino Romano cheese
- Zest of one lemon

1. Preheat the broiler on high. Arrange the asparagus in a single layer on a baking dish, sprinkle lightly with salt, pepper and oil. Broil until lightly browned but still crisp, turning the asparagus once if necessary (6 to 8 minutes total). Cut diagonally into 1 ½ inch pieces.

2. Brush the mushrooms clean, and cut into bite-sized pieces. Heat 1 tablespoon of oil in a skillet over medium-high heat. Toss in the mushrooms and sauté with a pinch of salt and pepper until soft. Remove to a plate to let cool.

3. Shred the Duck Confit meat.

4. Mix the arugula, duck shreds, asparagus and mushrooms in a large bowl. Dress lightly with the oil, vinegar and lemon zest.

Serve on individual plates, top with shaved Pecorino Romano, and finish with freshly ground black pepper.

Sarlat, the "capital" of the Périgord region in South-Western France, is renowned for its duck. It is a popular touristic destination for French people.

Moussaka

All the components in this interpretation of a Greek favorite are seasoned individually for the best flavor blend. As always, spices can be modified to suit your personal taste.

The egg brings richness to the sauce. The Pecorino Cheese adds sharpness and character. The meat can be kept on the chunky side for texture.

The flavors blend best when each component is divided between two layers (as opposed to one thick layer of each). Don't do it sloppily and you can serve it in the cooking dish.

Leaving a little space around the cheese layer allows the moisture from the moussaka to escape cleanly.

Serves 4 ~ ⧗ ⧗ ⧗

Meat Sauce:

- 1 lb ground lamb or beef
- 1 tablespoon olive oil
- 1 medium onion, diced
- 2 cloves garlic, minced
- 1 teaspoon allspice
- 1 teaspoon cinnamon
- 1 teaspoon black pepper
- 1 tablespoon dried oregano
- 1 tablespoon tomato paste
- ¼ cup red wine
- 2 tablespoons fresh lemon juice

Moussaka:

- 2 medium globe eggplants
- ¼ cup salt
- 4 cups water
- Olive oil
- 1 cup Pecorino Romano cheese

Cream Sauce:

- 2 oz butter
- 2 tablespoons flour
- 2 cups whole milk
- ¼ teaspoon ground nutmeg
- 2 egg yolks

1. **The meat** - In a large skillet, heat the oil and brown the meat; season with salt; add the onions, garlic, spices and tomato paste. Mix well. Add the wine and simmer for 15 minutes. Add the lemon juice and adjust seasoning.

2. **The eggplants** - Dissolve the salt in the water. Cut the eggplant into ½-inch thick circles and place in the brine for 20 minutes. Dry on paper towels. Dispose on a baking sheet, brush with oil and place under the broiler until golden brown, 3 to 4 minutes. Turn and brown the other side. Set aside.

3. **The sauce** - In a small saucepan, melt the butter then gradually add the flour whisking constantly, cooking the flour mixture to a light tan color. Gradually add the cold milk, very slowly in the beginning to avoid lumps, whisking until all the milk is added. Season with nutmeg.

In a small bowl, whisk the egg yolks until smooth. Temper them by adding a half cup of the warm milk from the saucepan. Then slowly pour the eggs into the pan. Keep cooking the sauce, stirring continually until it thickens. Turn off heat as soon as you see a bubble.

4. **The finish** - Preheat the oven to 350 °F. Oil the bottom of a casserole dish. Place a layer of eggplants, spread a layer of meat mixture over the eggplant, sprinkle with half the cheese; ladle some sauce. Repeat so you have two layers of each ingredient, ending with a thick layer of sauce sprinkled with cheese.

Bake for 30 to 45 minutes, until the top is lightly browned.

⚠ *Gluten*

This recipe, like several others, uses flour as a thickener, which is perfectly acceptable in light of the result. However, be aware that gluten intolerance is much more prevalent than what was thought before, a serious problem for those suffering from it.

For people with celiac disease, gluten causes osteoporosis. But even when the intolerance doesn't reach the level of true celiac disease, it is associated with measurable harmful effects.

Not everybody has it, but it is a real concern: for people at risk, one spoon of flour is enough to trigger a reaction. For those, use cream to thicken instead of flour.

Shepherd's Pie with Cauliflower

A classic English fare, Shepherd's Pie is essentially a lamb or beef stew topped with a layer of mashed potatoes, and then baked. Our version includes a healthful serving of greens and mashed cauliflower as an alternative to the potatoes.

Any greens can be used: cabbage, spinach, chard, kale or collard. The meat can also vary: ground beef, ground lamb or lamb stew meat all work well. You can add mushrooms to the meat, in which case you should reduce the quantity of broth since the mushrooms will produce both flavor and liquid.

&

Feel free to replace some of the broth by wine: alcohol evaporates during cooking, so it is not a concern in this dish.

Serves 6 ~ ⌛ ⌛

- 1 medium head of cauliflower
- ¼ cup flat-leaf parsley, minced
- 6 tablespoons butter, divided
- 2 tablespoons heavy cream
- 1 ½ lb beef or lamb (ground or stew)
- 2 tablespoons oil
- 1 medium onion, diced into ¼-inch pieces
- 2 teaspoons dried thyme
- 1 tablespoon flour (optional)
- 4 cups chopped greens (spinach, kale)
- 1 cup beef broth

Cauliflower can be substituted as a low-starch alternative in almost any dish requiring mashed potatoes.

Turnips can also replace potatoes. Although they are a root vegetable, their glycemic load is low, thanks to their fibrous structure.

Carrots are in the same league: don't live on carrots, but include them in your diet!

For the rare people who are so insulin-sensitive that they need to incorporate some starch in their diet: pick starches with a lot of nutritional value such as colorful root vegetables.

1. Separate the cauliflower florets. Place them in a saucepan, cover with water, bring to a boil; reduce heat and simmer for 10 minutes or until soft (but not soggy).

3. Preheat the oven to 375 °F. If using stew meat, chop into bite-sized pieces. In a large skillet, heat the oil over medium-high heat. Brown the meat for 5 minutes. Add the onion and thyme, season lightly with salt and pepper.

5. Transfer the meat mixture to a baking dish. Carefully top with the cauliflower preparation, making sure not to disturb the meat below. Cut the remaining butter into small pieces and dot them over the top of the dish. Bake, uncovered, until the cauliflower is lightly browned, 15 to 20 minutes.

⚠ **Alcohol**

Well conducted studies show that any amount of alcohol[*] increases women's risk of breast cancer. Studies showing cardiovascular benefits in men all have serious flaws.

2. Drain the cauliflower and return to the pot. Mash with the parsley and ⅓ of the butter. Add cream as needed to obtain a creamy consistency. Season with salt and pepper. Set aside.

4. Optionally add the flour and stir for 3 minutes. Deglaze by adding a little beef broth, scraping to release the browned bits from the bottom. Pour in the remaining broth, reduce heat to low, add the greens, combine and cover. Cook until the greens are thoroughly wilted, about 5 minutes. Adjust seasoning.

REMARKS

As a special treat, sweet potatoes can replace the cauliflower, providing a caloric, nutritious alternative for those who are not afraid of sugar!

Before baking, you can sprinkle the surface of the dish with grated Parmesan for an extra golden finish.

Spicy Lamb Stew

This dish by itself can constitute a whole meal, provided you adjust the quantity of vegetables to be three times that of the meat.

At time of writing, lamb is more often grass-fed than other meats (it was once always grass-fed, but recently has become more industrialized and less healthy). Grass-fed lamb is a rich source of the essential omega-3 fatty acids.

Roasting the cauliflower prior to adding it in the stew brings out a rich, sweet flavor.

Spices and herbs are radically under-used in Western cuisine. This is unfortunate because they are a wonderful tool for adding variety and nutrition in your diet. They are full of flavonoids, whose aromas are the expression of many different nutrients.

Serves 6 to 8 ~ ⧖ ⧖

- 3 lb boneless leg of lamb, cut into 1-inch cubes
- 3 tablespoons pure oil
- 1 large onion, diced into ¾-inch pieces
- 2 red bell peppers, diced into ¾-inch pieces
- Pinch of crushed red pepper flakes
- 2 cups red wine
- 1 can (28 oz) diced tomatoes with juice
- 3 cups mushroom broth or quality beef broth
- 10 cloves garlic, crushed and peeled
- 1 large head of cauliflower
- ¼ cup extra-virgin oil
- 2 tablespoons ground cumin
- ½ cup chopped flat-leaf parsley

⚠ Pay attention to the freshness of your spices. Don't keep them for years in your spice cabinet. (Time flies!) Although they are usually not a threat to your health, old spices oxidate and become less nutrient-dense. They are also much less fragrant.

1. In a medium stock pot, heat half the oil over high heat. Add the meat in 2 or 3 batches, making sure not to crowd the pan. Sear the lamb cubes until browned on all sides, about 5 minutes per batch. Remove and set aside.

2. Reduce the heat to medium-high. Add the remaining oil to the pan, then the diced onion, red bell pepper and pepper flakes. Sauté until soft and golden brown, about 5 minutes. Pour in the wine and bring to a boil. Using a wooden spoon, scrape the browned bits from the bottom of the pan.

3. Return the browned lamb and juices to the pot. Add the tomatoes, garlic and ⅔ of the broth. Cover and simmer on medium-low for 45 minutes, stirring every 10 minutes. (If you wish the lamb to be very tender, the stew can simmer for up to 2 hours on low heat. Add broth as needed if the cooking liquid becomes too thick).

4. **Roasted cauliflower:** while the stew is simmering, roast the cauliflower. Preheat the oven to 400 °F. Discard the core of the cauliflower, cut the florets into large bite-sized pieces. Place in a bowl with the oil, sprinkle with ground cumin, salt, pepper and toss to coat. Arrange in a single layer on a baking sheet and roast in the oven for 10 - 12 minutes until tender-crisp and lightly browned. Remove and set aside.

5. Fold the roasted cauliflower and chopped parsley into the stew. Season with salt, freshly ground black pepper and more red pepper flakes to taste. Simmer for an additional 10 minutes and serve.

Curry mixes, a staple of Indian cooking, carry an array of health benefits. Although its composition varies, curry usually includes turmeric, a member of the ginger family. Turmeric contains several compounds, including curcumin, the substance that appears to account for curry's health benefits.

⚠ Beware, though, that curry powder can be a serious source of contamination in the diet. Check where it comes from; for want of better information, buy the most local possible.

Braised Lamb Shanks

With the addition of gremolata, the very British "Lamb with Mint Sauce" acquires an Italian accent.

It is easy to make but beware: allow enough time for cooking! The long simmering attenuates the meat's strong flavor, a plus for some people, a minus for others. Even kids like it.

This dish provides a much needed respite from muscle meat, which is so prevalent in today's diet. Shanks are rich in fat and tendons; the long cooking in liquid allows you to extract nutrition also from the bones.

You can ask the butcher to saw the shanks in half so they are easier to handle (or to allow for smaller portions).

Omega-3 deficiency

Pastured grass-fed lamb is high in ω-3 (an important characteristic of lamb is that it is efficient at converting a good grassy diet into long-chain ω-3 fatty acids.)

Among the meats in the store, we are more likely to get ω-3 from lamb than from steak.

In today's diet, there is a real risk of ω-3 deficiency: it doesn't hurt to try to restore some balance. But we don't advocate taking supplements[*] because, while their benefits are not proven, they can for sure be harmful.

Check your lamb's pedigree

Even when they are grass-fed, animals are often finished and fattened up on grain. Australian lamb used to be grass-fed, but is not any more. Today, most grass-fed lamb is imported from New Zealand.

Also look for locally produced grass-fed lamb: there are hopefully some good sources in your area. Support you local farmer and rancher!

Serves 4 ~ ⏳ ⏳ ⏳

- 4 small lamb shanks, about 1 lb each
- 3 tablespoons olive oil
- 1 onion, peeled and coarsely diced
- 2 carrots, peeled and coarsely diced
- 2 celery sticks, coarsely diced
- 2 cloves garlic, peeled
- 6 oz tomato paste,
  or 1 can (28 oz) diced tomatoes
- 2 cups red wine
- 1 tablespoon finely chopped rosemary
- 2 bay leaves

Gremolata:

- 2 tablespoons toasted pine nuts
- 2 tablespoons toasted hazelnuts
- Zest of 2 lemons
- ¼ cup chopped flat-leaf parsley
- ¼ cup chopped mint

1. Heat up the oil in a large, thick pot. Season the lamb shanks with salt and pepper and brown them well on all sides (about 3 minutes per side), then remove from the pot and reserve.

2. Coarsely mix the onion, carrots, celery and garlic in a food processor. Add them to the pot and sauté for about 10 minutes until they become fragrant. Season to taste with salt and pepper.

3. Add the tomato paste, wine, rosemary and bay leaves. Return the shanks to the pot. Cover with water. Bring to a boil, then lower heat, cover tightly and simmer for 2 ½ to 3 hours, adding a little liquid once in a while to cover.

4. In the meantime, combine all the gremolata ingredients in a food processor and blend to get a coarse mix. Reserve.

Serve one shank per person: surround with the sauce and sprinkle some gremolata on top.

NOTE

Instead of simmering on the stove top, you can transfer the covered pot to the oven (preheated to 400 °F) and cook for the same amount of time. The oven provides an even, low temperature for braising.

Rosemary can be replaced with other herbs such as thyme or oregano.

Pork Roast with Rosemary

An Italian classic... Picture yourself in a garden, on a sunny afternoon, enjoying food and conversation with a group of lifetime friends...

Buy a pork roast with the bone in, the pork equivalent of a rack of lamb: figure about 2 chops for 3 people (or for 2 people with a large appetite).

Ask the butcher to leave all the fat on, as it is tasty and will keep the roast from drying out during the long, slow cooking. (Ironically, the fear of fat is such that nowadays, pork, traditionally one of the fattest and succulent meats, is raised to be too lean.)

Cuts of meat

For the same animal, protein quality is pretty much the same for the different cuts of meat. The less expensive cuts are at least just as nutritious as the expensive ones.

Generally, the more expensive the cut, the less fat it contains. Another consideration is that grass-fed meat is leaner: it makes sense to select a more fatty cut when buying grass-fed meat than you would when getting grain-fed.

Don't "French" too much!

Frenching is a butcher's technique where all the fat and meat at the end of the ribs are removed to give the rack roast a cleaner look.

The amount of fat taken away varies, but in general, too much is removed because of the misguided fear of fat and cholesterol. In fact, in many other countries, including France, a lot more fat is left on the roast.

Serves 6 to 8 ~ ⌛

- 4 lb bone-in pork roast (about 5 chops)
- 8 sprigs fresh rosemary
- 4 cloves garlic
- ½ tablespoon salt
- ½ teaspoon pepper
- 2 tablespoons olive oil

1. Preheat the oven to 350 °F.

   Reserve half the rosemary sprigs. Discard the hard stem from the other half and chop the leaves. Mix them with the minced garlic, salt and pepper.

2. Using a good butcher's knife, separate the bone, cutting as close to the bone as possible, but leaving the meat and bone attached along one edge of the roast.

3. Using a sharp knife, punch a longitudinal slit throughout the center of the roast.

4. Stuff some rosemary mixture in the central slit and spread the rest in the space between the bone and meat.

5. Turn the meat bone-side down, arrange the rosemary branches on top, tie the roast with kitchen string.

6   Place in a baking dish, bone-side down; pour the oil all over and bake for 1½ to 2 hours.

   The cooking time depends on the oven and the size of the roast. It is safer to check with a meat thermometer that the internal temperature has reached 170 °F.

Take the meat out of the oven, cover to keep warm, let rest 5 minutes before carving.

First separate the roast from the bone; then carve slices. The bones make a nice portion of ribs!

Fat quality

Consume a large spectrum of fats to get a variety of molecule lengths and the essential fatty acids that our body cannot synthesize.

Once the potential issue of ω-3, ω-6 deficiency has been taken care of, remember that the quality of fat is mainly determined by the health of its source, not by its ω-3 / ω-6 ratio[*], or its saturated / unsaturated composition.

A (too) Frenched rack of lamb.

Calf Liver alla Veneziana

Serves 4 ~ ⏳

- 1 lb calf's liver
- 1 large onion
- 2 tablespoons butter
- ½ cup dry white wine or broth

Pamper your digestive system!

When nutrition is addressed, the digestive system (stomach, intestine, etc.) is often neglected, even though the food we eat has important repercussions on its health.

Eat things that are rich in digestive enzymes: for that, nothing beats liver!

Beware of false certainties and "magic" foods though:

The microbiome (the ensemble of the micro-organisms that live in our body) definitely has a strong impact on our digestive system; it is tempting to try to influence it, or to improve the mix of microbes in our gut.

But at this point, the microbiome is many orders of magnitude more complex than we can comprehend. The beneficial effects of fussing with it might have unexpected serious side effects[helicobacter].

Don't overcook

Overcooking denatures proteins in general, enzymes in particular:

- Digestive enzymes present in food facilitate the absorption of micronutrients. Overcooking alters the shape of these enzymes, preventing them from performing their function, thus diminishing our ability to absorb nutrients.

- Most of the minerals in our body are not free-floating, but attached to proteins instead (the free-floating minerals are mostly calcium, sodium and potassium). Denaturing the protein impairs the absorption of the associated mineral.

Believe it or not, in France, calf's liver is more expensive than the best cut of beef!

One good feature of liver (except for those who already have too much iron in their diet, a fairly uncommon situation) is that it is a great source of iron.

Liver is also rich in enzymes that aid digestion.

To preserve the nutritional value of liver, don't overcook. The liver is also tastier when still pink inside, with a slightly firm consistency.

1. Slice the liver fairly thinly, and then cut into medium size sticks.

2. Mince the onions and sauté them in half the butter until they turn golden. Add the wine, season with salt and pepper. Cover and simmer until the onions are translucent and tender. Remove from the pan and set aside.

3. In the same pan, heat up the remaining butter. Add the liver and cook briefly over high heat, 2 to 4 minutes at most. The inside should be just barely cooked.

Mix in the onions, season to taste and serve hot!

Bone Marrow with Leeks

Whether as one of the many constituent of Pot-au-feu or by itself on toasted peasant bread, bone marrow is a ubiquitous bistrot fare in France and a highly appreciated treat. It can also be used to give a hearty flavor to broth. It enters in the composition of elaborate modern dishes.

Marrow bones can be boiled or baked. Baking is preferable because this prevents the marrow from escaping in the cooking liquid. For that method, it is necessary to ask the butcher to split the bones lengthwise so that the marrow is exposed to the heat. Sprinkling with salt before baking helps the marrow stay in the bone.

Serves 4 ~ ⧗

- 4 beef marrow bones, each about 5-inch long, sawed up lengthwise

- 1 teaspoon coarse salt

- 1 lb leeks

- 2 tablespoons butter

- 2 tablespoons lemon juice

- Freshly ground peppercorns

- 2 tablespoons Parmesan cheese shavings (optional)

Bone marrow

The marrow, a fatty tissue inside the bones, is a manufacturing site for many types of the animal's cells: the fats, proteins, minerals and vitamin arrays contained in the bone marrow are remarkable. They are, like stem cells, a kind of primordial soup.

1. Preheat the oven to 425 °F.

2. Wash the leeks: cut them lengthwise halfway through the core and rinse well to remove any soil trapped between the leaves. Slice thinly.

3. Melt the butter in a pan. Add the leeks, cover and cook over low heat, stirring occasionally, until the leeks become tender and translucent, about 20 minutes. If necessary, add a tablespoon of water once in a while so that the leeks don't brown. Add the lemon juice towards the end of the cooking process.

4. Place the split bones on a baking tray, marrow side up. Sprinkle with a little coarse salt.

5. Bake for about 10 minutes, until the marrow doesn't show pink areas anymore. Make sure to remove from the oven before the marrow becomes runny.

6. On each individual plate, place a bed of leeks. Scoop out the marrow from a bone, cut into pieces and place on top of the greens. Sprinkle with freshly ground peppercorns and optionally some Parmesan cheese shavings.

Fatty acid length

It helps our metabolism if the length of the fatty acids we eat is in the range of our needs. Long fatty acids are the most commonly useful for structural purposes in our body, contrary to the common belief that the omega-3 / omega-6 fats are the only useful ones.

Although we can build these fatty acids, we might as well eat some. The longer ones are all animal derived: we can't get long-chain fatty acids from vegetal sources; and, with the exception of dairy, all animal-based fatty acids are at least medium to long-chain.

But don't choose your food solely based on the length of the fatty acids it contains!

LIQUIDS

Hydration

Our body is constituted of about 65 % water. Our ability to distribute nutrients and to clear waste is very dependent on how well hydrated we are.

Needs vary depending on age, activity level, climate; also, as always, we must pay attention to our individual conditions. For these reasons, it is not possible to give precise instructions on how much to drink. However, to put things into perspective:

- *We lose 2 to 5 % of our body weight in fluids during the day and night, through all our metabolic functions.*

- *A deficiency in fluids of as little as 1 % of our body weight can mean dehydration[*]; that's not much when you think of it: for an average person, it translates into 1 or 2 pounds only.*

The several pounds of lost fluid must be replenished through what we eat (vegetables contain a lot of water) and drink.

Water

Our most natural source of hydration is water. It is not necessary, though, to drink during the meals: drinking a lot while eating dilutes the digestive enzymes; it might also make you eat faster, thus impairing digestion and nutrient absorption.

Drink throughout the day, even if you are not thirsty. Thirst is not a good enough indicator that you are dehydrated; in particular, with aging we might lose the thirst drive, but not the need for water.

Energy production at the cellular level also involves water. Active people need to drink more, and not only because of sweat, but also to replace what was used for producing energy.

If you are drinking tap water, pay attention to the quality of your municipal water supply.

Vary your bottled waters (especially the carbonated ones) for mineral content.

Coffee and Tea

Drink as much coffee[*] and tea as you want, as long as it doesn't disrupt your sleep, upset your stomach or make you nervous.

Coffee and tea are associated with a lower incidence of serious diseases, and this is true of all types of teas, not only green tea.

Although there is no proof at this point that it is as beneficial as coffee or tea, there is some evidence that cocoa[*] is healthy. Unfortunately, cocoa usually comes loaded with sugar.

Milk

Milk is a good source of minerals and vitamins. Lactose intolerance is a false problem: lactase can be induced[*], even in the populations reputed to lack it, simply by drinking milk regularly.

Several studies found that milk did better than sports drinks for post-exercise hydration and returning to electrolyte balance.

Drink whole milk:

- Fat is necessary to absorb vitamins, which are in turn required for us to absorb calcium. Low-fat milk can even be considered dangerous[milk].

- Removing fat changes the natural balance of the food and adds a layer of processing: always a bad thing.

- The missing fat in low-fat products is replaced by sugar to compensate for taste and texture.

Drink milk from healthy animals: milk, being the only food for a young mammal, is a concentrated source of all nutrients, purified from naturally occurring toxins; however, the animal is incapable of filtering unnatural toxins: make sure the cows have been fed no antibiotics or hormones.

Drink milk that was processed as little as possible: pasteurization, a heat treatment, destroys valuable enzymes; homogenization[*] creates other health risks.

There is currently some hype around everything fermented. Fermented milk is a good addition to the diet, but it is not the advertised universal solution: it might help the biome[*], but it brings only ten species, as opposed to the trillions present in our biome.

Blended drinks

Be careful with the sugar content of your blended drinks. Stay away from low-fat, sugar-laden smoothies. Otherwise, there is nothing wrong with juicing. Juicing helps release nutrition from raw vegetables.

⚠ **Fruit juice** should be only occasionally used because of the sugar content.

⚠ **Soy milk** is not recommended for the same reasons that soy is not recommended: the phytoestrogens present in soy mimic human hormones, causing imbalance in both men and women.

⚠ **Sports drinks** are supposed to help replenish electrolytes and minerals. It is true that by sweating, we deplete ourselves of sodium, calcium, magnesium... But sports drinks are a chemistry project, not a real food: they contain artificial sweeteners, fructose, dyes and an artificial ratio of minerals.

Milk (or exotic variations such as lassi or kefir) works better than sport drinks.

⚠ **Soft drinks** are obviously to be avoided: they are full of sugar and possess none of the redeeming value of the nutrients found in fruit juice.

⚠ Wine and alcohol

Concerning wine and alcohol[*], most of the claims of cardiovascular benefits are questionable. In particular, the cancer risks in women are an argument against using wine for health benefits.

The body's ability to detoxify alcohol is limited and varies from person to person. For the many people who lack the liver enzyme alcohol-dehydrogenase[*], or don't have enough of it (a telltale sign is that they turn red when consuming alcohol), alcohol is a cellular poison. For those who have adequate levels of the enzyme, it is not as toxic.

The social value of alcohol is undeniable. For those who can metabolize it, drinking once in a while for pleasure is not too bad.

⚠ Beer

With its high glycemic load, combining grain and alcohol, beer is one of the worst drinks possible. In spite of some extravagant health claims, beer[*] is not advised until further notice.

> - Drink plenty of water (but not necessarily with the meals).
> - Drink tea, herbal tea and coffee.
> - Drink whole milk, coming from healthy animals, with a little processing as possible.
>
> Minimize the consumption of anything else, especially sweetened beverages.

Poached Fish with Caper Sauce

This dish demonstrates the technique of poaching, which gently cooks the food in liquid just below the boiling point, imparting some of the broth's flavor to the food.

Fish is usually poached in "court-bouillon," which produces a very delicate aroma. With greens and a tart caper sauce, it is a great way to serve fish.

The cooking method and the sauce are two recipes that can be used independently for many different dishes. You can even poach a whole fish, like a Petrale sole.

Serves 4 ~ ⏳ ⏳

- 4 thick, firm fish fillets 6 oz each (for example salmon or true cod)

Court-Bouillon:

- 1 carrot, sliced
- 1 stalk celery, sliced
- ½ medium onion, sliced
- 3 sprigs lemon thyme
- 2 sprigs flat-leaf parsley
- 3 cups water
- ½ cup white wine
- 3 teaspoons salt

Caper berries make tasty pickles.

Buds are the most common way to enjoy capers.

Fish should be an important part of our diet: it can constitute at least 25 % of our protein intake.

Fish fat has different properties than meat fat. Eating fish is a good way to balance our sources of fat.

The mineral content of fish is also different from that of land animals. For example, fish is rich in **iodine** that helps fight thyroid problems.

Caper sauce:

- 3 tablespoons capers, rinsed
- ½ cup packed fresh flat-leaf parsley leaves
- ⅓ cup extra-virgin oil
- 2 tablespoons minced shallot
- 1 teaspoon Dijon mustard
- 1 clove garlic, minced
- 1 tablespoon red wine vinegar

1. Poached fish

Combine all the court-bouillon ingredients in a non-reactive skillet large enough to hold all the pieces of fish side-by-side with room to spare. Bring to a simmer for 5 minutes to draw out the flavors of the ingredients.

Place the fish in the cooking liquid for about 6 minutes for cod, 10 minutes for salmon. Check the doneness of the fish using a small knife on the underside, if necessary.

2. Caper sauce

In a food processor, combine all the ingredients for the sauce and process until finely minced. Set aside.

Serve the fish over a bed of sautéed leafy greens, topped with some caper sauce.

Pan-Seared, Oven-Finished Fish

This method for cooking fish is almost identical to the one used for chicken breast, and although it works particularly well with salmon, it is suitable for any firm fish fillet including halibut and swordfish.

Once you have made pan-seared salmon, you have an unlimited horizon of meals. The more elaborate recipes are good, but they are merely an example of what you can do with a few basic techniques: searing, poaching, baking...

You can sear salmon fillet or chicken breast ahead of time and save them in the refrigerator. They will keep for a few days (longer in any case than completely raw ones). Then, just oven-finish before serving.

Do not overcook salmon: if you want to ensure a moist, flaky result, don't exceed 8 minutes in the oven.

Salmon

⚠ *Farmed Salmon vs. Trout*

Avoid farmed salmon at all cost: the conditions and additives (dyes and antibiotics) used nowadays are absolutely toxic. If wild caught, salmon is a healthy fish.

Most trout is also farmed, but in a healthier way, so trout is the best among farmed fish. Sole is good too: although farmed, it is not as contaminated as salmon.

Rainbow trout

Serves 4 ~ ⧖

Fish:

- 4 salmon fillets, skin on, 4 to 6 oz each
- 1 tablespoon oil

Greens:

- ½ lb fresh English peas
- ½ lb asparagus spears
- ¼ lb sugar snap peas
- ¼ lb green beans
- 1 cup arugula
- A few basil leaves
- 2 tablespoons oil

Serve with:

- 1 cup Asparagus Pistachio Pesto*
- Zest of 1 lemon

Greens

1. Wash all the greens. Shell the English peas. Trim the beans, sugar peas and asparagus spears diagonally into ¼-inch pieces.

2. In a medium skillet, heat the oil over medium-high heat. Add the asparagus, snap peas, green beans and peas. Sauté stirring frequently for 2 - 3 minutes.

3. Gently fold in the arugula, basil leaves and season with salt and freshly ground black pepper. Toss to combine until the arugula is slightly wilted. Turn off heat.

Salmon

4. Season the skin side of the salmon with salt and freshly ground pepper.

5. In a non-stick skillet, heat the oil until almost smoking. Place the fish skin side down and sear for 1 minute. Season the "non-skin" side and turn, searing the other side for another 30 seconds. Transfer to a baking dish. Set aside.

6. Just prior to serving, place the seared fish in the 450 °F preheated oven until done (8 minutes exactly for salmon), then remove from the oven.

To serve: place the cooked greens on individual plates. Top with a piece of salmon and a generous serving of asparagus pesto. Finish by grating a little lemon zest over each plate.

Salmon skin

For this cooking method, definitely leave the skin on. Like chicken skin, salmon skin is full of nutrients that are particularly suited for our own skin, tendon, cartilage and joint health.

Have peas only once in a while as they are fairly starchy.

Pan-Cooked Salmon

Serves 4 ~ ⧖ ⧖

Salmon:

- 4 wild salmon fillets, skin and bones removed

Asian Dressing:

- ¼ cup soy sauce
- ⅓ cup water
- 1 teaspoon honey
- 2 tablespoons rice vinegar
- ¼ teaspoon ground ginger
- ⅛ teaspoon garlic powder
- 2 teaspoons cornstarch, dissolved in 1 tablespoon water

Vegetables:

- Vegetables of various colors, for example:
  - 1 carrot
  - 2 Swiss chard leaves
  - 1 yellow zucchini
  - 1 red bell pepper
  - 1 leek
- 2 tablespoons sesame oil
- 2 tablespoons toasted white or black sesame seeds

⚠ **Soy sauce**

The general advice against soy also holds for soy sauce: because of the phytoestrogens contained in soybeans, an excessive consumption of soy sauce can cause hormonal imbalances in both men and women.

Use it once in a while, but don't make it the seasoning by default!

Salt

Hypertension linked to salt[*] consumption is less of a risk than was previously thought, and in fact, new food guidelines have loosened the salt restriction. The truth is that too little or too much salt are associated with diseases.

It is rare that people who eat a real food diet consume too much salt: if you prepare fresh food and salt it to taste, you are not at risk.

There is no reason to fear salt and extrapolate to the whole population the problems of a minority.

⚠ *However, if you eat a large quantity of salty foods (salted nuts for example, or, heaven forbid, potato chips) every day, then you could be at risk of too much salt.*

Eating large quantities of the same ingredient daily is always potentially dangerous.

Asian Dressing

1. In a small saucepan, whisk together all the dressing ingredients minus the cornstarch. Bring to a boil. Whisk in the cornstarch and stir until thickened. Transfer the sauce to a bowl and let cool.

Fish

2. Heat a non-stick skillet over medium heat. Dip the salmon fillets in the sauce, turn to coat, then place in the skillet, presentation–side down. Cook for 4 minutes.

3. Turn, cover the pan, reduce heat to low and cook for another 4 minutes until firm. Remove the fillets to a plate and cover to keep warm.

Vegetables

4. Wash and cut all the vegetables into very thin, 2-inch long strips.

5. In the pan that was used for the salmon, heat the sesame oil over medium heat. Add the julienne vegetables and toss until just cooked, about 2 - 3 minutes. Add a couple of tablespoons of the dressing to the vegetables and toss to coat.

To serve, place the vegetables on a platter or individual plates, top with a salmon fillet, additional sauce and a sprinkle of toasted sesame seeds.

Fish Papillote with Vegetable Julienne

Serves 4 ~ ⧗ ⧗

- 4 cod fillets (or fish of your choice), 4 oz each
- 1 carrot
- 1 small bunch "pencil" asparagus
- 1 small leek
- 2 tablespoons oil
- Juice of one lemon
- 2 oz salted butter
- 4 large fresh basil leaves

A dish with two French words in its name... had better be good! "Papillote," a piece of paper used as a wrapper, clearly refers to the parchment paper. "Julienne" is a way to cut the vegetables, and even for the French, its etymology remains obscure.

This elegant dish, suitable for entertaining dinner guests, is simple enough to prepare for an everyday family treat. One nice feature is that the individual portions can be prepared ahead of time and baked at the last minute.

As the food bakes and lets off steam, the parchment puffs up into a dome. Most fishes present well using this method including salmon (remove skin), cod, tilapia, halibut, sea bass, rockfish and snapper. The vegetables and flavorings can be adapted to suit your personal taste. Parchment paper is now commonly found in all supermarkets.

Cold water fish *such as cod is rich in long-chain omega-3 fatty acids (one of their functions is to act as "anti-freeze" for the fish).*

In the good old days, cod liver oil was given as a source of vitamin K and D.

Other good cold water fish are wild salmon and mackerel.

This picture doesn't constitute an endorsement of the method...

1. Preheat the oven to 450 °F. "Julienne" cut the vegetables, that is, slice them into thin, two-inch long pieces.

A beautiful "rainbow" of nutrition

2. **Basil butter:** leave the butter to warm at room temperature; in a small bowl, cream the butter, add the finely minced basil and combine well. (Or if you feel lazy, skip the basil, just use plain butter.)

3. Prepare the parchment paper: fold 12" x 16" pieces of parchment paper in half. Beginning at one end of the fold, cut a point, then go round into as wide a semicircle as possible, ending at the opposite end of the fold with a rounded shape. When opened out, the paper should be heart shaped.

4. Brush one side of each paper heart with oil.

- Center some vegetables on the oiled parchment.

- Place a fish fillet on top of each bed of vegetables.

- Top with a squeeze of fresh lemon juice and season with salt and pepper.

- Spoon a nice dollop of basil butter on top of each fish fillet.

5. Fold the second side of the paper over the fish. Starting at the rounded end, make a small, tight fold toward the center and continue making small folds around the open edge. At the end, fold the paper several times on itself to close tightly and tuck the point under the packet.

Bake on the center rack of the oven until cooked through, about 10 - 12 minutes, depending on the thickness of the fish.

Transfer the papillotes to serving plates, cut open and enjoy immediately.

Salmon Tartare

For this recipe, you need super fresh wild caught salmon. Sashimi quality fish is of course preferable.

Wild salmon is famously rich in good fats. Farmed salmon is fed a grain-based diet (which is even more unnatural for fish than it is for humans) and generally exposed to all kinds of diseases due to the prevalent raising practices.

Here is a good opportunity to use fancy salts. The raw fish and simple seasoning constitute a propitious environment to open our taste buds to new tastes.

Serves 4 ~ ⧖ ⧖

- 12 oz wild salmon fillet, skin and bones removed
- 2 shallots
- Chives, dill, green onion or other herbs to taste.
- Juice of 1 lemon
- 4 tablespoons of very good olive oil
- Fancy coarse salt (optional)

Don't fear raw meat!

Tartares and Carpaccios are nutrient-rich meals that are easily digested and enrich the body.

Both are prepared with raw meat or fish, cut in tiny dice for Tartares, thinly sliced for Carpaccios. Lemon juice can be used to cure the meat (note however that this has no real cooking effect and doesn't increase safety if the fish is not fresh). The added oil and raw allium contribute great nutrition.

Contrary to common perception, our body is better equipped at digesting raw meat than raw vegetables! Meat doesn't require as much cooking as vegetables to release its nutrients.

It is just not true that we digest[*] vegetables better.

Although we don't advocate eating most of our food raw (especially vegetables), uncooked meat once in a while provides variety and allows access to enzymes present in raw meat that might be gone from cooked meat.

Sourcing

This is where sourcing really makes a difference: you want the finest piece of fish or meat.

Historically meats needed to be cooked well for fear of parasites. Even today, when most of this concern is gone, sourcing must be reliable.

It will save you a lot of effort if the seller can remove the skin and bones from the fillet for you. Generally they are nice about it, so it's worth it because this operation is harder than it looks.

1. Dice the fish into tiny, ⅛-inch wide cubes.

2. Dice the shallots and the herbs very finely and mix them with the fish. Keep in the refrigerator.

3. Half an hour before serving, season with salt and pour in the lemon juice and the oil. Mix, and then garnish with a few herbs.

Serve as an appetizer or as a main course. Depending on your taste, let the fish marinate in lemon for a longer of shorter time: the longer, the more "cooked" the consistency will be.

Scallop Carpaccio, prepared in a similar way, is equally delicious.

1. Instead of dicing, slice each scallop to obtain translucent circles that are as thin as possible.

2. Spread the circles on a single layer on the serving platter, sprinkle with thinly diced shallots and herbs, salt, pepper, lemon juice and oil.

You can serve almost immediately.

The coral (the red crescent-shaped part) is a delicacy seldom available in America. It is good to sauté it quickly as its taste can be a little too strong for some people. (It might also be more susceptible to contaminants than the rest of the scallop).

"Breaded" Fish Fillets

This recipe replaces the usual bread crumbs with nut meal, an easy way to limit starches. Use your favorite one: almond and hazelnut meal are the more commonly available.

Farmed vs. wild

Always attempt to get wild caught fish because farmed fish is often raised in a contaminated environment. This danger is particularly acute for salmon.

Smaller is better

Small body fish have a shorter life and therefore have less time to accumulate toxins, such as mercury and other heavy metals, from the environment.

It is best to avoid the largest, long-lived fish that are high in the food chain such as swordfish, shark and large tunas (some can be 100 years old!)

Excellent in that respect and many others are: sardines, mackerel, anchovies... The smaller yellowfin tuna is safer than the large bluefin or the slightly smaller albacore.

Among the freshwater fish, catfish, a bottom feeder with a long life, is a "dirty fish." Trout on the other hand is much cleaner.

Any thin fish fillets can be used: sole, catfish, halibut. This is a good way to make kids and grown-ups eat fish!

This cooking method is perfect for an everyday meal and also works well with thin, flat cuts of white meat: veal, chicken breast, turkey breast, or whatever you happen to have in the refrigerator!

Watch the heat as the nut meal will darken quickly if the pans get to hot. Reduce heat or temporarily remove pan from heat, should this happen.

Frying has been demonized, in large part due to the fear of fats. As long as you fry reasonably (with fresh oil, not oxidized or rancid, and below the smoke point), there is no need to fear fried foods.

Serves 4 ~ ⧗

- 4 tilapia (or other firm fish) fillets
- 1 cup almond (or other nut) meal
- 1 egg
- Oil for sautéing

Garnish:

- Parsley
- Lemon

1. Wash and dry the fish fillets well with a paper towel. It is important that they be dry so the egg can stick. Season the fillets with salt and freshly ground black pepper.

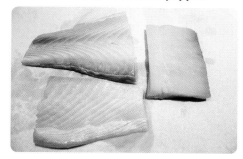

2. Dip the fillets in the egg so that they are entirely coated. Shake off the excess.

3. Dredge each fillet into almond meal, making sure it is covered all around.

4. Heat a large, non-stick sauté pan over medium heat. Add enough oil to coat the bottom of the pan. Have the oil heated, but not smoking.

5. Cook the fillets over medium heat until lightly browned, about 3 minutes. Turn and cook on the other side for another 3 minutes.

Finish with fresh lemon juice and a sprinkle of chopped parsley. Serve immediately.

Mediterranean Seafood Stew

Don't be put off by the large number of ingredients. This dish is quite easy to make, and if you skip an ingredient or two, it will be just as tasty.

Although this stew has classic Mediterranean flavors, the seafood and fish selection can change with season or preference, the wine can be red or white, the herbs can vary and the amount of spices is up to the cook.

Serves 6 to 8 ~ ⧗ ⧗

Seafood:

- 1 ½ lb cod fillet, cut into 2-inch pieces
- 24 fresh clams, scrubbed
- 18 raw medium shrimp, peeled and deveined
- ½ lb bay scallops
- 18 mussels

Broth:

- ¼ cup extra-virgin olive oil
- 2 medium onions, diced into ½-inch pieces
- 4 cloves garlic, finely minced
- 1 can (28 oz) diced tomatoes in juice
- 2 cups dry red wine
- 24 oz fish broth or clam juice
- 1 tablespoon tomato paste

Herbs:

- 2 teaspoons fennel seeds
- 2 teaspoons dried oregano
- 2 bay leaves
- ½ teaspoon dried crushed red pepper flakes
- 3 teaspoons grated orange peel
- 3 tablespoons chopped fresh flat-leaf parsley

Shellfish

Wonderfully flavorful, shellfish brings variety in your diet.

Like all seafood, it provides a good source of iodine and minerals.

However, shellfish possesses no unique properties among seafood, so in case of intolerance or allergy, other types of seafood offer fine alternatives.

Stew base

1. Heat the oil in a large, heavy stock pot over medium heat. Add the diced onion and minced garlic and sauté until the onions are tender, but not browned, about 5 minutes.

2. Add the herbs and spices, tomatoes with juice, wine, fish broth or clam juice, tomato paste, red pepper flakes and orange peel. Bring to a boil. Reduce heat and simmer, uncovered, for about 30 minutes.

Seafood

3. Add the clams to the cooking liquid. Cover the pot and cook until the clams open, about 10 minutes. Discard any clams that are still closed. Add the rest of the fish and seafood. Simmer until the seafood is just cooked through, about 5 minutes.

4. Add the chopped parsley and season to taste with sea salt and freshly ground black pepper.

Serve immediately.

NOTE

The stew base can be prepared one day ahead, cooled, covered and refrigerated. When ready to eat, heat the stew to a simmer, and then start adding the seafood and the fish.

Coconut Shrimp

Devein the shrimp!
The so-called "vein" is in
fact the shrimp's digestive tract.

Some people are
concerned by the shrimp's
high cholesterol content. If
you vary your proteins, you don't have
to worry: the benefits of eating some shrimp
outweigh the concerns.

With exception of some genetic variant in the
population, dietary cholesterol[*] doesn't affect
blood cholesterol. The vast majority of our
cholesterol is manufactured by the liver.

Serves 4 ~ ⧖

- 16 large shrimps
- 1 egg
- ¼ cup finely shredded unsweetened coconut meat
- ¼ cup almond flour
- 1 cup coconut oil for frying

Coconut

Young and old coconuts are very different things,
and, as is the case for most vegetables (young vs.
mature spinach, fresh vs. mature chard), taste
different and have different nutritional properties.

Despite previous popular belief, coconut is good for
us under all its forms:

- *Green coconut, mineral-rich and not too sweet,*
  contains mostly water; it becomes oilier and
  sweeter as it matures. But even the sweeter milk of
  a mature coconut is much less sugary than a soda.

- *The oil is extracted from the "meat" of the mature*
  coconut. Its high smoke point (450 °F) makes
  it suitable for frying. Its fats are very healthy,
  consisting of long chains of natural saturated
  fatty acids that are not harmful at normal cooking
  temperatures. Coconut oil also contains an unusual
  blend of short and medium-chain fatty acids.

Fortunately times have changed, and now the
goodness of coconut oil is being acknowledged.

The bad rap was due to the fact that coconut oil
contains predominantly saturated fat. We now
know that saturated[*] fat is not a problem. (But
it will take a few years until the media and
institutional medicine acknowledge it.)

Coconut oil does impart
a special flavor to
food though, some
like it, some don't...

1. Wash, peel and devein the shrimp, leaving the tail on for presentation and easier handling. Dry extremely well: this will help the batter to stick.

2. Beat the egg with a pinch of salt and pepper. In a separate bowl, mix the shredded coconut and almond flour.

3. Dip each shrimp into the egg, then into the almond flour and coconut mixture until well coated. Place on a board and allow to cool in the refrigerator. This also helps the batter to stick.

4. In a large skillet, heat the coconut oil to frying temperature. Place the shrimp on one level. Cook until golden brown, about 3 minutes per side, without disturbing until it's time to turn them over.

Serve hot with lemon or a sweet and sour sauce.

Breakfast, Snacks and Condiments

Eat real food, not pills!

Ingredients interact in complex ways, and nutrients only work within the context of the whole food symphony. Focusing on any given property of an ingredient is a mistake.

Don't rely on supplements: at best, supplements don't work; at worst, they have very negative impacts on your health.

- Eat fresh, real food that is the closest possible to what nature created.

- Eat nutrient-dense colorful vegetables; proteins of all kinds; plenty of natural fats, either saturated or unsaturated.

- Avoid sugars, flours, starches, grains and cereals.

- Avoid processed food.

- Eat enough to have the energy to sustain your level of activity. Do not count your calories!

- Question any ingredient that you eat regularly in large quantities.

Condiments

When used in a smart way, condiments, relishes and sauces are potent allies. Consumed in small quantities, they enhance the food experience by bringing diversity, excitement and nutrition to the meal.

- **Vinegar** can be either brewed or distilled; both methods involve some heat processing, but brewing yields a more complex taste, and therefore richer nutritional composition.

- **Soy sauce** is made with soy! Don't overuse it.

- **MSG** (Monosodium Glutamate) has been demonized out of proportion. However, enough people have serious adverse reactions to it that it is better to avoid it.

- **Mustards** are often such complicated mixes of chemicals that most people don't realize mustard is, in fact, a plant. Pick a mustard that is as simple as possible, all it needs is crushed seeds and vinegar.

- **Mayonnaise -** Make your own! Since there is no heat issue, this gives you a chance to experiment and benefit from many different healthy oils.

- **Sauces -** Beware of industrial sauces and check their ingredients: they often contain sugar, undesirable additives and low-quality oils.

- **Chili peppers** belong to a different plant family than peppercorns; they have different properties, but similar effects. In the chili family, cayenne pepper is commonly used as a folk remedy against nose congestion.

Chili[*] and spicy foods have the reputation of hurting the stomach: but in fact, cultures that consume this kind of hot food have less gastrointestinal disease.

It is true that chili upsets some people's stomach. The same mechanism that fights congestion caused by nose mucus applies with negative effects on stomach mucus; but rather than being a cause, the symptom indicates that the stomach is already damaged.

As always, pay attention to your personal tolerance.

- **Salt -** If you eat a real food diet, there is no need to fear salt[*]. Nowadays, gourmet salts are available in most grocery stores: use various salts to benefit from a diversity of minerals and tastes.

- **Pepper -** Peppercorns give birth to a family of spices that includes black pepper (the most ubiquitous), white pepper and green peppercorns.

It is an example of food that is not colorful but nevertheless potent: pepperine, responsible for the pungency in pepper, promotes gut health by facilitating nutrient absorption. It also has anti-inflammatory and immune activator properties.

Fumigation, used to treat regular pepper against pests, is a source of contamination in the diet. Select organic, non-fumigated pepper.

Chili[*] peppers have medically proven effects on arthritis and autoimmune diseases.

Fall Fruit Caponata

Caponata is a Sicilian eggplant dish with a sweet and sour seasoning. In this variation, pears, apples and persimmons give the caponata a fall sweetness, making it a unique treat for the holiday season.

Consider this preparation a condiment. In our nutrient-rich diet, we can have fruit on a fairly regular basis, but not too much, in order to reduce our sugar consumption.

In limited amounts, such fruit relishes are an amazing way to bring nutrition and variety to the table.

Fruit

We have been told time and again that fruit is good for us. And indeed, given the choice between a doughnut (or even Cheerios) and fruit, one should definitely go for the fruit. However, in the context of a nutrient-rich, real food diet, fruit[*] is not as important, since it contains no nutrient that you couldn't get elsewhere, while packing a fairly large quantity of sugar.

In our setting, fruit becomes an adornment, the small treat, the occasional dessert after dinner.

Now, if you eat fruit, definitely eat the skin: most of the nutritional value of the apple is in its skin. The red apple is dramatically more nutrient-dense than the green one; its quercetin is one of the best naturally occurring antihistamines.

Serves 6 to 8 ~ 🕴 🕴

- 2 eggplants
- 1 firm but ripe Bartlett, Comice or Bosc pear
- 1 Fuji apple
- 1 Fuyu persimmon
- 1 yellow onion
- 4 garlic cloves
- 2 tablespoons capers
- 2 teaspoons salt
- 4 tablespoons extra-virgin olive oil, divided
- 1 can (28 oz) diced tomatoes in juice
- ¼ cup currants
- 1 tablespoon balsamic vinegar
- ¼ cup minced flat-leaf parsley, divided
- 2 tablespoons pumpkin seeds, lightly toasted
- 1 cup chicken broth (optional)

Persimmons come in many varieties. For this Caponata, use the hard, crunchy type (its sugar content is also lower).

1. Cut the eggplants, pear, apple and persimmon into ½-inch cubes. Do not peel any of them! Peel and dice the onion into ½-inch cubes. Mince the garlic. Rinse the capers.

2. Place the eggplant pieces in a colander and sprinkle liberally with salt. Let stand for 30 minutes. Rinse and pat dry with paper towels.

3. In a sauté pan, heat half the oil over medium heat. Add the eggplant cubes and sauté, stirring frequently for 3 minutes. Cover, reduce heat to low and cook until the eggplant is very soft, about 10 minutes. Remove the eggplant from the pan and set aside.

4. Heat the remaining oil over medium heat. Add the onion and garlic and sauté until golden, about 3 minutes.

5. Add the tomatoes, pears, apples, persimmons, capers, currants, balsamic vinegar and cooked eggplant. Simmer until the liquid has evaporated, about 10 minutes.

Optionally add a little bit of broth as needed to increase the level of moisture of the dish.

6. Fold in the minced parsley and garnish with the toasted pumpkin seeds. Adjust seasoning.

Olive Tapenade

Makes 1 cup ~ ⌛ ⌛

- ½ cup finely chopped flat parsley
- 6 anchovy fillets
- 4 oz mixed olives, pitted and minced
- 1 shallot, minced
- 3 tablespoons extra-virgin olive oil
- 1 tablespoon red wine vinegar
- 2 garlic cloves, finely minced
- 1 teaspoon minced lemon zest

Serve with:

- Parmesan Crackers*
- Raw vegetables: celery, cauliflower, carrots, endive, radicchio...

Tapenade originates from France's Provence region and usually mixes olives, capers, anchovies and garlic in a paste-like condiment. This hand chopped version stays on the chunky side, letting each individual flavor express itself fully.

It is best to use meaty olives such as Kalamata, Picholine and California black. If pitted olives are not available, do it yourself by crushing them with the back of a wooden spoon.

The Parmesan Crackers offer an interesting vessel for serving the tapenade.*

1. Finely chop the parsley.

2. Finely chop the anchovies. Add the olives and shallots. Continue to chop until the mixture is very fine and well mixed.

3. Place the preparation in a small bowl. Add the oil, vinegar, garlic, parsley and lemon zest. Season with freshly ground black pepper and mix well.

There is no need to add salt, the anchovies are salty enough.

Serve with Parmesan Crackers*, or as a dip with raw or cooked vegetables.

⚠ Labels

Don't trust labels[*] blindly. While label laws are necessary to exert some control over what ingredients are included in processed foods, the result is not always foolproof.

Use your judgment. Labels are often misleading:

- "Whole grain" products can contain as much as 49 % of non-whole grains (not that whole grain is much better than refined grain).

- "Cold pressed" means that the oil was processed under lower temperature than regular press. It doesn't mean that it was pressed at room temperature.

- A nutrition label reports "0 g trans fats" if there is less than 0.5 g of trans fat per serving. Foods, such as cooking sprays, which have a minuscule serving size can proudly boast "Trans Fat 0 g," while consisting almost exclusively of trans fats.

- Beware that sugar and starches can be disguised under many different names.

- The FDA allows the use of such words as "healthy," "heart-healthy," or "natural" on labels. While these words sound nice, they don't have a legal definition and therefore mean nothing.

⚠ Keep in mind that real food doesn't come with nutrition labels!

When buying processed foods, select those with the fewest ingredients.

Nutrition Facts

Serving Size 1/4 sec spray (0.25g)
Serving Per Container About 600

Amount Per Serving		
Calories 0	Calories from Fat 0	
		% Daily Value*
Total Fat 0g		0%
Sat Fat 0g		0%
Trans Fat 0g		
Polyunsat Fat 0g		
Monounsat Fat 0g		
Cholesterol 0mg		0%
Sodium 0mg		0%
Total Carb. 0g		0%
Protein 0g		0%

Not a significant source of dietary fiber, sugars, vitamin A, vitamin C, calcium and iron.

*Percent Daily Values are based on a 2,000 calorie diet

Your typical cooking spray

Collard & Olive Relish

This unusual relish can accompany anything, from roasted vegetables to meat or fish.

Serves 4 to 6 ~ ⧗ ⧗

- 1 bunch (about 1 lb) collard greens
- 2 oz (about 18) Kalamata olives
- 2 garlic cloves, chopped
- 1 teaspoon balsamic vinegar
- ¼ teaspoon Cayenne pepper
- ½ cup freshly grated Dry Jack cheese
- 2 tablespoons extra-virgin olive oil
- Juice and zest of ½ lemon

Thyroid issues

Cruciforms have been accused of causing goitre, a disease of the thyroid gland.

Thyroid failure is more common nowadays than it once was, and some believe that cruciforms are responsible for the problem because they can bind iodine. (Iodine deficiency is a cause of thyroid disease.)

This claim has yet to been proven. At this point, it would be a bad bet to give up the well known spectacular nutritional value of cruciforms against an unproven claim. (Fluoride in toothpaste is more likely to be the culprit.)

And if iodine is a concern, eat more fish! Fish is a good source of iodine.

Other than being flat, collard greens look very much like cabbage leaves.

In the family of the dark leafy greens, they are among the milder tasting, at the same time possessing the nutritious qualities common to the cruciferous vegetables: in particular, for vitamin K they are the closest second to Kale, the superhero.

1. Remove and discard the center ribs of the collard greens; pit and coarsely chop the olives; peel and chop the garlic.

2. Bring a 4-quart pot of water to a boil. Add the greens and simmer uncovered, stirring occasionally, until tender (about 10 minutes). Drain, gently pressing on the greens to extract excess water. Chop coarsely.

3. In a food processor, combine the chopped greens with olives, garlic, vinegar, Cayenne pepper and grated cheese. Pulse until finely chopped.

4. Transfer the mixture to a bowl. Add the oil, lemon juice and zest. Season with salt and freshly ground black pepper to taste.

Cauliflower can be baked at fairly high temperature (400 °F) without losing too much of its superpowers because it is protected by a very fibrous structure.

A better way still, is to bake at 300 °F, then finish under the broiler.

Roasted Cauliflower

You can use this preparation in many ways, for example as a sauce for roasted cauliflower:

- Preheat oven to 400 °F.

- Remove the core of a head of cauliflower, cut the florets into large, bite-sized pieces.

- In a bowl, toss the florets with ¼ cup oil, sprinkle with salt and pepper.

- Place florets in a single layer on a sheet pan and roast on the top rack of the oven, for 10 to 12 minutes until tender-crisp and lightly browned.

Roasting the cauliflower brings out its natural sweetness. It can then be seasoned it with a variety of condiments.

Asparagus Pistachio "Pesto"

Real pesto is only found in Liguria, a region of northern Italy, and in my friend Sonia's kitchen! This variation with fresh spring asparagus is a great complement to grilled fish or spring vegetables.

Be careful not to over-process the mixture: it should remain coarsely chopped and chunky.

Eat a large variety of nuts!

Nuts are nutritionally very beneficial. Because they are the most studied so far, walnuts and almonds are also the most supported for health benefits; but while they differ slightly, all nuts are nutrient-dense and packed with beneficial fats.

Nuts consist mostly of fats, plus some proteins and a small amount of carbs. Their strongest suit is that they are extremely high in wonderful medium to long-chain saturated fats.

- *They are also rich in the omega-3 and omega-6 essential fats.*

- *They are rich in protein: their protein completeness is not perfect but pretty good anyway.*

- *They are rich in elements, in particular copper, manganese and magnesium. (Magnesium helps with muscle contraction and heart regularity.)*

Well conducted studies have shown that both tree nuts and peanuts have cardiovascular benefits statistically comparable to those of statins[*].

Makes about 3 cups ~ ⏳

- 1 lb asparagus, trimmed and cut into 1 inch long pieces

- ½ cup toasted pistachio nuts, coarsely chopped

- 8 medium fresh basil leaves, coarsely chopped

- ½ cup crumbled Pecorino Romano cheese, or grated Parmesan cheese

- 2 tablespoons extra-virgin olive oil

- Zest of one lemon

1. **Blanch the asparagus**

   Bring a small pot of water to a boil. Add the asparagus pieces and let boil gently until bright green and tender crisp, approximately 1 minute. Remove the asparagus and place in a bowl of cold water. Rinse a couple of times with cold water to thoroughly cool. Drain well and dry on paper towels. Set aside.

2. In a food processor, place the shelled and toasted pistachio nuts, asparagus pieces, basil and cheese. Pulse the processor several times until the mixture is coarsely chopped.

3. Transfer to a bowl. Add the oil and fold to combine. Using a microplane zester, zest the lemon directly into the bowl and fold in until just combined. Season to taste with salt and freshly ground pepper.

Almonds - Their strong point is manganese and magnesium. New discoveries also show that almonds help with cardiovascular disease.

⚠ If possible, roast the nuts yourself and salt them to taste. Commercially roasted nuts might contain unhealthy oils, added sugar or too much salt.

⚠ If you eat a lot of salted nuts, you could end up being one of those people that have too much salt in their diet.

⚠ Vary the nuts and consume them in reasonable quantities if you have them for snacks.

⚠ Nuts and seeds are often paired with dried fruit: a tasty combination, but rich in sugar.

Walnuts & Pecans - Those nuts have different properties, but they are similar in terms of providing high amounts of good fats.

Pistachio - Since they are almost always sold roasted and salted, they do present a risk of adding to much salt to your diet. They are also a little heavier on the carb front.

Pine nuts - They are present in many ethnic cuisines, and an indispensable ingredient in pesto.

Cashews - Although a little heavier on carbs than the others, they are a very good nut, contrary to popular perception, with the best amino acid profile of all the nuts and also one of the better mineral content.

Peanuts

Peanuts or "ground nuts" are not nuts: they are in fact a legume growing in underground pods, and as such they are controversial. However, for the general population, their benefits outweigh their inconveniences.

The distinction between tree nuts (all the other nuts) and ground nuts is particularly important when allergies are concerned.

Tomato & Bell Pepper Relish

This is a very adaptable dish that can be used for breakfast with eggs, as a side to soups, or served with fish, meat and poultry.

❧

The relish is best when using ripe, summer tomatoes picked at their peak, sweet and flavorful. But in colder months, seasoning properly with salt helps bring forward the sweetness hidden in the winter tomatoes.

Bell peppers belong to the family of septate nightshades. They are extremely high in potassium and carotenoids and deserve to be used more often!

Depending on their color, bell peppers display a different balance of micronutrients, so include them all! The red ones have a better micronutrient score; the yellow ones stand out for minerals and amino acids. And enjoy the green ones too!

Serves 8 ~ ⏳ ⏳

- 2 cups assorted cherry tomatoes, halved
- 1 red bell pepper, finely diced
- 1 orange bell pepper, finely diced
- 1 yellow bell pepper, finely diced
- ½ teaspoon crushed red pepper flakes
- 1 medium red onion, finely diced
- 3 garlic cloves, minced
- 4 tablespoons chopped fresh flat-leaf parsley, plus whole leaves for garnish
- ½ cup extra-virgin oil
- 4 tablespoons red wine vinegar
- 2 tablespoons fresh lemon juice

The mix of colors says it all, this dish is replete with micronutrients: yellow to red carotenoids, red to purple "cyans," allium, fats...

❧

Malnutrition[*] *(micronutrient poverty) can sometimes have worse consequences than* **undernutrition** *(not enough food):*

The effects of not having enough food can be reversed with food, whereas micronutrient deficiency has longer term effects.

1. Combine all the ingredients in a medium-sized bowl.

2. Season to taste with salt and freshly ground black pepper.

Serve as a side dish to any protein course, or use to create a salad (filling the hollow part of a half avocado for example).

Understanding sugar information

Food labels display total carbohydrates and, immediately below, dietary fiber and sugars. For example:

Total Carbohydrate	37 g
Dietary Fiber	4 g
Sugars	1 g

How are these mysterious figures related?
Do you add something to something?
Or subtract???

Here is how to decode the information:

- **Total Carbohydrates** *include: dietary fiber, starches, natural sugars and added sugars.*

- **Dietary Fiber** *has no or little impact on our blood sugar level.*

- **Sugars** *are the simple sugars, mono or disaccharides.*

The labels single out simple sugars, but in fact we know that starches or complex sugars are no better than simple sugars: if the food is not very fibrous, starches will pass to the blood as quickly as simple sugars.

By taking the	Total Carbohydrates
and subtracting the	Dietary Fibers
we get the	Simple Sugars + Starches
	(that is, the total amount of sugar that has an impact on our blood.)

In the example above, the label[*] should state:

Total Carbohydrate	37 g
Dietary Fiber	4 g
All Sugars 37 - 4 = 33 g	

Nutrition Facts

Serving Size 2/3 cup (55g)
Servings Per Container About 8

Amount Per Serving	
Calories 230	Calories from Fat 72

	% Daily Value*
Total Fat 8g	**12%**
Saturated Fat 1g	**5%**
Trans Fat 0g	
Cholesterol 0mg	**0%**
Sodium 160mg	**7%**
Total Carbohydrate 37g	**12%**
Dietary Fiber 4g	**16%**
Sugars 1g	
Protein 0g	

Vitamin A	10%
Vitamin C	8%
Calcium	20%
Iron	45%

* Percent Daily Values are based on a 2,000 calorie diet. Your daily value may be higher or lower depending on your calorie needs.

	Calories:	2,000	2,500
Total Fat	Less than	65g	80g
Sat Fat	Less than	20g	25g
Cholesterol	Less than	300mg	300mg
Sodium	Less than	2,400mg	2,400mg
Total Carbohydrate		300g	375g
Dietary Fiber		25g	30g

⚠ **Sugar in disguise**

Be aware that sugar can be listed under many names, among others: dextrose, cane crystals, cane sugar, caramel, corn syrup, evaporated cane juice, fructose, fruit juice concentrate, high-fructose corn syrup, honey, invert sugar, lactose, malt syrup, maltose, maple syrup, molasses, raw sugar, ribose rice syrup, rice malt, sucrose, syrup...

Less common names include: disaccharides, erythritol, galactose, glucitol, glucosamine, hexitol, inversol, isomalt, maltodextrin, mannitol, pentose, sorbitol, sucanat, xylitol, xylose...

*And don't forget that things such as **corn starch** or even **wheat flour** are also hidden sugar.*

Mixed-Greens "Pesto"
with Pumpkin Seeds

Pesto is traditionally an uncooked sauce that blends basil, garlic, pine nuts, Parmesan cheese and olive oil. Today it is not uncommon to prepare "pesto" from a myriad of non-traditional ingredients.

Experiment with various seeds and nuts (walnuts, pistachio, cashews and even, why not, pine nuts!)

Try different herbs: if you like your food with a little more bite, try an all arugula version.

As a nutrient-dense addition to any meal, this pesto provides essential fatty acids from the pumpkin seeds, varying amounts of carotenoids, vitamins and minerals depending on the herbs used.

Use it to garnish fish, poultry or vegetable dishes.

Phytonutrients

Phytonutrients or phytochemicals are chemicals produced by plants and are responsible for many of the plants' attributes such as color or smell.

Although these chemical compounds have evolved for the benefit of the plant (as a defense against predators for example), not ours, they constitute a treasure for us too.

At the same time, their pharmacological properties confer on them a potential for harm. Like medicines, the effect is dependent on the dose taken.

Think of food as medicine: the way to achieve the right dosage is by variety. This is another reason for consuming seasonal vegetables: it provides a "back door" path to the right mix and dose.

Makes about 2 cups ~ ⏳

- 6 tablespoons extra-virgin olive oil, divided
- 1 cup unsalted hulled (green) raw pumpkin seeds
- 2 garlic cloves, minced
- 1 pinch of red pepper flakes
- 2 cups coarsely chopped fresh greens and herbs (cilantro, parsley, arugula, mâche, mint, spinach, watercress...)
- 2 scallions, minced
- ¼ cup water or as needed
- 2 tablespoons fresh lemon juice

Eggplants are great, but you don't want to feed only on eggplants, because of the powerful phytochemicals they contain.

1. Heat one third of the oil in a skillet over medium heat. Add the pumpkin seeds with a bit of salt and pepper. Stir constantly until the seeds turn light brown, puff up and begin to pop; this takes about 4 minutes.

2. Add the garlic and red pepper flakes. Cook, stirring, for another minute. Remove from heat and allow to cool.

3. Chop all the greens coarsely.

4. Once the seed mixture has completely cooled off, transfer to a food processor with the chopped greens, scallions and remaining oil. Add water as needed and pulse until the mixture forms a coarse paste.

5. Season to taste with lemon juice, salt and freshly ground pepper.

Fresh herbs contribute to our nutritional completeness.

They are a convenient way to enhance our food, while increasing variety and flavor.

Rather than focusing on any single attribute, appreciate the herbs for their diversity.

The visual representation below is an illustration of the nutritional richness of fresh herbs, each spoke representing a different micronutrient. This only gives an overall idea, since the number of micronutrients is too large to be represented.

(Pasta data is provided for comparison.)

Parsley   Dill   Basil   Chives   Rosemary   Pasta

Preserved Lemons

There are many recipes for preserving lemons. This one is different because it targets the rind of the fruit, instead of its pulp.

Preserved lemons are used in many Mediterranean dishes, Moroccan Chicken Tagine* for example.

For a 1 quart jar ~ ⌛

- 1-quart Mason jar
- 6 medium organic lemons, washed
- ¾ cup salt
- ½ cup olive oil, divided

Optional spices:

- 4 garlic cloves, peeled and bruised (smashed lightly with the side of a chef's knife)
- 4 bay leaves
- 8 cloves
- 1 stick of cinnamon
- 1 teaspoon peppercorns
- 1 teaspoon coriander seeds

⚠ Citrus fruits

Citrus fruits[*] are loved for their vitamin C content. People tend to use them in excess.

In reality, they should be used sparingly because their sugar content overweighs their nutritional value. There is a lot more vitamin C in a tomato than there is in a lemon.

Don't think of them as unique, but feel free to use them in small quantities for flavoring, color preservation, etc.

Cinnamon

Cinnamon is supposed to help with insulin sensitivity. Without falling prey to fad, we can say that there is some weak evidence of that. In any case, cinnamon is nutritionally complex and a good addition to our food.

1. Spread ⅓ of the salt in the bottom of the glass jar.

2. Cut half the lemons through the "belly." In a large bowl, toss them with another ⅓ of the salt and all the spices. Firmly pack the mixture into the jar.

3. Cover with the juice from the remaining lemons, top with the remaining salt and half the oil.

4. Close the jar tightly, turn and shake gently to mix the salt. Then pour the remaining oil in the jar to cover the lemons. Close the jar.

5. Leave at room temperature. Every other day, gently turn the jar upside-down a few times. (It will take a few days for the salt to completely dissolve.)

The lemons will take approximately 4 to 6 weeks to cure. They are ready when the pith and pulp are soft and can easily be removed from the rinds with the fingers. Check and, if still too firm, replace and re-seal.

When the lemons are ready, remove and discard the fleshy pulp (keep the rinds!). Rinse the rinds well to remove the salt.

Remove all the lemons when they are ready: if they are over-cured they will become mushy.

The cured rinds can be packed in fresh olive oil and kept for up to one year.

Cooking Oils

Manufacturing oil involves extracting it from its source (seed, nut, fruit) and refining it to modify its taste, aspect and shelf life.

Extraction can be achieved:

- Mechanically, by decanting and centrifugating, or by pressing, the expeller press being the most common. (Note that "cold press" extraction is misleading; it is a legal term that actually allows some heating of the product.)

- Chemically, using solvents, most commonly hexane.

Refining usually involves heat (up to 500 °F) and further chemical processing.

The heating destroys some of the oil's nutritional value and can create harmful "trans" molecules. The chemical solvents are toxic and carcinogenic[oils].

Unrefined oils, mechanically extracted under lowest possible heat, retain the most nutritional properties. They are the best. Whenever possible, seek these characteristics in the extra-virgin oils you buy.

However, sometimes you'll need pure oils, which can be used at higher temperatures. By definition, pure oils require additional processing in order to remove the impurities. Look for **oil that was purified by filtration**. That might prove difficult. Coconut oil is a good refined oil. Pure olive oil refined reasonably might be available too.

⚠ Smoke Point

Heating oils and fats in general beyond their smoke point (the temperature at which the fat decomposes and smoke becomes visible) degrades them with unhealthy consequences.

The smoke point depends on what the oil is made of and also on how it was processed. "Virgin" oils have a lower smoke point than the more refined (purified) oils. This explains, in part, the variations in the numbers found in the literature: for olive oils, smoke points range from 320 °F to 470 °F.

Rather than relying on generic data, it is useful to observe and recognize when the oil's temperature is too high. Symptoms include:

- Smoke (by then, it's too late; discard the oil and start over.)

- Burnt smell (by then, it is usually too late also.)

- Color (might be hard to tell in a black pan.)

- The shimmer that appears in the oil is a good indication that it has reached its maximum, and that you can safely cook in it.

This is easier to see when using a stainless steel pan. The bubbles, produced when you throw shallots in, are not a problem; they are simply caused by the release of water present in the ingredient.

Modern processing

Use natural oils. Avoid man-made trans fats (natural occurring trans fats are OK, though).

For each cooking method, select an appropriate type of oil:

- For cooking at high temperatures and frying, choose oils that have a high smoke point such as coconut oil, pure olive oil, filtered peanut oil, refined safflower oil...

- Other oils we want to use, but not cook with, include: virgin olive oil, non filtered peanut oil, sesame oil...

- Don't use: Canola or soybean oil.

- Vary your oils.

To protect it from rancidity, keep your oil in a closed container and store it in a cool, dark place.

Homemade Mayonnaise

Making your own mayonnaise is simple and easy if you respect a few principles: all the ingredients should be at room temperature, and the oil should be incorporated slowly to ensure a proper emulsion whether using a food processor or whisking by hand.

Unlike commercial products, which can be stored for an almost indefinite amount of time, the home-style version, if refrigerated properly, will only keep for 3 to 4 days. This recipe can be used as a spread, or as a base for other dressings, aïoli or remoulade.

For **Aïoli**, add a crushed clove of garlic to the ingredients.

> ⚠ **Mayonnaise** - Today, store-bought mayonnaise is prepared almost exclusively with soybean oil. Regular consumption of soy products is not advised because the heavy quantity of phytoestrogens they contain can affect and destabilize your hormones.
>
> If you consume a lot of mayonnaise, it's easy to make your own, using different oils to increase the diversity of fatty acids in your diet.
>
> Since the preparation is not heated, this is a great opportunity to try varied oils, even the more fragile ones. Use extra-virgin oil with the least processing possible: mechanically extracted, without heat treatment or solvents.

Makes 1 cup ~ ⧗

- 1 egg yolk
- 1 teaspoon Dijon mustard
- 1 teaspoon lemon juice or vinegar
- 1 pinch of salt
- 1 cup extra-virgin oil of your choice

1. Let the egg sit at room temperature for at least one hour.

2. Whisk together the egg yolk, mustard, lemon juice and salt (and optionally the crushed garlic). Set aside half of the preparation, it will be useful for making more, or for a second try, should you miss the first time around.

3. Using a whisk or a fork, add the oil to the mixture a few drops at a time, turning constantly and rapidly in small circles.

   The trick is to add the new oil in a corner and mix with the rest only when it has been completely absorbed. When the mayonnaise begins to thicken, you can start adding oil a little faster.

Getting Organized

Let's face it: it is more time consuming to feed yourself and your family a nutrient-rich, real food diet than buying ready-made frozen dinners or boiling pasta. But, with a little bit of practice, it is not that hard.

Here are a few tips to make things easier:

- Clean the vegetables in bulk, trim them, cut them up and store them in re-sealable plastic bags, ready to be cooked.

- Sear chicken breast or salmon ahead of time; they will be ready to be oven finished when needed.

- Keep portions of raw or cooked meat or fish in the freezer. Freeze duck confit!

- Prepare larger portions than necessary and be creative with the leftovers (see below)!

A few ingredients that you should always keep in stock:

- Onion, garlic, shallots, scallions
- Oils of all kinds
- Cream, butter, yogurt
- Grated Parmesan (can be frozen)
- Eggs
- Bacon
- Broth, store-bought or homemade (can be frozen)
- Nuts and seeds
- Herbs and spices

Anchovies

Have a supply of various specialty items that keep. Combine them with fresh ingredients (tomatoes, cucumber, avocado, salad leaves, cooked vegetables) or leftovers to create a tasty dish that is different each time.

(Note that we do not suggest that you fill up your refrigerator with a multitude of industrial ready-made sauces, ketchup, or mayonnaises.)

Choose only the tastiest, closest to real food preparations and use them creatively!

Vegetables in vinegar: pickles, capers, baby onions...

Fancy mustards

Cheese, including feta, crumbled blue cheese, Parmesan...

Vegetables in oil: sun-dried tomatoes, bell peppers, olives...

Also consider:

- fried onions
- guacamole, spreads
- pesto
- roasted garlic...

Vinaigrette Dressing

Vinaigrette can easily be prepared by hand using a whisk; the luxury of a food processor ensures a proper emulsion. The same result can be achieved by putting all the ingredients in a jar with a tight fitting lid and shaking vigorously.

If vinaigrette is to be stored for a while, only add the fresh shallots just before using.

If you find that extra-virgin olive oil makes the vinaigrette bitter, try blending it with pure olive oil or with different oils altogether.

You can also experiment and make vinaigrettes with different types of vinegar and fresh herbs such as chives, tarragon, etc.

Makes 1 cup ~ ⏳

- ¼ cup champagne vinegar
- 2 teaspoons Dijon mustard
- Salt and pepper to taste
- ¾ cup extra-virgin olive oil
- 2 tablespoons minced shallots or fresh herbs

1. Blend the mustard, vinegar and salt. Season to taste with freshly ground black pepper.

2. Slowly drizzle in the oils and keep mixing until fully incorporated.

3. Add the minced shallots or fresh herbs.

SNACKS

So our body can function optimally, we need to observe cycles of eating and fasting that reflect the catabolic and anabolic phases of our metabolism[*]. Snacks allow the benefit of a fasting state without the negative effects of an actual, prolonged fast.

For growing children that are always hungry, or those practicing a sport, emphasize the snacks, both in size and in quality: the easy way out would be to load them with carbs, but nutrient-rich food will ensure peak performance and best recovery.

- Snacks must be small, about 2 to 4 oz total.
- Ideally, snacks should combine protein, fats and nutrient-rich carbohydrates, just like the other meals. In our culture, it is harder to get the vegetable part in the snack: fruits are acceptable because the small portion size limits the amount of sugar.
- Snack should be timed in such a way that no more than 3 hours elapse between eating: have your snacks at well defined times and do not munch in between!

Other than that, snacks can consist of pretty much anything. Below are some ideas, but feel free to be creative!

Yogurt

(About ½ cup)

Yogurt brings dairy proteins and fats (make sure to get whole milk yogurt).

For a more complete snack, add nutrient-rich carbohydrates such as:
- a few berries, seeds or nuts
- or a teaspoon of nut butter

Or, for a change, try a savory version with chopped fresh herbs, garlic even; season with salt, pepper and a little oil. Yogurt goes with everything!

Cheese and fruit

(¼ apple, a little piece of cheese)

Cheese can be considered the quintessential sports snack thanks to its caloric density, fats, proteins and ions, which are related to muscle functioning.

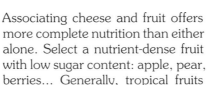

Associating cheese and fruit offers more complete nutrition than either alone. Select a nutrient-dense fruit with low sugar content: apple, pear, berries... Generally, tropical fruits (mango, banana, pineapple, papaya) have a higher sugar content.

Celery sticks and nut butter

(4 sticks, 1 or 2 tablespoons nut butter)

This is quite a complete snack with proteins, fats and a nutrient-dense vegetable.

Nowadays, you are not limited to peanut butter: there are all kinds to select from, including almond, walnut, cashew, hazelnut, sesame...

Soy nut butter is not recommended for the same reason that soy is not recommended. Also avoid hydrogenated oils, chocolate flavored, or sugar added (or anything added, actually). The nut should be the only ingredient.

Blended drinks

(½ to 1 cup)

Blended drinks offer endless possibilities. Combine:

- Yogurt, milk, cream, whipping cream. As always, use whole milk dairy and avoid creams with added carrageenan (another sugar).
- Vegetables
- Fruits: the usual berries and seasonal fruit.

Nuts and seeds

(a small handful)

When you are in a hurry or travelling, a handful of nuts is a handy snack! Avoid the mixes with dry fruit because of the sugar content.

Nuts and seeds contain fat, protein, some useful carbohydrates and a lot of micronutrients. The balance between the macronutrients is not ideal, but for a quick, no fuss, on-the-go snack, it's about as good as it gets!

Olives and cheese

(2 oz cheese and 4 olives)

Olives are cured in many different ways; try them all for variety! Taste various cheeses (little mozzarella balls, little cubes of feta, ewe's cheese...), for extra indulgence, add Parmesan Crackers*.

Smoked fish

(2 oz of fish)

Smoked[*] fish has similar nutritional value to fresh fish. For salmon, select wild fish if possible. But don't limit yourself to salmon, try mackerel, white fish, trout, eel, herring, etc.

Cream and butter are a nice complement to smoked fish. For the vegetable portion of the snack, include asparagus spears, celery or cucumber sticks. Add Parmesan Crackers*, and you have a luxurious treat!

Vegetables and dips

Why stop at celery and nut butter? Try:

- Carrots, cauliflower, cucumber, radishes, bell peppers...
- Cream cheese, guacamole, tapenade, butter, Crab Dip*...

And...

Canned sardines in oil, canned salmon or tuna, fish roe, cod liver, Cheesecake* (see our sugarless recipe), Swiss Cheese Cookies*, Deviled Eggs*...

Peanuts

Contrary to the other common nuts, peanuts[*] grow in underground pods. They are legumes and contain lectins and phytic acid. They also are a source of aflatoxin[*], a potentially toxic substance. For these reasons, some people advise against eating any peanuts at all.

But in fact, the benefits of peanuts outweigh their negative aspects:

1. It's a question of proportion: true, legumes are not so desirable because of their antinutrients; but legumes are normally eaten in much larger quantities than nuts.

2. We should limit lectins, but we can't eliminate them entirely, they are in everything. Note that roasting the peanut helps diminish the lectins.

3. The risk of aflatoxin[*] is overblown. However, since aflatoxins increase over time, freshness of the peanuts is important.

As part of a diverse diet, peanuts provide good nutrition. Pay attention to individual response such as intestinal tolerance or allergic reactions (even non life threatening).

Yogurt and fermented foods

Many health properties are attributed to fermented foods in the public's mind. True, fermentation can alter nutritional properties, add flavor and variety (many dairy products are fermented); it helps detoxify legumes; it also makes food more digestible, especially for soy. (In fact, it's the only way to make soy[*] edible.)

Don't think of fermenting as a magic, miraculous process, though. Most of the time, the initial properties of the food prevail: fermenting soybean doesn't make it healthier for men.

Fermenting, most of the time, simply makes food more palatable.

Swiss Cheese Cookies

These treats constitute the perfect snack, packing a lot of good fats and proteins with very little starch.

These most *addictive* "cookies" are surprisingly crunchy when you bite into them, yet they melt on your tongue... Success is assured with your guests. You should however resist the temptation to make them too big as they are quite filling.

❧

Like pastry crust, the less you knead the dough, the better the result.

Here is a great opportunity to use the fancy gourmet salts that are in fashion nowadays.

Makes 20 cookies ~

- 4 oz butter
- 4 oz Swiss cheese
- 3 oz almond meal
- 1 oz flour
- 1 egg
- ¼ teaspoon nutmeg
- Ground black pepper
- ¼ teaspoon coarse salt

Butter and the Brain

Other than water, the brain is almost exclusively made of fat, and replenishing that fat should be one of our goals.

Long molecules cannot cross the **blood-brain barrier,** which separates the blood flow from the inside of the brain: this is the case for most of the saturated fats and a large number of the other fats.

Dairy fats, butter in particular, are rich in medium and short-chain fatty acids that can cross the blood-brain barrier. Once inside, they are re-assembled into longer chains as needed to provide energy and building material for the brain.

On the other hand, the heart can use any length of saturated fat. The rest of the body can also use fatty acids of virtually any length.

1. Cut the butter into small pieces and let it warm up at room temperature: it needs to be very soft so it can easily blend with the rest of the ingredients.

2. Grate the cheese finely. It is easier if you let it harden for a little while in the freezer before doing so.

3. Quickly mix all the ingredients except the egg, working with your fingertips, as you would prepare a pastry crust. Make sure no pieces of butter remain visible.

4. Add the egg and mix. If the dough is too sticky, use a spoon. Then refrigerate until the dough can be handled easily.

5. Spread a large elongated spoonful of dough on a piece of plastic wrap. Fold the wrap over and shape a roll, about 1 inch thick.

6. Place in the freezer for at least 1 hour, until frozen stiff. This is necessary so the cookies won't melt and spread out while cooking. You can, therefore, prepare the rolls ahead of time and store them in the freezer until you need them.

7. Preheat oven to 400 °F.
Unwrap the frozen rolls and cut into ¾-inch long sections. Place them on a cookie sheet, spacing them so they have room to spread a little bit. Bake for about 15 to 20 minutes.

Take out of the oven when the cookies are slightly golden, but don't let them burn!.

NOTE: You can vary the proportions of almond meal to flour: the 1 to 3 proportion used here works well. For a sturdier cookie, use 2 oz flour and 2 oz almond meal. It is even possible to make a flourless cookie using 4 oz almond meal: it will be more fragile, but delicious and starch free!

Parmesan Crackers

These super crispy crackers are made of 100 % cheese! They are perfect as a protein-and-fat snack, a nice treat with your morning eggs, a crunchy addition to a salad, or on the side of a soup. They can replace chips for dips.

They can also be shaped into elegant serving bowls for serving snacks or appetizers.

The shredded cheese has more moisture and helps the cracker stick together. The grated cheese gives crunch. In most cases, a half and half mix works well. But if the cheese pancake is too sticky and difficult to turn over, it's probably because it contains too much moisture. In that case, increase the proportion of grated cheese.

Makes 30 crackers ~ ⏳⏳

- 8 oz shredded Parmesan cheese
- 8 oz finely grated Parmesan cheese
- Optional spices: freshly ground black pepper, cayenne pepper, paprika, etc...
- Seeds (optional)

Seeds

Pumpkin seeds are the kings of seeds as far as nutrients are concerned, thanks to the array of good fats they contain and their omega-3 content.

Since modern diets tends to overwhelm our system with omega-6, having omega-3 rich food is a way to improve our food diversity.

Oven method

1. Preheat the oven to 375 °F. Line a baking tray with parchment paper.

2. Mix the two cheeses, optionally adding the spices.

3. Place tablespoons of the mixture in little mounds on the parchment paper. Spread them with the back of the spoon to obtain 4-inch wide discs. Allow for at least ½ inch of space for the crackers to spread during cooking.

4. Bake for about 6 minutes or until golden. Detach with a thin spatula (this is easier after they have cooled off a bit).

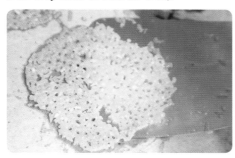

Let cool before serving. The crackers can be kept in an airtight container, although nobody ever had a chance to test how long they could last...

You can drape a Parmesan pancake over an upside-down glass and press gently to shape a bowl (it helps if the cracker is a little less cooked than usual).

Serve salads or snacks in these fancy edible bowls.

Stove top method

This method works well too, allowing to produce larger crackers or smaller batches without fuss.

1. Heat a non-stick skillet over medium-high heat. The pan should be hot enough for the cheese to melt, but not so hot that it burns. This might take a little experimenting.

2. Spread a handful of cheese mixture in a thin 6-inch disk in the skillet. The thinner the layer of cheese, the crispier the result.

3. Let it cook for 3 to 4 minutes, until the bottom turns golden brown. Flip over with a spatula and let cook for about a minute, until the other side is golden too.

For fancier crisps, sprinkle seeds in the skillet before adding the cheese.

Crab Dip

This preparation works well as a dip for raw vegetables. You can also accompany it with Parmesan Crackers*.

෴

Crab is a good source of several minerals, but its biggest claim to nutrient fame is vitamin B12 (although in that respect, egg yolks do even better).

Makes 3 cups ~ ⏳

- 1 cup fresh crab meat
- 1 cup Homemade Mayonnaise*
- 1 cup cheddar cheese, grated
- ½ cup scallions, minced
- Freshly ground black pepper

⚠ **Freshness** is important for all seafood, but even more so for shellfish: spoiled shellfish[*] has a high toxicity.

1. Mix the crab meat, mayonnaise and grated cheese.

2. In a double boiler, cook over medium heat until melted through (you can simply place a heat-proof bowl in a pan of water).

3. Stir in the scallions and black pepper.

Serve hot as a dip with raw vegetables: celery, asparagus, cucumber, carrots...

Flavonoids

A large family of pigments synthesized by plants, flavonoids have in common a chemical structure with a 3-ring carbon backbone.

Anthocyanidins are a subclass of flavonoids.

Plants particularly rich in flavonoids include: parsley, onions, tea, bananas, citrus fruits, legumes, cocoa and all of the ones that are rich in "cyans," recognizable by their red-blue color.

Flavonoids claim many health benefits that, for most, overlap those of anthocyanidins.

Their characteristic taste is bitterness.

Nomenclature

One reason why nutrients are so confusing is that there are many possible ways to classify them. This results in a lot of different families that partially overlap one another; any given nutrient generally belongs to several families.

For instance, nutrients can be sorted out by:

1. Stereo-chemical properties: *this way of classifying examines the 3-dimensional shape of the molecules and the effect of their spatial arrangement on our metabolism.*

For example, flavonoids are substances that share a common molecular structure. This shape confers them common properties for taste and health benefits.

2. Physical and chemical properties: *this classification is based on how the nutrients react physically and chemically.*

For example, "salts" are defined as ionic compounds resulting from the reaction of an acid and a base. They can dissociate into ions that become free to bind with other nutrients: some salts can thus impair nutrition and the functions (muscle contraction, kidney function...) that rely on the presence of unbound ions.

3. Function in a biological system: *for example the class of "antioxidants" groups various substances that have a similar effect on our body, in this case inhibiting the oxidation of other molecules.*

৵

Do not get lost in the maze of nutrient families; don't try to dig into the nomenclature: the way to attend to the categories is to eat colorful, diverse food!

Deviled Eggs

A classic dish, easy to prepare and easier still to eat!

Add ingredients in the yolk mixture according to your taste:

- Minced shallots
- Chopped pickles
- Tabasco sauce
- Worcestershire sauce...

Garnish with toppings of your choice:

- Capers
- Avocado
- Olives
- Parsley...

Macronutrients

Our "ideal plate" has a built-in way to limit the total intake of food by imposing a fixed 3 to 1 proportion of vegetables to proteins. While the 3/1 ratio was determined empirically, for most people, observing these rules will make them feel full before they overeat.

The "ideal plate" limits addictive foods by removing sugar and starches, making the body more responsive to its satiation signals. If you obey these principles, your body will not develop hormonal resistance, and it will be able to tell you reliably when to stop eating.

⚠ **Calorie restriction** may lead to missing nutrients, that is, malnourishment.

Calorie restriction has many other potentially negative effects, depending on the nature of the restriction: if food intake is limited across the board, it is probably OK. But, if the restriction concerns mostly protein or fat, as is the trend today, it is harmful because the proportion of carbs in the diet is increased. Low-fat-low-carb diets are equally dangerous because they can result in burning muscle for energy.

If you eat right, you don't need to restrict your calories to achieve a good, healthy body shape.

The quality of the calories is more important than their quantity: the impact of our food on our blood sugar and insulin production is more important than its caloric value.

Makes 12 pieces ~ ⧗ ⧗

- 6 large eggs
- 2 tablespoons Homemade Mayonnaise*
- 1 teaspoon white vinegar
- 1 teaspoon Dijon mustard

Garnish:

- Paprika

1. **Hard boil the eggs:** place them in a saucepan; add enough cold water to cover the eggs by 1 or 2 inches. Bring to a boil. Cover, turn heat off and let stand, covered, for 15 minutes.

2. Drain immediately and rinse for 1 minute under cold running water. Tap the eggs to crack the shells all over and peel. Slice the eggs in half lengthwise; carefully extract and reserve the yolks.

3. Mash the yolks with a fork. Add the mayonnaise, vinegar, mustard and optional ingredients; season to taste with salt and pepper and stir well.

4. Spoon the yolk mixture into the half egg whites. For cleaner results, you can make a piping bag out of a plastic bag by cutting open one of the corners.

Garnish with paprika and the toppings of your choice.

Breakfast Scramble

Scrambled eggs are a quick and easy breakfast fix with unlimited possibilities. The combination presented here offers a base from which anything can be substituted. Use your imagination and your leftovers!

Cook the ingredients that take longer separately (raw meat, hard vegetables) so they can be done properly without overcooking the rest of the dish.

Eat a lot of eggs

The dark ages of egg restriction are over!

It has been proven that dietary cholesterol[*] (the one in the food) does not affect our health. We can eat as many eggs as we want, as long as it doesn't threaten the variety of our diet.

Eggs provide a great source of proteins, fats and vitamin B12.

Eggs yolks are a good source of iron in ferrous (Fe^{2+}) form. In the vegetables, iron is often present in ferric (Fe^{3+}) form, which is harder for the body to absorb.

Serves 2 ~ ⧗

- 1 tablespoon butter
- ½ zucchini, diced into ½-inch pieces
- ½ yellow zucchini, dices into ½-inch pieces
- 6 crimini mushrooms, quartered
- ½ cup blanched broccolini
- 1 handful baby arugula leaves
- 3 tablespoons grated cheese
- 4 eggs

1. Heat the butter in a sauté pan over medium heat until it becomes frothy.

2. Add the meat or vegetables that take longer to cook (bell pepper, zucchini, mushroom...) and sauté until soft, 2 to 5 minutes.

3. Add the pre-cooked vegetables (broccolini) and wait for a minute or two for them to warm up.

4. Throw the fresh greens on top, wait until they are a little wilted and mix with the rest.

5. Beat the eggs.

6. Fold the eggs into the vegetables, cooking until just set. Season to taste with salt and pepper.

7. Top with grated cheese. Cover and wait 5 minutes until the cheese is melted.

Variations are endless, anything goes, especially leftovers from the night before!

MEAT	VEGETABLE	CHEESE
Cubed or shredded (pork, beef, chicken...)	Blanched or steamed (asparagus, broccoli...)	Hard (Cheddar, Gruyere, Gouda, Jack...)
Ground (pork, beef, turkey, sausage...)	Sautéed (eggplants, leeks, mushrooms, onion, scallion...)	Soft (Mozzarella, blue cheese, goat cheese...)
Seafood (shrimp, crab, canned fish...)	Fresh (avocado, tomato, salad mix, leafy greens, parsley, cilantro, herbs...)	Grated or shredded (Parmesan, Pecorino, Swiss...)

Eggs Benedict with "Polenta"

Polenta, a traditional food in many parts of the world, is prepared with corn meal. The version presented here substitutes cauliflower and produces a very satisfying result.

Serve for breakfast in small portions, or make it a complete meal with larger portions.

Breakfast for 4 ~ ⧖ ⧖ ⧖

- 4 eggs
- 2 teaspoons white vinegar
- ½ teaspoon salt

Greens:

- 1 bunch green leafy vegetables
- 2 tablespoons oil

Hollandaise Sauce:

- 1 egg yolk
- 1 teaspoon water
- 1 teaspoon lemon juice
- 4 oz butter

Cauliflower Polenta:

- 2 ½ cups grated cauliflower
- 1 egg
- 2 large tablespoons sour cream
- 2 oz shredded Swiss cheese

Hollandaise Sauce

1. Mix the egg yolk, water and lemon juice in a small narrow bowl.

2. Melt the butter in a separate container, until frothy.

3. Place a handheld blender in the bowl containing the egg mixture. Turn the blender on and slowly pour in the butter. Keep blending until all the butter has been incorporated. The sauce should be thick, coating a wooden spoon. Season to taste.

Cauliflower "Polenta"

4. Separate the cauliflower into large florets; grate them using the large holes of a box grater.

   Measure the required quantity. Reserve the rest for another usage, such as Cauliflower Crust Pizza*.

5. Bring to a boil a half inch of water at the bottom of a pot. Insert a steamer basket with the grated cauliflower. Cover and steam for 5 minutes. Remove the basket from the heat. Let cool and air out the steam from the cauliflower.

   Preheat the oven to 350 °F.

6. Mix the steamed cauliflower with the rest of the "polenta" ingredients, season to taste with salt and pepper. Place the mixture in small buttered individual molds or on a large baking tray, in a layer about 1-inch thick. Bake in preheated oven for 40 minutes.

Poached eggs

7. Heat a saucepan filled with water within 1 inch of the top. Add the salt and vinegar.

8. When the water is boiling, turn off the heat. With a spoon, stir the water in one direction to create a spinning vortex in the center of the pan. Crack 1 egg into a small cup and very gently, drop the egg in the center of the vortex: this will help the egg stay together.

9. Cover and let the egg poach for 4 minutes. Remove carefully from the water with a slotted spoon; reserve in a bowl of warm water.

   Poach the other eggs in the same way. To save time, you can poach all the eggs together: in that case, don't spin the water. The eggs might not be as pretty but they will be ready faster.

Assembly

Sauté the greens in the oil over medium heat until wilted.

On each plate:

- Place a portion of polenta.
- Top it with a bed of greens.
- Place a poached egg on top.
- Finish with a generous serving of Hollandaise sauce.

Serve immediately.

Quiche

Quiche Lorraine is named after a region in the North East of France.

This savory open pie, with its filling of eggs and bacon, and a deliciously crunchy crust, seems to have been created for breakfast. Since it is a pie after all, it might be an easier morning fare for those people who miss a breakfast pastry.

This version uses almond meal for the crust. Some recipes call for ham instead of bacon. Cooked vegetables, such as spinach or broccoli, may be added to the filling, making this dish a complete meal.

Although it is a little more elaborate than most breakfast dishes, it can be prepared in advance and reheated in the morning.

Almond meal (sometimes called "almond flour") is a great non-starchy substitute for flour in many cases. It is made from pure almonds, so its nutritional properties are those of almonds.

Since it doesn't contain gluten, it is not as structurally strong as flour. Adding butter and eggs helps.

When used to replace flour, the finely ground, white almond meal from blanched peeled almonds works best. For "breading" or dishes like this one, a coarse, less processed version works well.

Serves 4 ~ ⧖ ⧖

Crust:

- 4 oz unsalted butter
- 6 oz fine almond meal
- 1 egg

Filling:

- 1 small onion, minced
- 5 oz bacon, cut into small pieces
- 3 large eggs
- 1 cup heavy cream
- 6 pinches of grated nutmeg
- 1 oz butter

1. Preheat the oven to 425 °F.

   Melt the butter for the crust and mix with the almond meal and egg.

2. Butter a 9 or 10-inch pie dish thoroughly. Press the almond meal mixture into the dish to form a crust, going about 1 inch up the sides. Reserve in a cool place.

3. In a heavy skillet over medium heat, cook the bacon and onion, stirring occasionally, until the onion turns translucent and golden yellow, about 10 minutes.

4. Spread the bacon and onion mixture over the "crust" in the pie dish.

5. Whisk together the eggs, cream and nutmeg. Season to taste with salt and pepper. Pour in the dish, leaving ¼ inch for the mixture to expand. Dot the butter on top.

⚠ Vegetarians and vegans are at particular risk for B12 deficiency:

For vegetarians, the only natural source of B12 is in egg yolks, as real B12 is produced only by animals.

Bake on the center rack of the oven, until the top is golden and the quiche is set in the center, about 30 minutes. Let cool slightly before serving.

Vitamin B12

Although we don't like to put any particular nutrient in the spotlight, vitamin B12 is especially important:

- *The entire neurological system (nerves and brain) is deeply dependant on B12. Without B12, it does not function.*

- *Our bone marrow cannot make red cells and transport oxygen without B12.*

- *Methionine, an essential amino acid (no way around it), poses a threat for a part of population (genetically deficient in the enzyme methylene tetrahydrofolate reductase) because it causes a build-up in homocysteine, a toxic derivative. Vitamin B12 is essential for clearing that build-up.*

Desserts

Limit sugar consumption

Dessert should be an occasional treat, not a routine. Choose the best and enjoy it mindfully. Make it worth the trouble!

All the natural sweeteners have pretty much the same effect as table sugar on your body.

While there are essential fats and essential amino acids, there are no essential carbohydrates: the body can manufacture all the carbs it needs.

But in fact, the diet we propose is not a low-carb diet: by eating a lot of colorful nutrient-dense vegetables, you do consume a good amount of carbohydrates.

Sugar is addictive for hormonal reasons. It is also addictive for psychological reasons. It's worth trying to break the habit.

Sweeteners

Our sweet tooth evolved at the dawn of mankind, when sugar was scarce. Now that sugar is ubiquitous, this fondness has become a liability: it is part of an ancient signaling system that is completely unadapted to the modern world.

- **Glucose** is a simple sugar. Our body processes most of the carbohydrates we eat into glucose.
- **Fructose**, also a simple sugar, is naturally occurring, predominantly in fruit.
- **Sucrose**, or table sugar, is a disaccharide; its molecule is a combination of glucose and fructose.

Sucrose, glucose and fructose are sparsely spread in nature; therefore our body is not equipped to deal with an over-abundance of either.

The main problem with glucose is that it triggers the production of insulin. Excessive sugar and insulin are toxic to our body. For a detailed discussion of the nefarious effects of glucose, see section *The Hormonal Effects of Food*.

⚠ Fructose

Our body processes fructose differently than glucose. However, fructose[*] doesn't solve the problem of the physiological harm of sugar.

Fructose is more readily converted into triglycerides, which are easily converted into body fat. Fructose decreases the diameter of our LDL particles, which increases their ability to migrate through the arterial walls and damage our arteries. Fructose carries an array of negative hormonal effects, different from those of glucose, but as deadly.

If you consume fructose in its natural environment, such as a whole fruit, it is not so nefarious. When extracted and super concentrated, it becomes very toxic.

⚠ High fructose corn syrup

Never, ever, ever, ever, ever, use it! Although there is nothing uniquely bad about it, this is highly concentrated fructose. Its introduction is responsible from a lot of modern evils.

Eating whole corn? Once a month is OK. As with all starches, the main drawback of corn is its high sugar content.

⚠ Artificial sweeteners

For a lifetime of food enjoyment, we must re-train our palate. Once we are able to appreciate natural flavors, the pleasure in food will increase exponentially; food will once again be thrilling!

In order to do so, we have to get away from seeking the sugary tastes of our childhood. This is one of the reasons why we should avoid artificial sweeteners: their usage will only reinforce a bad habit and prevent our palate (and brain) to re-train.

Additionally, artificial sweeteners, even though they may not contain actual sugar, will trigger some brain and body chemistry associated with a response to sugar. The artificial sweetness will disrupt the neuroendocrine system that regulates hunger and activity[sweeteners].

⚠ Agave nectar

This is another manufactured sugar. It has more nutrient value than plain table sugar, but it is still highly concentrated sugar.

⚠ Honey

Honey has a high glycemic load, but it also has some redeeming properties: it contains small amounts of minerals, enzymes and micronutrients; it might also have some anti-viral effects.

For these reasons, honey is preferable to other sweeteners: if you're going to use a sweetener, use honey.

However, it is still is a concentrated, manufactured sugar (albeit by the bees). Use it sparingly.

> Sugars occurring in their natural context come with other nutrient values, and thus we can endorse their *occasional* use.

Nutrition and Exercise

Nowadays everybody agrees that exercise is necessary. Motivations differ from person to person: health, weight loss, strength, body build-up, athletic performance...

In this section, we will examine how nutrition affects and complements exercise.

ENERGY PRODUCTION

Exercise and energy are tightly connected, so first, we need to understand how the food we eat is stored and used to produce energy.

Our body's ability to produce energy all boils down to ATP production: ATP molecules are the immediate source of energy that enables us to move our body around.

Our cells hold a small amount of ready-to-use ATP that can be consumed in a matter of seconds and must be replenished. This replenishment is achieved in three manners:

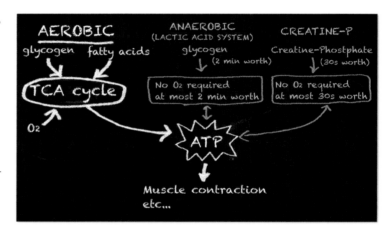

1. **Aerobic (TCA cycle)** - An important characteristic of this system is that it requires oxygen to operate: that's why our capacity to extract O_2 from our breathing is important (VO_2max). This system can generate large amounts of ATP, but its rate of production is relatively low.

2. **Anaerobic (Lactic Acid System)** - This method is engaged when oxygen is too scarce for the needs of the aerobic system: it produces ATP quickly, but its capacity is limited to less than 2 minutes' worth of effort. It is accompanied with the production of lactic acid, hydrogen ions and the well known sensation of muscle burn. Its fuel is primarily muscle glycogen.

3. **Creatine-Phosphate** - This system can replenish ATP quickly but it is only good for up to 30 seconds of exertion: its function is to supply very high intensity, short bursts of energy; its fuel is a chemical (phosphocreatine) present in limited quantity in our cells.

All three methods come into play at some point during athletic activity, but one will be predominant depending on the intensity and duration of the exercise:

- The Aerobic System is important for sports emphasizing endurance, from a 5-minute run to a marathon.

- For events requiring a maximal energy output for 30 to 120 seconds (200 to 800 meter run), the Anaerobic System will come into play.

- Athletes such as weight lifters or sprinters, producing short, intense efforts, take advantage of the Creatine-Phosphate System.

While very important under specific circumstances, the last two systems can be considered as specialty items. In this section, we will focus on the aerobic process, since it produces the bulk of the energy for most of us common mortals.

FUEL STORAGE AND RELEASE

Although proteins are also used under special conditions, the major sources of fuel for the TCA cycle are fats and sugars (numbers given as a rough estimate):

1. In the blood, as circulating sugar (mostly glucose, 5 g total) and fats (mostly triglycerides, 8 g). These are immediately available.

2. In the liver, as glycogen (100 g = 430 Calories) and a small amount of triglycerides. Glycogen can be viewed as short term energy storage.

3. In the muscles, as glycogen (350 g = 1500 Cal) and triglycerides (250 g = 2500 Cal).

4. In the fat cells, as triglycerides (10 kg = 95,000 Cal). Fat is longer term energy storage.

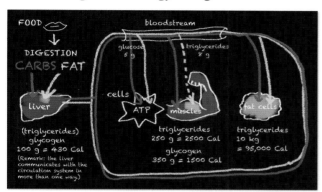

The carbs we eat are broken down during digestion and circulated through the blood (after a passage through the liver). When blood sugar is high enough, sugar is taken into our cells to produce energy immediately, or stored as glycogen in the liver and muscle cells. When glycogen tanks are full, sugar is stored as triglycerides in fat cells: fat cells are by far our largest energy reservoir.

The fat, after being digested, first goes into the lymphatic system, but eventually ends up in the bloodstream. It can then be used for energy production or pass into the muscle and fat cells to be stored as triglycerides.

When needed, glucagon enables the release of glycogen (as glucose) and triglycerides from their storage: after some conversion, they are circulated into the blood and can be grabbed by our cells everywhere to produce energy. One exception is for muscle glycogen that cannot circulate in the blood but must be consumed "on site."

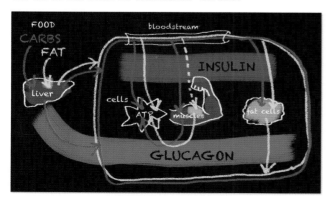

Armed with this basic technical knowledge, let's examine how nutrition can enhance exercise. For a given athletic activity, the problem is to start generating ATP fast enough and to have enough fuel to sustain the production of ATP for the whole duration of the activity.

1. Very low level of activity

At rest, our energy expenditure is very low: our glycogen tanks are easily filled up, any excess food is stored as fat. In the course of the day, glycogen and fat reserves get slowly depleted to provide energy for our basal needs and must be refilled through meals.

Our eating patterns should be cyclical. Grazing (eating very small amounts) all day long to avoid insulin spikes would be a mistake. Our biological machinery is supposed to work in cycles: constant insulin and sugar levels can lead to resistance (the body quits paying attention). We want to trigger our insulin/glucagon cycles by alternating periods of eating and fasting that will deplete our glycogen reserves.

Periodicity also governs the anabolic (building) and catabolic (tearing down) states of our body. Catabolic mode (happening during the fasting time) is needed to get rid of old stuff.

2. Exercise for health

The first benefit of exercise, even for those with no particular health problems, is increased well being and enjoyment of life.

Exercise substantially improves our hormonal response to food, making us less prone to hormonal resistance. It enables the harmonious regulation of the cycles of hunger and satiation, as well as blood sugar and insulin. It improves cellular health and leads to a vibrant energetic personality.

We make a distinction between "health" and "fitness." Fitness is usually interpreted in terms of performance, the training and eating being optimized for a specific goal to the detriment of long term health. Health is a global concern of the whole body and mind.

For exercise to be effective we need not only enough circulating energy in the blood, but also micronutrients and elements (for example, calcium and magnesium are required for muscular movement). We want a fresh supply of those in the blood in times of demand.

- Eat 30 to 60 minutes before exercising: this allows time for some nutrients from the meal to pass into the blood. After exercise starts, the body shifts to a mode in which digestion and absorption of nutrients are impaired.

- Try to eat again 30 to 60 minutes after exercise: this is the time window where the cells are more efficient at taking up nutrients, helping the body to recover and repair itself.

If you can, time exercise to fall between two meals. Otherwise, eat relatively small snacks: you don't want to disrupt the rest of your energy cycles. Focus on proteins, fats and micronutrients!

⚠ *In terms of decreased injuries and improved hormonal environment, the optimal time to exercise is early to mid-afternoon.*

3. Trekking

This sounds fine for everyday life, you'll say, but what about if I am about to embark on a week of trekking? Don't I need carbohydrates?

No. If you have been eating properly, you have created a flexible capacity to exploit your energy sources. You don't need the extra carbs because your body has the ability to use fat for energy.

Your endurance is already much better than if you had been relying on sugar and starches: heavy carb eaters train their bodies to use only carbs, and, in our view, that is a sign of malnourishment.

The body also needs many micronutrients for muscles, tendons and ligaments to be supple and the lining of the arteries to be compliant.

4. Fat loss

Plain weight loss is not the goal. It's not even generally desirable. Being too thin is rarely healthy: lean muscle mass and bone density are associated with greater longevity. Healthy weight loss is *fat loss*.

There are two kinds of fat: *subcutaneous* (right under the skin) and *visceral* (around the internal organs). They respond differently to food.

Subcutaneous fat is fairly harmless. Internal fat, the most dangerous health wise, is the body's preferred site for depositing[LPL] fat resulting from eating starch, sugar and alcohol, so it is important to restrict these. Internal fat is a warning sign of excess in the diet.

For internal fat loss, favor short, high power interval training, which improves insulin sensitivity and increases the benefit from this dietary restriction. Long, low intensity exercise raises cortisol levels and interferes with fat loss.

Here again, don't skip the pre-exercise meal: micronutrients are necessary to the efficiency of the workout. If you don't eat well, you don't get your bang for your exercise buck!

FAT MYTHS

Myth #1 - *To be thin, you should focus on burning more calories than you eat.*

This line of thought is dangerous because its logical conclusion is calorie restriction, which generally is not a good idea: it can lead to malnourishment; it slows down your metabolism; it makes you smaller but not thinner.

If fat loss were a simple accounting problem, where expenditures must balance income, it wouldn't be so hard to lose weight.

Of course exercise consumes energy, and as a result, you are more likely to be trim. But this won't happen if you can't burn fat because of your hormonal and enzymatic condition.

Myth #2 - *Exercising on an empty stomach will make you burn fat right away.*

No. When blood glucose is low, the body dumps its glycogen first: all you achieve is earlier depletion of your glycogen. This doesn't make you access your fat any better and impairs your workout.

Myth #3 - *Eating fat makes you fat.*

No. In fact, eating a larger proportion of fat helps stir your body's preference toward burning fat instead of sugar. And if you don't create the enzymatic environment that allows you to burnt fat, you can exercise all you want, you will not lose fat!

Myth #4 - *To burn fat, do low intensity exercise.*

It might be true that lower intensity activity uses a higher percentage of fat for fuel, but since it burns very little energy, it's a higher percentage of not much...

5. Athletic performance

The general advice applies here too: pay attention to your micronutrients and elements. Eat before training.

Insulin can be anabolic under the right conditions. (But not for most people: most of the time, for most people, it just signals storage.) That's the one time you could use carbs to get the insulin spikes: an athlete could have a potato or another starchy nutrient-rich vegetable with his protein. Note that this is different from carb loading.

CARB LOADING MYTH

As everybody knows, endurance athletes do what's called "carb loading." Although there is more to it, this is understood by the general public as a carb binge the night before a race.

The idea is to create a greater reserve of glycogen. Seems like a reasonable idea but...

- Glycogen tanks are pretty small. It doesn't take much to fill them up, and most of the time our glycogen capacity is full.

- Carb loading doesn't expand the capacity of the glycogen tanks.

- When the glycogen tanks are full, the ingested carbs get stored as fat.

- High blood sugar and insulin shift the body's energy preference toward sugar and impair our capacity to use fat. The people that cannot switch to fat when their glycogen is exhausted are those who crash at the end of the marathon.

Instead, it's a much better idea to create an environment where the body can use fat, of which we have a nearly infinite supply, whereas we only have about 2000 Calories of glycogen.

MICRONUTRIENTS AND ENERGY

It is obvious that insufficient *macronutrients* will result in fatigue during exercise by lack of glucose, glycogen or fats.

Less obvious is the essential role played by *micronutrients* in energy production: a huge flux of micronutrients, electrolytes and minerals is required in order for our metabolism to function properly. Deficiency in those will be the source of many ailments, including fatigue.

One key factor to athletic performance is the ability to replenish ATP: this capacity depends on the ion gradient across the mitochondria membrane; that is in turn dependent on the presence of elements and electrolytes. The quality of nutrition improves the efficiency of the whole energy production chain.

In conclusion, the dietary advice for athletes is pretty much the same as for the rest of us:

- Build your plate around protein: the daily target for most people is between 1 and 3 g of protein per kg of body weight. This quantity should be increased based on the activities for the day, when more repletion or repair is needed, and for younger or older people. For an athlete, it can be increased to 2 to 5 g.

- Sports that depend on muscle mass and focus primarily on strength and power, are more protein intense. For those, double the protein throughout the day, before and after exercise.

- Sustained sub-maximal exercise such as jogging requires no additional protein.

- The scale of vegetables is defined by the scale of protein. The protein sets the agenda: it could be a 3-oz buffalo steak, or an 8-oz salmon fillet; the vegetable portion of the meal is still 3 times that of protein by weight, based on raw weight.

Bananas with Coconut Cream

This is a low-starch adaptation of a Vietnamese classic. The original version adds tapioca pearls and sugar. But in fact, when there is no added sugar, the pinch of salt brings forward the sweetness of the banana and coconut.

Choose bananas that are ripe just so: too ripe and they turn black, not ripe enough and tart, the dessert will be bland.

For this recipe, use canned coconut extract, not the clear juice for drinking.

Sesame

Sesame seeds contain unique nutrients: the prickly sensation on the tongue is the manifestation of anti-inflammatory effect of the oils they contain.

⚠ Bananas

Bananas don't enter in the northern fruit category. As a general rule, sub-tropical and tropical fruits are higher in sugar: this is the case for bananas, mangos, papayas, pineapple...

Common wisdom has it that bananas are a great source of potassium, yet tomatoes are richer in potassium.

Keep in mind that this use of bananas in a dessert is not an endorsement of eating bananas on a regular basis... This being said, bananas here are a nice way to bring sugar in its natural environment.

Coconut

Coconut extract brings good saturated fats.

Banana blossom

Serves 6 ~ ⏳

- 6 large ripe bananas
- 400 ml coconut extract
- 2 tablespoons sesame seeds
- ½ teaspoon salt

1. Carefully open the container of coconut extract without shaking it. Scoop up and set aside 3 tablespoons of the creamy part on top.

2. Peel the bananas, removing the strings that run alongside the fruit. Cut each banana into 4 pieces.

3. Place them in a pot. Pour in the rest of the coconut extract; add a pinch of salt. Bring to a boil over high heat so that it boils quickly; turn heat down, let boil gently for 3 minutes and turn off heat.

4. In a small pan, roast the sesame seeds until they turn golden (but not black), stirring continuously so that they don't burn. Add the salt. Crush lightly to release the aroma.

In each individual bowl, place a few pieces of banana, cover with the cooking liquid.

At the last moment only, put a spoonful of the creamy coconut and a pinch of roasted sesame seeds on top of each serving.

Baked Apples

The quintessential dessert of yesteryear! The traditional recipe calls for brown sugar, but when you are used to real food, the natural sweetness of the apple, enhanced by baking, is more than enough.

⚠ Don't seek food only for their fiber content. We get plenty of fiber with the all the nutrient-rich vegetables in our diet!

Dietary fiber

Dietary fiber[*] is a special type of carbohydrate that does not turn into blood sugar.

- **Insoluble fiber,** such as cellulose, passes through the body, absorbing water in the process. Its claim to fame is to facilitate transit. Fiber is the reason why broccoli must be cooked to release the nutrients it traps.

- **Soluble fiber** breaks down in water. It can absorb water to become a gelatinous substance that is fermented by bacteria in our digestive tract, yielding physiologically active products.

The notion that "fiber cures everything" is oversimplistic: fiber is more than just transit. By putting too much focus on fiber, we deprive ourselves of nutrition (while absorbing water, insoluble fiber also pulls out nutrients.) Soluble fiber is less prone to that effect; on the other hand, it can cause negative gastrointestinal reactions.

There is such a thing as "fiber quality," determined in part by the soluble to insoluble fiber ratio. But again, don't become a fiber accountant!

Don't invest everything in fiber.

This being said, the fiber in the apple is a "good" fiber with a healthy soluble to insoluble ratio.

The apples that work best are the ones you'd use for baking a pie: the very common Golden Delicious works well; other more tart varieties are worth trying too.

Serves 2 ~ ⧖

- 2 organic baking apples
- 2 tablespoons unsalted butter
- 2 pinches of salt
- Cinnamon, nutmeg, or other spices of choice

Serve with:

- 2 tablespoons sour cream or crème fraîche

Nutritious, with a healthy fiber[*] composition, the apple is the poster girl of the northern seasonal fruits!

෴

Don't peel apples: the peel is a great opportunity to get quercetin, a natural remedy against allergies and colds. Red apples are the richest in that respect, but try others too!

⚠ It is especially important to pay attention to the way the apple was grown if you are going to eat the peel.

1. Preheat oven to 350 °F.

2. Scoop out the core of the apples, making sure you don't go all the way through, so you get a well that's closed at the bottom. Place the apples in a baking dish.

3. Fill the well in each apple with 1 tablespoon of butter and a pinch of salt; sprinkle with cinnamon.

4. Bake for 30 to 45 minutes, or until the apples are tender.

Optionally top with a tablespoon of cream and an extra pinch of spices before serving.

Biology vs. Free Will

The emotional attachment to food shouldn't be underestimated: it is obviously very hard to reject the foods you grew up on, the foods your mother fed you.

The psychological implications of food are strong: it's hard to give up sugar for physiological reasons (hormonal vicious cycles), as well as psychological reasons (the brain knows it will be rewarded with immediate pleasure by sweet food).

However, you can also make psychology work in your favor:

Surely, some people are endowed with "better" genes than others; everybody has a friend who can eat huge amount of any foods, apparently without adverse effects, whereas they must be permanently on guard. Genetic conditions can be the cause of hormonal resistance, with the effect that biological signals go unheard, in particular the "Stop eating!" signal.

If you suffer from such a condition, you must acknowledge it and move on. Although it's tougher, you still have freedom of choice.

Bad genes don't mean you are doomed and condemned to bad nutrition: you still have free will! Awareness of your biology should help your will's efforts: if you are leptin resistant, know that you must struggle more than others to stop eating and do it!

The physiological signals have authority but not dictatorship. Your behavior can win over them.

Chocolate Mousse

For this low-sugar variation of a French classic, you can select any chocolate. Since the only sugar of this recipe comes from the chocolate, this allows you to control the sweetness of the mousse: after you have tried the 70% "bitter" chocolate, sweet enough for most people, dare the 85 % or even the 90 % one!

Chocolate mousse can be prepared very simply with just chocolate and eggs, nothing more. However, this recipe is richer in good dairy fats, and the whipped cream makes the mousse smoother. But if you prefer it firmer, skip the cream.

Checking the ingredients when buying chocolate is a good occasion to learn what you are eating. Read the label: a lot of sophisticated chemistry goes into the production of a chocolate bar.

If your source is reliable, and the hens are healthy, raw eggs are not dangerous. Elsewhere, pasteurized eggs are safer to use in the mousse.

Since it's not cooked, don't keep the mousse for too long (a few days). However, it is interesting to note that, contrary to popular expectations, almost all animal products degrade in safer ways than vegetal products[decay].

Cocoa pods

Serves 6 ~ ⧗ ⧗

- 8 oz chocolate of your choice, broken into pieces
- 4 tablespoons unsalted butter
- 4 eggs, separated
- ¾ cup heavy whipping cream
- 2 teaspoons orange liqueur (Grand Marnier or Cointreau, optional)

1. In a bowl placed in a pot of simmering water, melt the chocolate and butter, stirring with a spatula until smooth. Remove from heat. (Actually, you can melt the chocolate and butter directly in the saucepan at very low heat, stirring constantly and removing from heat as soon as the mix is melted.)

Cocoa beans

2. Let cool until the bowl can be moved with bare hands. Add the egg yolks, one at a time, mixing vigorously and thoroughly after each one. Transfer to a large mixing bowl.

3. In a clean metal bowl, beat the egg whites with a pinch of salt to stiff peaks.

4. In another bowl, whip the cream until it becomes frothy. Optionally add the liqueur. Continue to whip to soft peaks.

5. Fold in a large spoonful of beaten egg whites into the chocolate mixture to loosen its consistency. Then fold in the rest of the egg whites thoroughly: use a gentle circular motion of the wooden spatula, lifting the chocolate mass from the bottom to the top.

6. Finally fold in the whipped cream.

Transfer to a serving bowl and refrigerate for at least two hours before serving. (Overnight is better.)

Serve with a dollop of whipped cream on top.

Cheesecake

Serves 8 ~ ⏳ ⏳

Crust:

- 4 oz unsalted butter
- 6 oz hazelnut meal
- 1 egg

Filling:

- 16 oz Philadelphia cream cheese
- 4 oz crème fraîche or sour cream
- 4 eggs
- ½ teaspoon vanilla extract
- Pinch of salt

The low sugar version of a classic: just add a little fruit, cream or cooked fruit.

Although you can use any nut meal for the crust, the hazelnut somehow has the "dessert touch."

⚠ ***Choose whole milk dairy!***

Low-fat dairy is a bad choice.

1) Your body needs fat: fat is necessary for optimal body function.

2) Butyric acid, a short-chain fatty acid, is an energy source. Trans-palmitoleic[*] acid is a good trans fat with beneficial metabolic effects.

3) The processing involved in removing the fat is bad to start with; then the fat is replaced by sugar to compensate for lost the texture and taste.

4) Fat improves the absorption of milk nutrients. Non-fat milk is no better than sugar water.

1. Preheat the oven to 355 °F. Melt the butter and mix with the hazelnut meal and egg.

2. Grease a non-stick round cake pan carefully. Pack the nut and butter mixture at the bottom to form a crust, pressing slightly, especially on the sides. Reserve in a cool place.

3. Mix all the ingredients for the filling (a hand held mixer is best to eliminate the lumps).

Take out and let rest in the refrigerator for at least half a day before serving.

Serve with fresh or cooked fruit.

4. Pour in the cake pan. Bake for 40 minutes, then turn off the oven and leave the cake inside the oven for another 45 minutes.

Banana Bread

This dessert is completely free of added sugar and flour, yet it looks (and tastes) like a cake!

Almond meal is a good substitute for flour in many cases, but since it doesn't contain gluten, it is not as good as flour at holding the cake together. It works best when the almond meal is very fine and white, with no skin.

But for this cake, coarse almond meal will, in fact, do fine.

Buy the bananas one week or two in advance and let them sit at room temperature. They are ready when the skin has turned black.

Vanilla beans

Eggs - *You don't need to restrict the number of eggs you eat for fear of cholesterol: dietary cholesterol[*] is irrelevant.*

But of course, even though egg is an excellent protein (and the only source of B12 for vegetarians), you need to vary your diet to ensure a variety of protein, fats and other nutrients.

Serves 8 ~ ⏳⏳

- 5 medium over-ripe bananas
- 3 oz unsalted butter
- 3 large eggs
- 4 tablespoons plain whole milk yogurt
- ½ teaspoon vanilla extract
- 7 oz almond meal
- 1 teaspoon baking soda
- 1 tablespoon baking powder
- Chocolate chips or nuts (optional)

1. Preheat the oven to 350 °F. Butter thoroughly a rectangular 9" x 5" x 3" cake pan.

2. Mash the bananas well, using a fork.

3. Melt the butter and let it cool a little. Beat the eggs.

4. In a large bowl, mix the bananas, butter, eggs, yogurt and vanilla.

5. Add the almond meal, baking soda and baking powder. Optionally add the chocolate chips or nuts. Mix well.

6. Pour the batter into the cake pan. Bake for about 55 minutes: a knife inserted into the center should come out clean.

Let cool for 10 minutes before inverting on a plate to unmold.

Chocolate Cake

*A cake
w i t h o u t
flour of any kind!
How does it stay together?
Not sure, but it does.*

As with the Chocolate Mousse*, you control the sweetness of the cake by selecting the chocolate.

Insulin and glucagon *are hormones that regulate our energy behavior: how we eat can either put us in "storage" mode or in "spending" mode.*

Eating sugar and starches stimulates insulin production and tips the body towards carb-based energy production and fat storage mode.

When blood sugar is low, glucagon allows the release of stored energy, promoting a higher, healthier metabolic rate.

Serves 8 ~ ⧗ ⧗

- 10 oz chocolate of your choice, broken into pieces
- 6 oz unsalted butter + ½ oz for buttering the mold
- 6 tablespoons whipping cream
- 5 eggs, at room temperature
- 1 pinch of salt

You can still build it...

1. Preheat the oven to 350 °F. Butter a 9-inch cake pan thoroughly. (Unmolding will much easier if you have a mold with a hinge.)

2. In a saucepan over very low heat, melt the chocolate and butter, stirring constantly with a wooden spoon until smooth. Remove from heat.

3. Beat the eggs, cream and salt together for a few minutes.

4. Mix the chocolate preparation and the egg mixture.

5. Pour into the buttered cake mold. Bake in the preheated oven for 45 minutes (check by sticking the tip of a knife in the cake to see if it comes out clean).

Let the cake cool off before unmolding.

Serve with whipped cream or a few berries on top.

Beware of sodas!

Fruit Cobbler

A nice feature about this treat is that it doesn't matter if the fruits produce a lot of juice: since the crust is on top, it won't get soggy. You can therefore use almost any fruit.

This dessert is best with juicy summer fruits, though. Select those with a high nutrient to sugar ratio, such as:

- Berries

- Apricots, peaches, nectarines, plums

- Cherries

Fresh figs work well too, but they are a little heavier in sugar.

Serves 4 to 6 ~ ⧗

- 1 lb fruit of your choice
  pitted and cut into pieces

- Pinch of cinnamon, ginger,
  or spice of your choice

- 1 oz butter for greasing the dish

Crust:

- 4 oz finely ground almond meal

- 2 oz unsalted butter
  at room temperature

⚠ **Fruits**

Fruits are delicious! But remember, there is nothing unique in them: you can find all the same nutrients, with less sugar, in the colorful nutrient-dense vegetables.

Contrary to the widespread belief that fruits are essential to our diet, we don't need fruit, provided we follow a colorful, nutrient-rich diet.

1. Preheat the oven to 395 °F. Mix quickly all the crust ingredients using the finger tips: do not over mix; the preparation must stay loose and crumbly.

2. Butter abundantly an oven-safe dish. Place the fruit on top, sprinkle with the spices.

3. Loosely crumble the crust mixture on top of the fruit.

Bake for 30 minutes, or until the crust is golden. Contrary to what you might think, if you use too much butter for the crust, it will be less crunchy.

Exotic fruits tend to be more loaded with sugar than the rest.

Chilled Peach Soup

This soup is best during the later summer months when peaches are ripe and sweet. There are many similar recipes: the particularity of this one is that it is blended.

Serves 8 ~ ⧗ ⧗

- 10 fresh, medium size, ripe peaches
- 1 cup white wine or sparkling wine
- 2 teaspoons chopped fresh mint leaves
- ½ teaspoon ground cinnamon
- ¼ teaspoon ground nutmeg
- 2 cups half-and-half
- ⅛ teaspoon cayenne pepper
- 6 oz crème fraîche or sour cream
- Fresh mint sprigs for garnish

Stone fruits include peaches, nectarines, apricots, plums, cherries and the lesser knows loquats.

Although they are more southern than apples, they can be considered "seasonal northern fruit" too. They have a higher sugar concentration than apples, but lower than exotic fruit. They tend to contain more carotenoids than apples.

(Mango is also a pitted fruit, but the areas where it grows make it different. The northern seasonal fruits concentrate nutrients in order to be attractive to predators.)

Cooking the fruit releases the sugar, making it taste sweeter.

1. Peel the peaches. This should be easy if they are ripe. Otherwise, bring a pot of water to a simmer. Score the skin by placing an X in the pointed end of each fruit. Place peaches in simmering water for about 1 minute. Immediately remove and put in an ice bath. The peel should come off easily – if not, another minute in the hot water should do it.

2. Remove the pits and slice each peach into wedges. Reserve 1 cup diced for garnish.

3. Place the wine, chopped mint leaves, cinnamon, nutmeg and half-and-half in a medium saucepan. Stir to mix well. Bring to a simmer. (Don't worry about possible curds.)

4. Add the sliced peaches and simmer over medium heat, stirring frequently to prevent scorching, for 15 minutes or until the peaches are tender. Remove from heat.

5. Add the Cayenne pepper. Let the mixture cool slightly. Blend until very smooth. Cover and refrigerate at least 2 hours.

Just prior to serving, beat the cream. Serve the soup cold in individual bowls. Garnish each bowl with reserved diced peaches, a dollop of cream and a sprig of mint.

Clafoutis

Serves 6 ~ ⧗ ⧗

- 1 oz butter for greasing the mold
- 1 ½ lb dark red cherries
- 6 eggs
- 3 oz almond meal
- 1 cup whole milk
- 1 pinch salt

This is a low-carb version of a French classic. In some places they make it with small tart cherries, but we prefer nice, large, juicy ones, such as the Bing variety.

Traditionally the cherries are left whole so that the juice stays inside the fruit, but the children object to that method, saying that the cake is easier to eat when they are pitted. (They have a point: the pits can be dangerous to the teeth of unsuspecting diners). On the other hand, even with a special tool, it is messy and tedious to pit ripe juicy cherries. Wear a large apron!

Cherries are very rich in carotenoids and "cyans." They are very nutritious, but no more than a thousand other vegetables, and they are very rich in sugar...

1. Butter an oven-safe dish generously. Preheat the oven to 390 °F.

2. Wash the cherries, discard the stems. You can pit them, or keep them whole. Place the fruits in a single layer at the bottom of the dish.

3. In a medium-sized bowl, beat the eggs, and then mix in thoroughly all the remaining ingredients.

4. Pour the mixture over the cherries.

Bake for about 30 minutes in the middle of the oven. Test as you would for any cake, by sticking in a small knife: if it comes out clean, the clafoutis is ready.

Serve warm or at room temperature.

Pumpkin Pie

Pumpkin, abundant in the fall, is naturally sweet, and this makes it particularly suitable for a seasonal dessert. This recipe helps to diminish the otherwise excessive amounts of starch consumed during the holidays.

Serves 6 ~ ⏳ ⏳

- ½ oz butter for greasing the dish

Crust:

- 4 oz unsalted butter
- 6 oz fine almond meal
- 1 egg

Filling:

- 1 lb pumpkin flesh
- 3 large eggs
- 1 cup heavy cream
- 1 teaspoon grated cinnamon
- ½ teaspoon grated ginger
- ½ teaspoon salt

Dessert spices, such as nutmeg and cinnamon, possess some kind of unique medicinal effect. Include them in your diet (but remember, they are not magical).

Vanilla is sometimes synthetic. Real vanilla is one of the most expensive spices after saffron. How it is grown and extracted matters: since it is fragile, pesticides are often used; in addition, a lot of processing is required. This is an example of how a straightforward ingredient must be processed enormously to be distributed.

⚠ Excessive carb consumption impairs the metabolic functions: the liver turns excess sugar, especially fructose and alcohol, into triglycerides. Those in turn clog the cells with free fatty acids.

1. Preheat the oven to 375 °F.
   Melt the butter for the crust and mix with the almond meal and egg.

2. Butter a 9-inch pie dish thoroughly. Press the almond meal mixture in it to form a crust, going about ¾ inch up the sides. Reserve in a cool place.

3. Cook the peeled pumpkin flesh in boiling water, until a fork goes in easily (about 15 minutes).

4. Drain and mash with a fork. Let it drain in the colander fairly long in order to extract a good amount of water.

5. Add in all the other ingredients and mix thoroughly. Pour into the dish, allowing ¼ inch for the mixture to expand.

Bake on the center rack of the oven for 45 to 55 minutes: the crust must be golden and the inside still a little soft. A knife must come out clean.

Serve with cream.

Peanut Butter Cookies

You don't need extra sugar for these cookies to be a delicious, nutritious treat. The chocolate provides the sweetness and also structural stability to this somewhat fragile cookie. Use chocolate with as little sugar as you can stand. Also omit the extra salt if the peanut butter is already salted.

Peanut butter's bad reputation was based on its fat content, but we know better than being afraid of fat... Peanut butter is a basic, very nutritious food.

Yes, it is rich in fat (that's a good thing) and protein. It is probably the healthiest "fall back" snack. Many studies show that peanuts[*] lower heart disease.

Watch the composition of your peanut butter: get the plainest one, making sure there is nothing other than peanuts (and possibly a little salt) in it. Look out for added sugar.

And vary: try almond butter, cashew butter, etc.

Makes 16 cookies ~ ⧗ ⧗

- 1 egg
- 4 oz unsweetened peanut butter
- 1 teaspoon vanilla extract
- 4 oz almond flour
- ½ teaspoon baking soda
- 4 oz bitter chocolate
- ½ teaspoon salt

1. Preheat the oven to 375 °F. In a large bowl, beat the egg; add the peanut butter and vanilla; stir well.

2. Add the almond meal, baking soda and salt. Using your fingertips, mix well, until the dough is homogeneous.

3. Taking 1 tablespoon of dough each time, make balls, pressing in the palm of your hands. Lay them out on a baking sheet lined with parchment paper. Flatten each cookie with a fork.

4. Bake for 11 minutes. Then carefully move the cookies to a cooling tray.

5. Melt the chocolate over low heat in a double boiler. Dip each cookie so half of the cookie is covered with chocolate. Let cool until the chocolate hardens.

Exercise

Replenish your nutrients by eating 30 to 60 minutes after exercising: nutrients are necessary for your body to heal, rebuild the torn down ligaments, muscles, etc.

You need not worry about replenishing the glycogen unless you just ran a marathon (and even then, if you are a "fat burner" you didn't burn that much glycogen either.)

A great 1-hour workout burns 600 calories: that's a glass of milk and an apple!

Appendix

Further Reading

Nutritional science is, at this point in time, very incomplete; the only certainty is that there is no certainty. You don't have to agree with all the ideas expressed in the books listed below, but they demonstrate clearly that the science behind our "certainties" is not as solid as we have been led to believe.

Denise Minger. *Death by Food Pyramid*. Primal Blueprint Publishing.

A witty account of *"How Shoddy Science, Sketchy Politics and Shady Special Interests Have Ruined Our Health."*

A very serious book, yet entertaining and humorously written, *Death by Food Pyramid* exposes the fallacies of several nutritional dogmas and the underlying motives.

The book is an eye opener with a detailed history of how incomplete science, scientific feuds and political battles led to the current dietary situation. After reading the book, it becomes obvious that nutritional beliefs don't rest on firm science, that the current dietary guidelines do not reflect the scientific knowledge, and that our health is not necessarily the foremost priority for policy makers.

Nestle, Marion. *Food Politics*. Berkeley: University of California Press.

"How the Food Industry Influences Nutrition and Health."

Marion Nestle chaired the New York University department of Nutrition, Food Studies and Public Health from 1988 through 2003. She was the editor of the 1988 Surgeon General's Report on Nutrition and Health.

In her own words, this is a book about "how food and beverage companies encourage us to buy and eat more, [...] how they lobby government agencies, forge alliances with health professionals, market to children, sell junk food as health food, and get laws passed that favor corporate health over human health."

Michael Pollan. *In Defense of Food*. New York: Penguin Press (2008).

A nice short read, this is a great book to promote eating real food and not food-like substances.

Although we disagree with the assertion that we don't need to eat meat, and although we don't share the dislike of saturated fats, the book is great at explaining the links between politics, business and nutrition. It also demonstrates how modern processing is depriving our food of its nutritional value.

While it is true that the average American eats too much meat, the moto ("Eat mostly plants") undervalues animal proteins that are necessary, albeit in smaller quantity than is currently the norm.

Gary Taubes. *Good Calories, Bad Calories*. New York: Knopf.

A very intelligent and well documented investigation on how bad science and politics conspired to establish the current dietary dogma. It is an engrossing book that reads almost like a mystery novel.

All the important health issues linked to nutrition are addressed in a systematic, chronological manner, unrolling the various processes that led to the current situation. It shows clearly how the exact same scientific data is interpreted by scientist in opposite ways.

You'll find the history of the research on: fat, cholesterol and heart disease; insulin and diabetes; diets and weight loss; and more... The complexity of the hormonal systems involved in nutrition emerges clearly.

This is a long, intense read, but it is well worth the effort for anybody who wants to understand nutrition beyond the clichés.

Nina Teicholz. *The Big Fat Surprise*. Simon & Schuster.

> *"Why Butter, Meat & Cheese Belong in a Healthy Diet."*
>
> Another convincing account of how fats have been unjustly demonized; how low-fat nutritional advice based on weak scientific evidence has created vast health issues.
>
> This fairly easy to read book contains a detailed investigation on nutritional research over the last 60 years. It exposes how false beliefs and misinformation took hold and spread through the scientific community and the public.

ও

PUBLIC POLICY

The U.S. Senate Select Committee on Nutrition and Human Needs. *Dietary Goals for the United States*. Washington D.C. (1997).

> Also referred to as the "McGovern committee," this committee was established to make urgent dietary recommendations in the face of the rising health problems caused by bad nutrition in the United States.
>
> At some point in the 1970's it was concluded that America's health was deteriorating and that congress should be doing something about it. Thus the Federal Government officially got into the nutrition business. Out of this was born the famous Food Pyramid.
>
> This document significantly propelled Keys's ideas on cholesterol and saturated fat from hypothesis to established fact.

ও

REFERENCE BOOKS

While the debate rages around food, and various parties push forward their arguments, an understanding of the body is necessary. These books make difficult reading, but without a wide view of the entire body, we easily get confused by "experts," who only look at parts of the body with a magnifying glass and focus on their pet issue.

David L Nelson; Albert L Lehninger; Michael M Cox. Lehninger principles of biochemistry. New York: W. H. Freeman.

> A good basic biochemistry book for those who really want to dig in!

Human Physiology: An Integrated Approach.

> Another large text book...

ও

VEGANISM, VEGETARIANISM

T. Colin Campbell. *The China Study*. Dallas: BenBella Books.

> This is the vegans' reference book. Its title refers to the China-Oxford-Cornell Project, a series of observational studies done in 69 counties in China (see reference below). *The China Study* book (not to be confused with the study itself) is a huge book, which covers a lot of ground. Its conclusion is that "plant-based foods are beneficial, and animal-based foods are not."
>
> There is heated controversy about this book. Several serious authors have pointed out that the assertions Dr. Campbell makes don't appear to be supported by the China-Oxford-Cornell data itself.

The China-Oxford-Cornell Project (data for *The China Study*)

> http://www.ctsu.ox.ac.uk/~china/monograph/
>
> The 1989 data for *The China Study* is available online for anybody to download, and attempt to verify the conclusions of the book. Analyzing the data, it becomes clear that the China-Oxford-Cornell Project doesn't prove that a vegan lifestyle is healthy, and that in fact the contrary is very likely.

Technical Notes

The notes below are intended as a starting point for those who want to explore the science behind nutrition. All the assertions found in this book are based on strong scientific evidence, thorough documentation and the continual study of the latest research. But, rather than engaging in a scientific papers "shoot-out," we have chosen to provide the reader with pointers that explain the main idea behind our assertions. We encourage people to critically examine the arguments from various sides, no matter how imposing or influential the authors or institution who proffer them seem to be.

The vast quantity of existing documents means that science can be quoted to justify any position: it is especially easy to selectively pick the data that confirms your point of view, and ignore the rest. It is hard for the public to judge the scope and validity of research papers. This is even truer for some articles found on the internet that disseminate false information under a most serious appearance. Scientific research needs to be examined with a broad knowledge of medical issues, and must be put into context. Only by examining all of the evidence can one form a valid, informed opinion.

If you have time and the interest, the following website provides links to research that is relevant and well conducted:

http://quantitativemedicine.net/bibliography/

Adaptation

"Humans coevolved with this kind of nourishment for several hundred thousand years and have genetically adapted to it."

If you believe in the theory of evolution in general, you have to believe that our body has adapted to certain types of food. Can nutritional engineering come up with better foods than what nature provides? Theoretically yes, but we are very, very, very far from being able to do so: it is way beyond our capacity at this time. In the meantime, eat real food!

Trans fats are a good illustration. Natural trans fats are healthy: dairy, for example, contains a lot of natural trans fat, and in larger amounts when it comes from grass-fed animals; trans-palmitoleic acid in dairy is associated with many benefits, in particular a lower incidence of diabetes. The health benefits of trans fats are seemingly connected to their "trans" feature. On the other hand, man-made trans fats are now widely known to cause serious health problems.

Provided we had the right information, it wouldn't be bad to eat as our ancestors did, especially with regards to the nutrient density and variety of their diet. However, beware, there is a lot of faulty anthropology out there!

We can look at adaptation on two levels: the first one is encoded in our genome, and has a time scale of 100,000 of years. The second one is the lifetime adaptation within each individual, and is measured in years: a person can evolve to be a fat burner, or a carb burner; lactase can be induced; muscles are built.

Aflatoxin

"The risk of aflatoxin is an overblown concern."

Aflatoxin is a fungus present everywhere, not only in peanuts. It is toxic in high doses. Aflatoxin has been labeled a carcinogen based on the flawed AMES test. The benefits of eating peanuts highly outweigh the dangers of aflatoxin.

Alcohol

"Well conducted studies have shown that any amount of alcohol increases women's' risk of breast cancer. Studies showing cardiovascular benefits in men all have serious flaws."

"Concerning wine, most of the claims of cardiovascular benefits are questionable. The cancer risks in women are an argument against using wine for health benefits."

Alcohol presents no benefit for women; it is possibly mildly protective against heart disease for men, at low levels of consumption (less than 20 g of pure alcohol per day). Red wine is higher in histamines (a draw back), but overall a little healthier than white wine because of the resveratrol and blue-red nutrients it contains.

However, epidemiology studies have associated wine consumption with various cancers, both in men and women (possibly in combination with other things): breast cancer seems the most sensitive, but a single drink a day also significantly increases the risk of esophageal cancer. In addition, alcohol consumption raises triglyceride levels as alcohol is directly related to the manufacturing of triglycerides in the liver.

The claims that alcohol is beneficial were based on comparing drinkers to non-drinkers. The methodology was flawed: a lot of non-drinkers are former drinkers who quit drinking for health reasons, so they appear in studies as "sick non-drinkers." Later studies that didn't count the reformed drinkers as non-drinkers found no benefit in drinking.

Consume alcohol prudently!

Alcohol-dehydrogenase

"For the many people who lack the liver enzyme alcohol-dehydrogenase, alcohol is a cellular poison."

Two steps are needed to fully detoxify alcohol. Alcohol-dehydrogenase is involved in the first step: when it is missing, the cells are directly exposed to alcohol; alcohol completely blocks the oxidative pathways of the cell, preventing the Krebs cycle from functioning properly: this kills the cell.

The alcohol flush reaction, frequent among Asians, is due to the lack of alcohol-dehydrogenase. This enzyme cannot be induced in those who don't have the genetics. If you suffer from that syndrome, alcohol increases your risk of liver cancer. (Contrary to lactase that can be induced because all mammals possess it at birth).

AMES Test

"Is grilling or frying meat carcinogenic? The testing that established a link with cancer was flawed."

There might be some danger at a certain level in frying meat, but the original thought was based on the AMES testing: this experiment, dating from the early 70's, was initially a bacterial study that tested the mutagenicity of substances, looking at chemicals that would cause mutations in the bacteria. (Mutations are involved in cancer, but don't necessarily lead to cancer.) The next step used rats, again very different from humans. The current version of the test is still not very good. The AMES test is not an appropriate research model for humans.

Antioxidants

"Our nutrition should not be all about antioxidants."

The protective effect of antioxidants was asserted in the 1980's and exploited by the pharmaceutical industry, the idea being that cells are damaged by oxidation, which is caused by free-radicals ("oxidants"). Since then we have been encouraged to consume as many antioxidants as we can. But in fact, oxidants are needed by our body for a lot of purposes, and now some research reports on the benefits of suppressing the antioxidants (thereby increasing the activity of the oxidants) in some cancer cases.

Beef

"Grass-fed beef brings essential nutrients that you cannot get from vegetal sources, no matter how much grain you consume."

Beef in general supplies efficient amino acids, fatty acids, and bioavailable minerals, as well as B12 (not available from vegetal sources) and iron (more bioavailable from beef than spinach).

Grass-fed beef supplies longer chain omega-3 (EPA, DHA) fats that are not readily found in vegetable sources.

Beer

"With its high glycemic load, combining grain and alcohol, beer is one of the worst drinks possible."

The alcohol in beer raises the triglycerides, and the carbohydrates trigger high insulin, which also raises triglycerides. High triglycerides mean bad LDL. (See "Triglycerides.")

The claim that beer is nutritious is based on the fallacy that grains are nutritious. Beer was a staple in ancient diets because there weren't many practical ways to preserve and distribute nutrition.

Bioavailability

Within our context, bioavailability is a measure of how much of a nutrient that we ate is absorbed into our blood and made available where we need it. The presence of certain chemicals impairs the bioavailability of the micronutrients contained in the food by binding to them.

There are wildly different capacities across the population for absorbing and utilizing nutrients: some people absorb vitamin D and B12 very poorly; some avariciously absorb iron.

Biome

"Fermented milk might help the biome, but it brings only ten species as opposed to the trillions resident in our biome."

The biome designates the bacteria resident in our body, or on it: we are host to around 100 trillion bacteria that perform a number of critical functions and identify us as precisely as fingerprints.

Not all bacteria is bad: the biome is an important part of our ability to digest food and fight off infections. Because of this broad array of biological functions, a healthy biome is a great friend. By the same token, an unhealthy biome can induce chronic diseases, autoimmune diseases and increase the risk of cancer.

There are a few simple rules for maintaining a healthy biome: minimize antibiotics (including antibiotic hand soap), don't be excessively clean, and eat a diet that includes animal ingredients, since these organisms have a biome similar to ours.

Bisphenol A (BPA)

"Another concern is BPA, a potentially toxic additive commonly used for lining the cans."

BPA was thought to have destabilizing effects on the endocrine system because of its hormone-like properties. This, however, was not confirmed by later studies. In any case, even though some of the BPA scare has gone away, it doesn't hurt to look for BPA-free cans.

Butter

"Previous studies attributing carcinogenic effects to cooked butter may have been flawed."

The negative effect of cooking butter is linked with the AMES test, whose applicability to humans has been debunked. Most studies of that kind were executed in the context that "saturated fat is bad," and therefore are tainted.

Calcium

Calcium supplements are advertised for fighting osteoporosis. Although they help in that respect, calcium supplements also show negative health impacts, in particular concerning heart attacks.

The problem with bones is much more complex than just calcium: bone mineralization requires hormonal drivers, but the primary driver is the piezoelectric field that occurs when pressure is applied to the bone (a strong argument for exercising with weights).

Although bones look inert, they are in fact a live tissue that has its own blood supply. Bones continually grow, tear themselves down and are rebuilt. Bones play an active role in our body's calcium regulation: the body secretes several hormones that will either cause the bones to store calcium or to release it. Deprivation of vitamin K accelerates ectopic calcium, a cause of hardening of the arteries.

In any case, good sources of calcium include: dark green leafy vegetables, milk and bones (in soup or from canned sardines for example).

Calories

See also "Energy." By convention: 1 Calorie = 1 kcal.

"Fat stores 9 Calories per gram, protein and carbohydrates roughly 4."

In practice, the caloric value of an ingredient is established by burning the said ingredient in an instrument called a calorimeter, and measuring the quantity of heat produced. Not surprisingly, this measurement doesn't reflect the biological reality very accurately; there is no tight correlation between the output of the calorimeter and our biological usage: calories from the calorimeter don't translate well into body calories.

The biology of digesting broccoli is different from that of digesting potatoes, and results in fewer calories available to the body because of the broccoli's fiber content and the amount of energy required to import the other nutrients it contains as well.

"Calories have different biological impacts. Calories are not interchangeable."

Conventional wisdom has it that "a calorie is a calorie," no matter where it comes from: fat, protein or sugar. This is not true! Calories are not created equal and this is another reason why counting calories backfires.

Fat calories have a positive biological impact, they give us more energy, turn our metabolism on; fat increases the metabolic activity of the cell more than protein or sugar because of the hormonal signaling involved: fat increases the thyroid output, sugar decreases it. (The thyroid is the thermostat for the human body: people with high thyroid output tend to be hot and thin, while those with low thyroid are colder and fatter.)

Canola oil

"Roast you own nuts and seeds if you can. Otherwise you are likely to end up with such crazy things as peanuts roasted in Canola oil!"

Despite its cheerful, fresh sounding name, Canola oil is a totally unnatural oil, made from genetically modified rapeseed. Ironically, it is touted as one of the most healthful oils.

But let's keep things in perspective, Canola oil is not that bad. When facing the choice in the modern supermarket, select Canola over soy oil. (The same goes for store bought mayonnaise: if you can find it, prefer Canola oil mayonnaise over soy mayonnaise.)

Carbohydrate

The sugar we eat is stored as glycogen, triglycerides and blood glucose. Excess sugar is stored as fat.

Our body also uses carbohydrates for many structural functions; however, these are not carbs derived from our diet, but manufactured by the body on demand.

Consuming a lot of carbohydrates causes high blood sugar, a problem in itself. It also triggers the over-production of insulin, which has a lot of health implications.

Chili

"Chili peppers have medically proven effects on arthritis and autoimmune diseases. Cultures that consume this kind of hot food have less gastrointestinal disease."

There are two elements to that:

- Chili peppers modify the Tumor Necrosis Factor (TNF) alpha involved in inflammation, which plays a role in autoimmune arthritis.

- Chili peppers act as a painkiller: the pain receptors are particularly sensitive to local inflammation and chili acts to block them.

China Study

"Enough reliable sources have pointed to serious deficiencies in The China Study."

"Using the China Study data itself, it can be shown that meat consumption lowers mortality."

Using the China-Oxford-Cornell data (available online at http://www.ctsu.ox.ac.uk/~china/monograph/) we attempted to reproduce the conclusion of *The China Study* (the book). The result was full of surprises, here is just one example:

We looked at all-cause medical mortality versus dietary choices. There are several reasons for using all-cause mortality rather than specific diseases, such as cancer or heart disease: first, there is a general agreement on the diagnosis (dead!); second, a food that decreases one specific disease is of limited interest if it increases another disease. Surprisingly, the data shows that people who consumed red meat had lower mortality than the rest. While we wouldn't use this result to advise people to eat large amounts of red meat, it is sufficiently significant to cast a shadow on the validity of *The China Study* (the book).

Also see the *Further Reading* section in this book.

Cholesterol

"The new U.S. Government recommendation states that dietary cholesterol is harmless."

The U.S. Department of Health and Human Services, and the U.S. Department of Agriculture have recommended that limitations on dietary cholesterol be removed from the 2015 edition of *Dietary Guidelines for Americans*. As everybody will realize, this is a huge turnabout.

"Dietary cholesterol does not affect your health."
"You can have eggs every morning without fearing cholesterol."
"Dietary cholesterol is irrelevant."

"Dietary cholesterol doesn't affect blood cholesterol."

The liver is going to maintain a fixed amount of cholesterol in our system, no matter what. If we eat no cholesterol at all, the liver will manufacture the full amount required. If we eat some cholesterol, the liver will use it, and make the rest as needed. Diet has little relationship to circulating cholesterol.

This has been known for 60 years. The original results from the famous Framingham Study proved very early on that dietary cholesterol had no effect on blood cholesterol. Unfortunately, the cholesterol hypothesis took a life of its own.

"The relationship between dietary cholesterol and heart disease in the general population has been disproved."

"Dietary saturated fat and cholesterol don't contribute to heart disease."

Cholesterol became implicated as a possible culprit in the early 50's when cholesterol was discovered in arterial plaque, along with various other substances. The hypothesis of cholesterol as the bad guy was in great part due to Ancel Keys's study, which has since been largely debunked.

To start with, here are some facts:

- Women have higher cholesterol than men but significantly less heart disease.

- Many countries with high rates of heart disease have low cholesterol, and vice versa.

Lowering cholesterol doesn't cure heart disease: there have been many studies published in top journals, such as one in the Journal of the American Medical Association, which concluded in 2008: "Our findings do not support the hypothesis that hypercholesterolemia or low HDLC are important risk factors for all-cause mortality, coronary heart disease mortality, [...] in this cohort of persons older than 70 years."

Or back in 1992, in the British Medical Journal: "Lowering serum cholesterol concentrations does not reduce mortality and is unlikely to prevent coronary heart disease. Claims of the opposite are based on preferential citation of supportive trials." This researcher's hypothesis was that the belief that cholesterol should be lowered was due to drug companies selecting only studies that supported such a conclusion. He found that trials showing no benefit were seldom, if ever, cited.

The JUPITER trial showed very supportive results for cholesterol lowering drugs. One researcher who checked it out states: "The results of the JUPITER trial are clinically inconsistent[...]. The results of the JUPITER trial support concerns that commercially sponsored clinical trials are at risk of poor quality and bias."

"HDL cholesterol is protective against cancer of all kinds, stroke, heart attack and all cardiovascular diseases."

Key papers identify amazing protective effects of increased HDL: a 10 mg/dl increase in HDL was associated with a 36 % reduction in cancer, a very powerful result. Papers can be found on HDL's tumor fighting properties.

HDL, the "good cholesterol" is in fact not cholesterol: High Density Lipoprotein is a particle, tinier than LDL, also manufactured by the liver and circulated in the blood. HDL vacuums left-over cholesterol, as well as other toxic debris from LDL particles and hauls them back to the liver for disposal, becoming HDL2b in the process. An elevated HDL2b, not just the total HDL, is a sign that a lot of desirable cleanup is going on.

As a conclusion, cholesterol is not a toxic by-product: it is an essential constituent of our cell walls, as well as the foundational molecule for all steroidal and sex hormones. It is important and necessary to our life and well-being; shortages are dangerous.

Pills can lower cholesterol by interfering with the body's natural regulatory processes. Except in the case of organ failure, meddling with the body's regulation is almost always a very bad idea. Side effects of lowering cholesterol with statins include diabetes, cataracts, depression of the immune system, liver and muscle problems. Alzheimer's is strongly linked to low total cholesterol.

So, what causes heart disease? Heart disease is caused by debris that gets stuck behind the artery walls. This includes sugar remnants, small LDL particles and other stray molecules that oxidize and become dangerous. The immune system attempts to get rid of them or wall them off. This involves the secretion of signaling chemicals, which result in inflammation and plaque.

Bad diets, dangerous levels of sugar and starches, stress, lack of exercise, smoking and excess alcohol play major roles in this process.

Compare

"If you compare whole wheat to asparagus, you will find that the asparagus is much richer in micronutrients and protein."

Many websites are dedicated to giving nutritional information about ingredients, here are a few:

- Self Nutrition Data: http://nutritiondata.self.com/tools/nutrient-search
- FDA: http://www.fda.gov/Food/IngredientsPackagingLabeling/LabelingNutrition/ucm063367.htm
- National academy of science: https://fnic.nal.usda.gov/dietary-guidance/dietary-reference-intakes/dri-tables-and-application-reports
- USDA National Nutrient Database: http://ndb.nal.usda.gov

Cocoa

"There is some evidence that cocoa is healthy."

A recent study (2015), that seems too good to be true, agreed, finds that people who consume a lot of chocolate have fewer heart attacks and strokes. The antioxidants in cocoa might help the cardiovascular system by reducing blood pressure; its flavonoids have antioxidant, anti-inflammatory and anti-clotting properties that can improve insulin sensitivity.

One thing is certain: if the cocoa and fats in chocolate may be good for you, the added sugar is definitely harmful, so look for chocolate with the least amount of sugar you can tolerate.

Coffee and Tea

"They are associated with lower incidence of serious diseases, and this is true of all types of teas not only green tea."

Some nutritional websites express reservations about drinking large amounts of coffee. However, so far, every piece of epidemiology has shown no harm at higher doses (up to five 8-oz cups a day). Well executed, large epidemiological trials have associated coffee and tea with a lower incidence of many diseases, from colon and pancreatic cancer to Alzheimer's, adult onset diabetes, stroke, heart attack and all-cause mortality.

What is responsible for coffee's properties is at this point uncertain. Like many other plants, coffee contains substances that would be toxic to its predators; luckily for us, these substances turn out to be toxic to our predators, too. Coffee, for one thing, is brimming with antioxidants. Also, caffeine seems to be a crucial component: decaf doesn't exhibit the protective qualities.

Decay

"Almost all animal products degrade in safer ways than vegetal products."

If the products were sterile to start with, the animal products degrade into biologically identical sub-units, which we can still use as food. Vegetal products degrade in a way that decreases their biological use.

In real life, the products are not sterile, and what happens depends on the nature of the contaminants. Again, these can be worse in vegetables than in meat. Problems in meat are usually linked to processing issues. For vegetables, the problems concern mostly produce contaminated in the fields.

Dehydration

"A deficiency in fluids of as little as 1 % of our body weight can translate into dehydration."

One way to spot dehydration is dark urine: in a well hydrated person, urine is light yellow.

We lose fluid through sweat, urine, feces. Producing energy also consumes water, so when exercising, you need additional water, not only because of sweat, but to replace the water used in the Krebs cycle.

Dementia

"Sugar is linked with dementia."

Many factors are involved in causing dementia. Low cholesterol and low fat intake are emerging as possible causes. Conversely, ketogenic diets have shown some effectiveness against Alzheimer's.

Glycation also plays a role by impairing the vascular function. (There is probably more to that: some intracerebral insulin dysregulation causing insulin toxicity.)

Dependency

"Sugar dependency can also be a symptom of malnutrition."

An example: tryptophan is an essential amino acid, which is converted to serotonin in the brain, creating a sensation of well being and happiness. Some people need sugar in order to feel good because malnutrition has created an environment where the action of tryptophan is impaired, due to the lack of other nutrients: sugar and the ensuing insulin help tryptophan cross the blood-brain barrier.

Tryptophan supplements might cure the tryptophan problem, but not the other problems linked to malnutrition. It is more sensible to address malnutrition directly instead.

Desaturate

"It is easier for us to desaturate a saturated fat instead of using a random PUFA."

"Saturated fats are more versatile than unsaturated fats: they can be viewed as the universal donor from which various structurally different fats can be built."

"Bacon provides good saturated fat, which our body can desaturate as needed."

Desaturase are ubiquitous enzymes that the body employs for the specific purpose of turning saturated fats into unsaturated fats: the chemical reaction removes two hydrogen atoms and creates a double bond between two adjacent carbons. There are many different desaturase enzymes in various cells, but at the chemical level, they are all similar.

For example, Δ9-desaturase produces oleic acid by desaturating stearic acid, a saturated fatty acid either synthesized in the body from palmitic acid or ingested directly.

Digesting

"Contrary to common perception, our body is better equipped for digesting raw meat than raw vegetables."

A ruminant's stomach is necessary for completely breaking down vegetation: we do not possess that! The nature of our digestive enzymes and the pH of our stomach are different than those of ruminants. Raw vegetables are not directly digestible by humans because of the cellulose and other structural constituents, whereas in the meat, everything is digestible.

Electrolytes

Electrolytes are ionized minerals, that is, minerals that once dissolved in our body's fluids become electrically charged particles (ions). They play a functional role in the electrodynamics of cells. They are essential cofactors, determining the function of molecules.

The intracellular and extracellular balance of electrolyte concentration is important: the osmotic gradient regulates the hydration of the body, the blood pH; nerve and muscle function are triggered by electrolyte activity.

Energy

Calories are not interchangeable. The foods that we eat are used or stored in our body in different ways. We can say that foods have different energy destinies:

- ATP, resident in the cells, is the immediately available energy. The time it takes us to replenish our ATP from various other sources is the main question when it comes to energy. The source of energy we'll use, and the delay required to produce ATP are a function of the "trained" pathways. ATP can be produced using sugar, fat or protein as input to the Krebs (TCA) cycle.

- Sugar is traditionally thought of as "immediately available energy." But in fact, glucose is not uniquely qualified to generate ATP; glucose doesn't even provide energy more rapidly than other functions such as ketosis.

- Fatty acids of different lengths have different energy destinies: the short-chain ones, such as butyric acid, provide straightforward energy.

Conversely, our body "partitions" the food we consume by storing the energy in different ways:

- Blood glucose and free fatty acids are short term storage, i.e. immediately available energy.

- Glycogen in the liver and muscles, and triglycerides can be considered as intermediate storage.

- Fat cells are longer term storage, and they can hold large quantities of energy, as we all know.

What we eat goes into one of these storage tanks, depending on many factors: the type of foods eaten, the metabolism of the individual, in particular the hormonal distribution, the insulin response, genetic or medical conditions, level of activity...

"Excessive presence of carbohydrates in the blood will shift the body's energy preference to burning sugar and impair the burning of stored fat."

"The selection between fat, sugar or protein is driven by the presence or absence of the enzymes necessary to enable the chemical reactions."

"We can train our body to predominantly use fats for energy by switching to a diet that is richer in fats and poorer in carbs: our body will start producing the enzymes that make it possible to burn our fat reserves for energy."

See considerations about energy in the *Weight Loss* pages of this book.

Enzymes

Enzymes facilitate one or more specific chemical reactions by lowering the required activation energy.

In our body, enzymes play a major regulating role: generally speaking, reactions occurring in an enzymatic environment are controlled and desirable. Reactions that happen on their own, without enzyme activation, such as glycation, are uncontrolled and dangerous.

Enzymes are primarily made of proteins folded in complex 3-dimensional structures. They bind to the substrate (i.e. the target) by fitting their geometrical shape to the substrate's complementary shape.

Enzymes have a cofactor, usually a mineral atom hooked onto the enzyme: for example, if an enzyme has a magnesium cofactor, an Mg atom is attached to it. The cofactor allows the enzyme to function by shaping the enzyme. If we cook too much, we might destroy the 3-dimensional structure of the enzyme and therefore inactivate it.

Essential

In nutritional jargon, "essential" means more than just "important". The nutritional definition of "essential" has shifted to the more specific: "Something that is necessary to our body, but that we cannot fabricate in sufficient quantities and must therefore be obtained through diet."

Fat

See also "Saturated Fat."

"Excess food, with respect to the level of physical activity, gets converted into fat."

The quality of calories is much more important than their quantity. If we concentrate on the quality of our food as prescribed in this book, there is little risk of overeating. However, when our diet is far from optimal, the risk of overeating is very real. We cannot lose weight by eating less and exercising more, but we can definitely gain weight by eating more and exercising less.

For most people with weight problems, overeating is not the main issue, though.

"Eating fat doesn't make you fat."

When we eat too much fat or carbohydrates, the excess gets stored in our fat cells. However, when body fat is a concern, it is easier to get rid of the accumulated fat when the blood sugar and insulin levels are low: insulin puts the body in storage mode, and triglycerides contribute to locking the fat inside the cells. It's easier to get rid of fat if you feed on fat than if you feed on carbohydrates.

The mechanisms that regulate appetite, energy expenditure and fat storage are very complex. Not all is understood yet, but for certain, it is much more complicated than the simplistic popular understanding.

Fiber

Fiber is an oversold commodity: new research shows that it doesn't have the function in gastrointestinal health that was previously thought.

"Dietary fiber (indigestible chains of sugar)"
"Dietary fiber is a type of carbohydrate that does not turn into blood sugar."

By some definitions, fiber is always indigestible. By others, there is digestible and indigestible fiber, soluble and insoluble fiber: these two classifications are related, but do not overlap completely.

If dietary fibers are carbohydrates that cannot be digested, why are they sometimes included in the calorie count on food labels? Out of sloppiness?

"With a healthy fiber composition, the apple is the poster girl of the northern seasonal fruits!"

Fiber has several effects on our body. It famously helps intestinal transit. Less known is the fact that fiber affects the water balance inside the colon, by oncotic pressure. (Oncotic pressure is a phenomenon by which a type of particle that cannot cross a membrane attracts water on its side of the membrane, so that the net effect is to lower the particle's concentration.)

Soluble fiber is a more effective oncotic agent than insoluble fiber. This is a desirable property because it helps bowel regularity. Soluble fiber can participate in fermentation (good in some respects, but not in others, think gas...) and affects our biome.

Insoluble fiber is more inert. This might also be a desirable aspect of fiber because if too much water is pulled, many nutrients might be pulled at the same time and eliminated in the bowel movements.

In conclusion, both types of fiber are beneficial and should be consumed. Apples contain a good mixture of various types of fiber.

Fructose

Our body does not appear to be equipped to deal with the large amounts of fructose that have appeared in the Western diet.

"Fructose doesn't solve the problem of physiological harm of sugar."

In the recent past, because of its low glycemic index, fructose has been mistakenly perceived as healthy and sometimes labeled as such by the health authorities.

Fructose is not glucose, but this doesn't mean that fructose eliminates the problems linked with sugar: the liver first uses fructose to replenish its glycogen. Once glycogen reserves are topped up, the liver converts the remaining fructose into triglycerides, which it packs into VLDL particles along with cholesterol and other particles. These VLDL particles are sent off into the blood stream, and, as their triglycerides are stripped off by the cells to be used for energy, the VLDL particles shrink, eventually becoming LDL, the infamous "bad cholesterol."

So beware. But, as a general rule, if your triglycerides are low, you need not be concerned by the amount of fruit in your diet

Fruit

While our ancestors must have eaten fruit whenever possible, fruit was not available year-round as it is today. Note also that modern cultivated fruit is a lot sweeter than its wild counterpart.

"Fruit doesn't contain nutrients that you couldn't get elsewhere, while packing a fairly large quantity of sugar."

There is a widespread fear of not getting enough vitamins if we don't eat fruit. This has historical reasons: when it was discovered that fruit contained beneficial vitamins, in the collective mind the sugar in the fruit was equated with vitamins.

"Citrus fruits are loved for their vitamin C content. People tend to use them in excess."

In fact, a lot of vegetables have more vitamins than fruit, with only a fraction of the sugar. To take the example of the popular vitamin C: chili peppers, bell peppers, tomatoes, dark leafy greens, broccoli and other cruciferous vegetables, all contain more vitamin C than any citrus fruit. However, don't make the same mistake of equating the carbohydrates in vegetables with vitamins.

Another potential problem with fruits is their high fructose contents.

Gelatinization

"Digesting starch requires a lot of fluid and can have a wash out effect that depletes the body of minerals."

This is an antinutrient action.

There are various types of membrane pressure: osmotic pressure is a force that pulls fluid one way or another depending on ion concentration; oncotic pressure is a function of not merely ion but also particle concentration: for instance, a dissolved protein on one side of a membrane will draw water to dilute it. This phenomenon drives fluids in or out of cell walls. Sugar drives oncotic dilution: water will go where the sugar is; diarrhea can be caused by indigestible sugar that draws all the fluid. Starch, being sugar, has that effect too.

Glucagon

"Elevated insulin impairs the action of glucagon, thus preventing the use of stored fat for energy."

"Insulin and glucagon are hormones that regulate our behavior regarding energy: how we eat can either put us in storage mode or in spending mode."

"Eating too much sugar stimulates insulin production and tips the body towards carb-based energy production and fat storage mode."

"When the blood sugar is low, glucagon allows the release of stored energy and a high metabolic rate that makes us healthier faster."

There are many hormones that regulate our energy storage, utilization and seeking behavior.

When we eat in a way that causes our dietary hormones to put us into a caloric storage condition, we are not as strong. When we eat in a way that puts us in a high metabolic state, we are healthier.

If you eat in a way that stimulates insulin above basal need, you are in a state of fat storage and low metabolic energy. When you eat in a glucagon-dominant mode, you are in a high metabolic state. Glucagon and insulin are in a reciprocal relation: when one goes up, the other goes down.

Sugar stimulates insulin, hunger stimulates glucagon.

Gluconeogenesis

Most people will tell you that the brain runs on glucose. This is usually the reason given as to why we need to consume sugar and starch. But in fact...

"Our liver can produce sugar entirely from virtually any source, including fat and protein."

"Contrary to popular belief, the brain can also use fatty acids as a source of fuel."

To start with, the glucose used by our brain need not come from our food: the liver, which is an amazing chemical factory, can make glucose from many things, including proteins, lactate, glycerol (the backbone of triglyceride molecules) and fatty acids.

This process is called gluconeogenesis: "gluco" means sugar, and "neo genesis" means making from scratch. This happens mainly in the liver. Gluconeogenesis is regulated by glucagon, which is released when blood sugar is low.

"The brain can produce its own glucose and insulin, and regulate its sugar level."

The brain has a backup regulation system (that can, however, be overwhelmed). Within certain limits, the brain can fabricate glucose by the same gluconeogenic process as the liver. It has recently been discovered that the brain also produces insulin.

Actually, the brain can do fine without glucose. The dietary recommendation of a minimum of 130 g of carbohydrates per day necessary for the brain assumes that all the brain energy comes from sugar: this is the case for people who eat a carbohydrate-rich diet, and thus are carbohydrate-dependant. If no carbs are present, the brain can get energy in part through ketosis; it also makes its own glucose, as explained above.

There are still groups of people who lead the hunter-gatherer lifestyle; these people consume almost no sugar or starch, yet this doesn't seem to affect their brain. For most of our ancestors, glucose shortages were the norm.

Also keep in mind that to run properly, the brain needs a lot more than sugar, and that excess sugar is now thought to be a likely cause of Alzheimer's.

Glycation

"Excessive sugar in the blood impairs the functions of our body machinery at the molecular level, causing glycation and the manufacturing of defective cells, hormones or enzymes."
"Chronic elevated blood sugar level is responsible for glycation."

Our body is constantly manufacturing parts: for example, proteins are produced on demand, when and where the need arises. Things must be manufactured in a clean room.

Glucose molecules have a tendency to stick (by covalent bonding) to other molecules, which are then said to be glycated. This is a non-enzymatic reaction. Sugar is more prone to that kind of reaction than fat molecules because its chemical structure is looking for a lower energy state. It happens with fat (lipase oxidation), but less because of the fats' bond state: glycation is in orders of magnitude greater than lipase oxidation; sugar is a lot more reactive.

Glycation modifies the 3-dimensional structure of the molecule. The resulting molecules are defective and do not function as they were intended to. The more glucose, the more glycation. Glycated hemoglobin in red blood cells can be measured in a standard blood test, as hemoglobin A1c. (This measure is used as a surrogate for average blood glucose level.)

"These effects can build up slowly."

Glycation results in the fabrication of what is known as Advanced Glycation End-products (AGE). This is an ongoing process; its dire consequences become clinically evident over years. While glycation might be reversed, in presence of high blood sugar the protein goes through more reactions, leading to AGE. The accumulation of AGE leads to a chain reaction of AGE sticking and binding to each other.

The accumulation of AGE in various parts of the body (eye, kidney, nerves, arteries) causes endless health complications and accelerates aging, hence the very appropriate acronym.

Glycation and oxidation are part of the cell's life and death. High blood sugar makes it worse, though.

"Molecules produced in presence of a lot of sugar will be defective. Glycation leads, in particular, to small vessel diseases."

In recent research, glycation has been linked with inflammation and cancer; glycation in the brain causes dementia; in the arteries, atherosclerosis; glycated hemoglobin was identified in patients suffering from diabetes.

Small vessel disease affects the organs that are farthest from the heart: finger tips, toes, eyes, penis, brain... These are the organs at the end of the blood flow, where the blood turns around and the blood vessels get smaller and smaller.

Glycemic Index

Glycemic Index has been "in" for some time. It seems to provide a convenient, scientific basis for selecting carbohydrates. But it is, in fact, a worthless guide to nutritional value.

Glycemic index is measured by administering only one food, the one being tested, to a subject after an overnight fast. Is this how we eat? Obviously not, and this alone cancels most of the value of the measurement.

But issues with glycemic index do not stop here. The glycemic index is actually doing harm, because people use it as a nutritional guide. By this measure, real food, such as carrots, comes out about the same as many breakfast cereals, when, in fact, they are in no way equivalent: carrots are full of micronutrients; breakfast cereals are empty calories.

Mung beans have a low glycemic index, and for sure they have more nutrient value than wheat. However, their glycemic load remains substantial: mung bean noodles are not the magic healthy substitute for pasta...

Gout

"People suffering from gout have trouble clearing the uric acid resulting from the break down of purines."
"However, the majority of people who have gout are also insulin resistant. For these people, diminishing the insulogenic part of their diet reduces the gout symptoms."

Gout is a problem at several points in the metabolism, with different genetic variants. Even though the common manifestation is elevated uric acid in the blood, "gout" is in fact several diseases.

Uric acid is produced when metabolizing purines. Foods rich in proteins can be rich in purines; many vegetables also contain a lot of purines.

In spite of the direct connection with protein, most forms of gout are also associated with insulin resistance: insulin resistance, for some reason, is genetically linked with a poor ability to clear purines. Fava beans are especially terrible for gout, since they are high in purines and starches, which can lead to insulin resistance.

Grain

"An increasing number of studies argue that whole wheat is no better than sugar."

Studies that looked at glucose and insulin levels found no difference after consumption of whole grain or refined grain.

"Many medical institutions emphatically insist that whole wheat is beneficial to our health."

Studies proving that whole grain is beneficial compare people who eat whole grains with people who eat refined grains. The fact that whole grain is better than refined grain doesn't mean that eating a lot of whole grain is good for you in the absolute. This is like saying that, since low-tar cigarettes are better than regular cigarettes, the more low-tar cigarettes you smoke, the better it is for your health.

By using the raw data from *The China Study* you can plot cereal consumption versus mortality and verify that mortality increases with cereal consumption! (If you look specifically at colon cancer, wheat is protective, but what's the point if it increases your chances of dying of something else?)

The high level of methionine in grains is another strong argument against them: our body metabolizes methionine into cysteine, with homocysteine as an intermediate step. Homocystein is directly neurotoxic and is harmful to the arteries of the brain and heart: high levels of homocysteine in the blood are a risk factor for cardiovascular diseases.

Grains are widely promoted by the food industry. Cereals are very profitable. The true statement is "whole grains are better than refined grains, and not by much."

Helicobacter

"At this point, the microbiome is many orders of magnitude more complex than we can comprehend. The beneficial effects of fussing with it might have unexpected serious side effects."

An example: Helicobacter pylori is an infection caused by the eponymous bacteria. Ulcers and stomach cancer are associated with that infection.

Helicobacter pylori is currently endemic in China, and, as a predictable consequence, people there have a much higher incidence of stomach cancer. The decision was made to treat large populations with antibiotics: this resulted a much lower incidence of stomach cancer, but higher incidences of asthma and reflux (that can lead to oesophageal cancer). This shows that a "harmful" bacteria can also play a beneficial role in our body.

Homogenization

"Homogenization creates other health issues."

Homogenization is needed so that the fat in the milk doesn't separate from the rest. This involves a fair amount of processing, which is never a good thing.

According to its detractors, homogenized milk contributes to many diseases by boosting the absorbability of xanthine oxidase, an enzyme present in milk. Xanthine oxidase is a complex molecule: it is potentially dangerous, but it also has important physiological functions.

In well-sourced milk, homogenization is fine; non-homogenized, well-sourced milk is even better. If the milk's source is not sound, homogenization is less of a concern than everything else that can happen to milk.

Hormone-sensitive lipase (HSL)

"Insulin impairs the action of hormones that release fat from cells."

Hormone-sensitive lipase (HSL) is an enzyme present inside the cells: it allows the break down of triglycerides into fatty acids, which can then exit the cell and be burned for energy. HSL is very sensitive to insulin: when insulin is high, HSL is inactivated, and the triglycerides stay locked in the fat cells.

There are other hormones that are involved in getting fat out of the cells by stimulating HSL. Their action is also impaired by the presence of insulin.

Imbalance

"Excess in any particular amino acid results in imbalance. Although our body can adjust within a certain range, it cannot deal with overwhelming imbalance."

Particularly at risk are people that feed on supplements, such as some bodybuilders. Food supplements might, for example, include a lot of tryptophan to help fight depression.

Inducing

"Although in some populations lactase disappears in adults, lactase can be induced, even in the populations reputed to lack it."

Lactose intolerance with its manifestations of belly ache and diarrhea is caused by the lack of the enzyme lactase, which is necessary to digest milk. Asians possess lactase at birth. They lose it later because they don't drink milk as a culture.

The notion of inducing is central to this book's philosophy: the entire genome consists of codes for proteins. These proteins are induced as a response to a need: for example, enzymes are functional proteins, muscle fibers are structural proteins. If there was a genetic capacity, this capacity stays. If Asian babies can make lactase at birth, Asians can still make it later in life. Their genes didn't change.

Industry

"Without guidance, nobody can resist food marketing and the food industry."

On that subject, see Marion Nestle's book *Food Politics*, in the *Further Reading* section.

Inflammation

"Inflammation is an important factor that we would like to control."

We all know that inflammation is bad. But what is inflammation, really?

Inflammation is a chemical environment: it is pro-coagulant, making everything sticky. This is similar to what happens in presence of sugar, and that's why insulin and sugar are inflammatory. Inflammation is a good thing: it is a chemical signaling process designed to attract healing (white blood cells).

Inflammation is how the body protects itself against cancer. It is how it responds to the initial cardiovascular disease. If you suppress it, you suppress the body's initial response to injury. After the initial response, in the healing and reparative stage, we want to turn down inflammation but not suppress it. The task is more wisely left to your body's intrinsic regulatory system than to man-made pills.

But when there is *chronic* inflammation, the white blood cells destroy (destroying is what they are supposed to do) healthy cells. Chronic inflammation causes obesity, cardiovascular disease, etc.

A proper diet should turn off improper inflammatory signaling. In particular, anything that stimulates insulin stimulates inflammation. Meat on the other hand, contrary to popular belief, is anti-inflammatory: it doesn't stimulate insulin as much as alternative foods; it is easily digested, therefore not a great oxidative load on the liver; it increases the production of IGF1, which is also directly anti-inflammatory.

Insulin

"High levels of insulin can lead to insulin resistance."

One mechanism is that high levels of insulin cause the body to turn down the sensitivity of its insulin detector, like you would block your ears with your fingers when subjected to a very loud sound. This is only one danger of insulinogenic diets (i.e. diets promoting the production of insulin).

"Chronically elevated insulin is bad because insulin directly increases arterial stiffness, which leads to high blood pressure and atherosclerosis."

Insulin impairs the inducing of nitric oxide synthase (NOS). NOS releases nitric oxide, which in turn increases the flexibility of the arteries.

"While no study has proven the negative effect of fat on cardiovascular health, many studies have linked insulin with cardiovascular disease."
"Elevated insulin also clearly increases cancer risks."

Studies find strong relationships between high sugar levels and various cancers in the liver, breast, pancreas.

Interests

"A number of recent books explain this situation as the unappealing product of a mixture of incomplete science, politics and business interests."

See the *Further Reading* section.

Ketosis

Ketosis is a state in which so little glucose is available that the liver needs to synthesize molecules, called ketone bodies, to supply energy to the brain. The rest of the brain energy is obtained by synthesizing glucose from amino acids found in our muscles (ouch) or in our diet, and from the glycerol of the triglycerides in our fat.

Ketosis is characterized by a pH shift in the urine and the presence of ketone bodies. Keto-sticks sold in drugstores allow you to test whether you are in ketosis. (We all run a little bit on ketosis, but it's a matter of proportion.)

In Ketosis, fats (dietary or from fat tissue) and muscle proteins are used to generate ketones. This can lead to muscle break down, unless your diet is rich enough in fats and proteins.

Another problem with ketosis is that the blood glucose threshold required to enter the state is extremely broad: some people need very prolonged fasting, others reach the state within an hour. A better long-term strategy is to eat healthy fats and oils, in order to become a "fat burner" without being in ketosis.

"Note that this is different from ketosis where the body is running on fat only."

Ketosis shouldn't be confused with the gluconeogenic pathway, in which the liver (mostly) makes sugar from fats or protein. It is also different from being a "fat burner," when the cells use a large proportion of fat for energy in the Krebs cycle. Ketosis is a different chemical process altogether; every cell can potentially run on ketones.

In fact, almost all cells are intermittently in and out of ketosis, depending on what demand is placed on the local cellular system. This normal and reoccurring cellular event should not be confused with the whole-body state of ketosis.

A pertinent question is whether we want to drive a higher percentage of cells into this state for prolonged periods of time. This is really the question of whether fasting and various dietary manipulation states have value. They probably do, but we don't know enough to manage these issues coherently at this point.

Switching to ketones is immediately possible if sugar is removed. Becoming a fat burner takes time to induce the enzymes. When you are in a hurry for ATP, ketones are good!

Keys, Ancel

"Various studies, most notably Ancel Keys's, have linked saturated fat, cholesterol and heart disease."

Keys's most famous contribution to nutritional dogma is that "eating saturated fat increases cholesterol, which in turn causes coronary heart disease."

Ancel Keys is often considered the father of the whole cholesterol saga. An influential policy maker of the mid-twentieth century (for whom the K-rations of World War II were named), Dr. Keys is also known for his Seven Countries Study, wherein he found that diets higher in cholesterol lead to higher rates of heart disease. This study has since been largely debunked. Among other things, Dr. Keys had data from 22 countries, not 7, and discarded the data that did not match his hypotheses.

See Denise Minger's extensive analysis of Ancel Keys's work in *Death by Food Pyramid* (see *Further Reading* section).

Label

"A label can state 'no trans fats' if the food contains less than 0.5 g of trans fat per serving. For some cooking sprays, where serving size is minuscule, this can amount to a large proportion of trans fats."

Guidance for Industry: Trans Fatty Acids in Nutrition Labeling, Nutrient Content Claims, Health Claims; Small Entity Compliance Guide:

(http://www.fda.gov/Food/GuidanceRegulation/ GuidanceDocumentsRegulatoryInformation/ LabelingNutrition/ucm053479.htm)

"For conventional food products (those products other than dietary supplements), declaration of '0 g' of trans fat is not required for such products that contain less than 0.5 g of total fat in a serving if no claims are made about fat, fatty acid or cholesterol content. In the absence of these claims, the statement 'Not a significant source of trans fat' may be placed at the bottom of the table of nutrient values in lieu of declaring '0 g' of trans fat."

"The FDA allows the use of such words as healthy, heart-healthy and natural on labels. While these words sound nice, they don't have a legal definition and therefore mean nothing."

Adjectives like "healthy," "heart healthy" or "natural" imply that the food is good for you, but they have no legal definition and can be used indiscriminately since they are not legally binding. The only things these terms are good for is revealing which foods are low in cholesterol or fat, or high in fiber. All things that we don't care about...

Sugar information:

The math to determine the real sugar content of a food is, in reality, a little more complicated: fiber can be classified as soluble / insoluble (it has to do with cleavage points in the molecule) or digestible / indigestible. The two classifications are related, but do not overlap completely.

"Digestible" only vaguely relates to "soluble." Companies exploit this fact for the labeling. All we can be sure of is that if you subtract the fibers from the total carbs on the label, this is the minimum amount of sugar in the ingredient, and you are likely to have more.

Lectin

Lectins can impair the nutritional properties of other foods by binding to nutrients; but, in spite of their antinutrient properties, we need not have a mortal fear of lectins.

Lectins are ubiquitous. The reason why we should pay attention to them is that, since their concentration is high in legumes, this becomes a consideration in our choice of foods: especially for vegetarians, the lectin contents add up.

Leptin

"Chronically elevated blood sugar can cause leptin resistance."

The role of leptin is to discourage energy seeking. The difference between the quantity of energy present in the blood and the quantity of energy stored is part of how the body knows to seek energy. Too much energy in the blood means that energy must be stored, therefore the leptin signal is inappropriate: the body induces a protein that binds to leptin and inactivates it. (*Lectins* present in legumes inactivate leptin in a similar fashion.)

Leptin resistance can lead to elevated insulin. Elevated insulin can lead to insulin resistance via the same protein-binding mechanism described above for leptin.

The known binding proteins are in the thousands: vitamin D binding protein (or gc-globulin), sex hormone-binding globulin (SHBG), thyroxine-binding globulin (TBG), etc. Literature on leptin-binding is emerging.

Lipoprotein lipase (LPL)

"Insulin activates the enzymes that enable fat storage."

"Internal fat is the body's preferred site for depositing fat resulting from eating starch and sugar."

Lipoprotein lipase (LPL) is an important enzyme for fat storage. LPL is attached to the cell membranes. Its action is to break the triglycerides into free fatty acids, which it subsequently pulls into the cell.

The variations of LPL distribution in our body explains why people accumulate fat differently.

Insulin activates LPL on fat cells, particularly in the abdomen, and that's where fat gets deposited predominantly.

Lycopene

"Out of that came the idea that lycopene prevents prostate cancer. But in fact, a well executed study found out that taking lycopene supplements increased the frequency and severity of the disease."

The first study came out of Italy (GISSI trials): a lot of data was collected, originally looking at heart attacks. What they found is that the more tomato sauce people ate, the less prostate cancer they had. For some reason, it was assumed that the effect was due to lycopene. But, in fact, subsequent trials found that supplementing with lycopene increased the incidence and severity of cancer. It is speculated that the cancer protection was not in the single chemical (lycopene), but in the conjugated action of a complex array of chemicals. This is one more argument against supplements.

Malnutrition

"But even in those situations, malnutrition is an important issue, concurrently with undernutrition."

Reports from health organizations state that malnutrition is starting to be a serious concern in countries that previously were only concerned with undernutrition.

"Malnutrition can be worse than undernutrition: the effects of not having enough food can be reversed with food, whereas nutritional deficiency has longer term effects."

For example, Kwashiorkor is a condition caused by protein deficiency; it can happen even when people have enough calories: that's malnutrition. Marasmus is caused by not having enough food, therefore undernutrition. The symptoms of the people afflicted are completely different: people in the second group have lost muscle mass; those in first group, which don't have the right nutrients, are bloated due to liver and gastrointestinal tract failure.

The cell's health depends on the integrity of its wall, which in turn depends on having enough proteins and fats. Osmotic and oncotic pressure play a role too: if there is not enough functional protein, all the fluid leaks out of the cells and ends up in the stomach.

The body can recover from insufficient calories better and faster, with less long-term consequences, than from lack of protein. There is solid overwhelming evidence of that, and this has been understood for a hundred years.

Matrix

"Fat is not an isolated ingredient: it comes within a matrix of other nutrients that must also be healthy for the fat to be healthy."

In real food, all nutrients come in a rich array, together with other nutrients. This makes the value of the food, and that's why eating the whole food is important.

The chemistry of nutrition is very elaborate. Everything is interconnected, participating as only one piece of a huge puzzle. For example, hemoglobin, a molecule in our red blood cells, carries oxygen from our lungs to the rest of our body, thus allowing aerobic respiration. Hemoglobin contains an iron atom, which is in the Fe^{2+} (ferrous) ionic state under normal conditions.

A slight change in the 3-dimensional structure of hemoglobin, a seemingly minor adjustment, can switch the iron atom to the Fe^{3+} (ferric) ionic state. This renders the hemoglobin molecule incapable of normal oxygen binding.

Let's also keep in mind that there is still a lot that we don't understand.

Meat

"At time of writing, the studies linking red meat to harm are all flawed."

The latest (2015) IARC meta-study is no exception (for starters, it picked only 800 studies out of the thousands available).

"The bad reputation of red meat is based on the outdated assumption that cholesterol and saturated fats are harmful."

Epidemiology was involved too. The food guidelines are based on standardized food diary surveys. For 50 years, the questionnaires only defined three categories: meat, poultry and fish. Included in "meat" were processed meats (ham, spam, bologna, hot dog, hamburger...), known to contain all sorts of bizarre additives; trans fats were lumped with red meat; and confounding variables (red meat eaters are disproportionately heavy drinkers and smokers) were ignored. The conclusion that meat is bad was based on these distortions.

There is very little data looking at beef alone, but what data exists points to decreased "all cause mortality" linked with beef consumption. On the other hand, processed meat is clearly linked with all sorts of negative health effects.

The data from the China Study (the *China-Oxford-Cornell Study* itself, not the book) associates red meat with a markedly lower mortality, an interesting result for a study that is claimed as the reference by people who want to prove that meat is bad.

As for colorectal cancer, there is no good study linking it to meat consumption. Red meat might present a toxicity problem in the bacterial and liver response. This could be a problem for people with family history, but this is true of all foods taken in excess.

Red meat is also accused of causing kidney damage: but in fact, unless the kidneys are already diseased, red meat is not a problem. One function of the kidneys is to eliminate the by-products created by eating proteins. On a high-protein diet, the kidneys will be busier, but the evidence shows that they can handle it.

For red meat and gout, see "Gout."

Membrane

"The altered shape of artificial trans fat molecules will cause structural defects in our membranes."

An example: when the fat molecule doesn't fit properly, a hole is created in the membrane. This changes the permeability of the cell wall, allowing transaminase proteins to leak out: this is the first stage in the development of non-alcoholic fatty liver disease (steatohepatitis).

Metabolism

"For optimal function, we need to observe cycles of eating and fasting that reflect the catabolic and anabolic phases of our metabolism."

Metabolism is the continual physical and chemical transformation that happens in the body, in particular, the transformation of food to energy and body tissue.

Anabolism is that part of the metabolism that is involved in building body components from the various nutrients. Body components can be cells, enzymes, hormones, etc. Anabolism requires energy.

Catabolism is the part of the metabolism that is responsible for the tearing down process. This process releases energy.

We are being torn down by the passage of time. The body must restore and repair, and it must have a clean space to do so. The catabolic phase is the clearing up of the debris. This is all driven by the energy produced by the body. The more biological energy available (ATP, high VO_2), the more competently the body can repair and restore, and the more active the immune surveillance. If you do not provide an environment to catabolize (this requires not grazing), you cannot properly build new components. That is one reason why eating cycles are needed.

Microbiome
See "Biome."

Milk

"Low-fat milk can even be considered dangerous."

This is going back to nutrient complexity: by taking fat out, you have lost the nutrient value of the fat, and have turned a great food into a sugared drink (sugar is usually added to compensate for the lost texture and taste resulting from removing fat).

"For most people, the benefits of milk outweigh its inconveniences."

Milk is a good source of proteins and fats. It contains lactose (a disaccharide) and galactose (a low "glycemic index" sugar), but no fructose.

Milk detractors point out, correctly, that milk is full of things appropriate for feeding a growing mammal, including growth hormones. The point is that all mammals, including us, use the same growth hormones, so there is nothing wrong about cow's milk in that respect. The problems arise when the animals are injected with hyperconcentrated, unnatural growth hormones.

Healthy milk, therefore, comes from a healthy cow.

It is true that dairy products stimulate insulin production. But, there are direct measures proving that dairy also increases insulin sensitivity: there are few things we desire more than that effect!

The CARDIA (Coronary Artery Risk Development in Young Adults) study was a large, multicenter, multiracial, multicultural trial. It examined variables (diet, behavior, etc.) associated with the early onset of various diseases, in a 20 year follow up. The finding was that the more dairy consumed (at high intake levels as well), the less insulin resistance and the lower fasting glucose. Consumers of dairy exhibited less obesity, less diabetes and lower blood pressure.

Another study checked levels of trans-palmitoleic acid (unique to dairy) over time, in a large cohort. It found that the more trans-palmitoleic acid, the less obesity and diabetes. The measurement was taken directly from people's blood, thus eliminating any guess work. (This is not the case when food diaries are used, since food diaries are subjective).

Focusing on a single property, good or bad, in a food group is not a good way to judge its merits.

Minerals

In our context, minerals are the chemical elements required by our metabolism. They are classified in a different category than the micronutrients. While the number of minerals we need is large, the most notable are: Calcium (Ca), Iron (Fe), Magnesium (Mg), Phosphorus (P), Potassium (K), Zinc (Zn), Copper (Cu), Manganese (Mn), Selenium (Se).

Minerals are essential for activating almost all the energy exchanges in the body. The function of minerals is not completely understood. We need as rich a source as possible.

Myplate

"The 'myplate' standard (http://www. choosemyplate.gov) that replaced the pyramid has reduced the recommended proportion of grains, but it still implies that grains are a basic food group."

We don't agree that grains are a food group, or that fruits are necessary at all. The proportion of proteins in Myplate seems reasonable, but the fats are missing from the picture. In our mind, dairy is not necessarily a glass of milk (as implied by the drawing), and not an add on: it is part of the protein and fats.

Oils

"The heating of the oil destroys some of its nutritional value and can create harmful 'trans' molecules. The chemical solvents are toxic and carcinogenic."

How bad is it? We don't have it quantified just yet, but all solvent extraction processes have the potential of leaving very toxic substances in the oil.

Omega-3 / omega-6 ratio

See "Ratio."

Organic

"Looking at organic food through the lens of old school nutrition, which doesn't pay much attention to micronutrients beyond a limited list of vitamins, one might conclude that 'organic' is not worth the price difference."

Our body will detoxify our food to some extent. However, we don't know at this point how much contaminant can be tolerated until it becomes noxious. People have the sense that if they don't see it, it's OK.

A Stanford study looked at the nutritional content of organic versus conventional produce. Unfortunately, it only checked the standard limited nutrient list. Lycopene or cyanodins, for example, were missing.

It found that organic food is lower in pesticides (as expected) and higher in vitamin C. Those were the only two significant findings, and from there came the conclusion that organic was not worth the price.

But, how about all the other nutrients? Organic food tastes different, looks different, and has different levels of nutrients. A clear study is, so far, lacking.

Oxalic acid

Oxalic acid is a substance that, similarly to phytic acid, can prevent the absorption of important minerals by binding to them. This binding produces salts (oxalates) that can be irritating to our mucus membranes. Oxalic acid is responsible for kidney stones.

While phytic acid, another antinutrient, has actual nutritional value to us, oxalic acid doesn't.

Pathway

A series of processes happening in our body.

Peanuts

Some people criticize peanuts for their fat profile (omega-3 / omega-6 balance, saturated fat contents): this is groundless in the light of modern nutritional science.

"Many studies show that peanuts lower heart disease." See "Statins."

"Contrary to the other common nuts, peanuts are legumes, with the lectin and phytic acid issue."

This is a strong argument for roasting peanuts, since cooking helps eliminate the antinutrients.

Predators

"These substances protect us against our own predators."

"Our predators" refers to the various viruses / bacteria / parasite infections that we are prone to getting from our food, the air, and so on.

Protein

"Higher protein diets raise HDL cholesterol."

This is a statistical fact that has been known for a long time in the literature. It has, in fact, passed into basic metabolic physiological teaching.

"Studies say protein of animal source is protective in many ways."

For example:
- June 11, 2014 online issue of Neurology: the more protein in the diet, the less stroke risk.
- The data from the China Study also proves it.
- There is research all over the place on this, the latest being that high-protein is clearly protective after age 65.

Recommendations

"Let's start by pointing out that government recommendations are, by necessity, not dictated by scientific truth alone. They can only be a trade off."

- See in *Further Reading* section Denise Minger's book *Death by Food Pyramid* and Marion Nestle's *Food Politics;* both books explain how the original expert recommendation was distorted to suit the day's agenda.

- In 1977 George McGovern headed the U.S. Senate Select Committee on Nutrition and Human Needs, with the urgent task to fight obesity. However, the science wasn't in yet, and the rush to make recommendations created the movement towards vegetable and grain-based diets. These hasty recommendations have had devastating long term consequences on the health of the population.

- For those who think the establishment can be trusted blindly: remember when cigarettes were advertised as being good for the lungs and advocated by some in the medical profession as healthy? Remember when the government was distributing free cigarettes to soldiers?

- Isn't there an obvious conflict of interest in the USDA setting dietary guidelines when you consider that "agriculture" (the "A" in USDA) really means "grains"?

In addition, official recommendations are very slow at reflecting the advances of science. For example, the government took the anti-tobacco stance only a long time after there was evidence that tobacco was dangerous; this allowed people to righteously poison themselves and those around them for years. In the same vein, the nefarious effects of trans fats had already been known for quite a while when the institutions started investigating.

Quinoa

Quinoa is sold as "not really a grain" because of its high protein content. Dr. Mike's empirical experience is that his patients' estrogen and triglyceride levels went up when they consumed quinoa. Buckwheat had similar effects.

Ratio

"The omega-3 / omega-6 ratio is fairly irrelevant, as long as there is no deficiency in any essential fatty acid."

Many people take omega-3 supplements: it has been said that using vegetal oils instead of the traditional shortenings raises the proportion of omega-6 in our body to unhealthy levels.

This issue of omega-3 / omega-6 ratio is very controversial: some research actually finds that omega-6 fatty acids are beneficial (particularly in reducing the risk of heart disease), and that excess in omega-6 is not harmful.

"Once the issue of potential omega 3, omega 6 deficiency has been taken care of, the quality of fat is mainly determined by the health of its source."

The body can cope with excess, but not with deficiency. It is therefore important to eat enough of the essential fatty acids that our body, by definition, cannot make.

"Omega-3 supplementation has never shown benefits and has been linked to some forms of harm: for example, high omega-3 levels in the prostate are linked with cancer."

This was an observational set of studies that is not well understood yet. One explanation is that some people following an alternative medicine wisdom were taking in so much omega-3 that they completely depressed the cancer fighting anti-inflammatory prostaglandins that are so necessary for a healthy prostate.

Salt - Sodium

Is sodium bad? People with high blood pressure need to limit their intake. For the rest of us, salt is a necessary substance that shouldn't trigger anxiety. Don't get your calculator out, don't hunt sodium, don't go out of your way to avoid it. Season mindfully, pay attention to how your food tastes. Don't fear salt.

"Hypertension linked to salt consumption is less a risk than was thought. The fact is that too little or too much salt are associated with diseases."

Too restrictive in salt is harmful too, we need some salt: a 1991 study indicates that people need about 1 1/2 teaspoons of salt per day. Anything less triggers the production of a cascade of hormones to recuperate sodium from the waste stream, with

one side effect that makes people vulnerable to heart disease and kidney problems. This is proven biochemistry. Yet, the FDA as well as the USDA want to drastically restrict sodium consumption to about 1/2 teaspoon per day.

Sodium is tightly regulated for the whole system by the kidneys, and locally by the cells themselves. Therefore ingested sodium is expected to have little effect.

Ion pumps need sodium to balance the potassium. Very few people, less than 1%, are actually sodium sensitive. The main American medical societies no longer offer sodium guidance; or if they do, they leave it vague, simply saying "minimize added salt."

Satiety, Satiation

Satiety (the feeling of being full) is subjective, it has a psychological context: this is how you feel. Satiation refers generally to a physiological state, where the body's need for food is met. A resistant person can reach satiation without feeling satiety.

Saturated fat

Saturated fats and trans fats are often associated for no good reason: by definition, trans fat is unsaturated, with at least one double bond in "trans" configuration. This erroneous association has contributed to the bad rap of saturated fats: earlier data on saturated fat often included trans fats.

How healthy the saturated fat is depends on its source: mother's milk, butter from healthy cows, meat from healthy grass-fed animals, palm oil, all contain healthy saturated fats. Not surprisingly, saturated fat from unhealthy animals is also unhealthy.

"It has been determined that saturated fat is not a problem."

"Current science has demonstrated that dietary saturated fat and cholesterol don't contribute to heart disease."

"Modern analysis of these past studies reveals that they are flawed. After re-examining them with rigorous mathematical analysis, no correlation was found between saturated fats and cardiovascular disease."

A recent, well conducted meta-study examined 70 past studies and concluded that there is no association of saturated fat with heart disease.

(A meta-study gathers the data from past studies concerning a certain topic. While it can also be subject to bias, it is more reliable than individual smaller studies; one reason is the size of the data examined, which gives it more statistical significance; in addition, the rules for including individual studies in the meta-study can be set as to minimize selection bias.)

"We now know that eating saturated fat increases HDL level and LDL particle size."

This has been known for a long time in the literature, together with the fact that increased protein intake raises HDL. LDL size goes at least back to the Framingham Study, at least its inverse (low saturated fat diet causing small LDL size).

Shellfish

"Spoiled shellfish has a high toxicity."

Shellfish contains toxins (scombroids) that become more active with time. Since scombroids also trigger the production of high levels of histamines, people might mistake their reaction as allergy to shellfish, when it is, in fact, a defense reaction to scombroid food poisoning.

There are several other toxins associated with shellfish. Shellfish has a higher incidence of toxic and allergic problems than fish.

Smoked fish

"Smoked fish has similar nutritional value to fresh fish."

Like fresh fish, smoked fish is a good source of proteins, fats and vitamins. One drawback is that smoked fish is usually quite salty. This could be a consideration for the small part of the population that needs to watch their salt intake.

There are also food safety issues because most smoking doesn't entirely cook the fish, potentially leaving harmful bacteria. It is therefore important that the fish doesn't come from a contaminated source.

Smoked fish contains a lot of nitrites and nitrates. These were associated in epidemiological studies with stomach cancer; however, this was before we knew that almost all "stomach cancer" was infectious and a result of H. Pylori. The association was incidental.

Carcinogenicity of smoked fish is not a concern, especially if you vary your diet and don't feed exclusively on smoked fish.

Soil

"If the source is reliable, there is no danger in eating a little soil."

The danger of eating soil would be in gastrointestinal parasites. Those shouldn't be present if the sourcing is reliable and the food was produced under good sanitary conditions.

(Note that if the source is unreliable, peeling the carrot will not save you anyway.)

In the U.S. there are almost no soil-based human gastrointestinal parasites. It might even be beneficial to eat dirt: there is some evidence that it might act as a probiotic, supporting our immune system and microbiome.

Sourcing

"Consuming ingredients that are recklessly produced can and will lead to elevated amounts of dangerous substances in your body."

Our liver can detoxify our food to some extent, but it cannot deal with an overwhelming amount of toxins. Organic foods are good in that respect.

However, an absence of toxins, such as in organic foods, is not a guarantee of nutrition: the richness of nutrients in an ingredient depends on how rich the soil is and on the rest of the agricultural practices.

Soy

"Fermenting makes food more digestible; it's the only way to make soy edible."

During fermentation, bacteria "pre-digest" the food by breaking down its macronutrients. Fermented foods also add digestion-friendly bacteria to our biome.

Fermented soy is drastically different from plain soy: fermentation reduces the soy's antinutrient properties. The break down of macronutrients enables the release of micronutrients, thus increasing their bioavailability.

Statins

"Tree nuts and peanuts have cardiovascular benefits statistically comparable to those of statins."

Nuts are associated with greater longevity and less cardiovascular disease. In fact, nuts are more effective at reducing heart attacks than statins with fewer side effects, except for allergies (admittedly, an extremely serious problem for those afflicted). The right "dose" seems to be a handful, 2 or 3 times a week.

At this point, it is not known exactly how nuts work: the property was initially attributed to their high content of monounsaturated oil. However, this cannot explain the benefit: the long venerated monounsaturated oil is turning out to be not particularly heart-healthy at all. Another possibility is that nuts contain a lot of arginine, which helps the tiny muscles surrounding blood vessels to relax. They are also high in magnesium.

This is a lesson: not a single component in the nuts appears to be dominant, yet their benefit is real. Rather than deconstructing nuts, eat the whole food (you can skip the shell)!

Supplements

"Studies show that supplements are useless at best, harmful a lot of the time."

Carrots are famous for their vitamin A content. But, besides vitamin A, other carotenoids are protective against a range of diseases: macular degeneration, prostate cancer, breast cancer... Simple vitamin A supplementation doesn't offer the same protective effect. Nowadays lutein, another carotenoid, is being pushed in pharmacies against macular degeneration, a disease that vitamin A doesn't protect against. But can we trust the science for lutein?

Why trust a supplement? Eat the real thing! Singling out a given property, such as vitamin A, in the carotenoids is like looking at things through a microscope that limits our view.

Consuming supplements is risky. Supplements, like any other pill, should be taken for a specific reason, not just because it might be a good idea.

People think that supplements are safe because they are available without prescription. However, the "over the counter" supplement industry is not controlled:

- The first reason to avoid supplements is that their manufacturing involves risky practices. Isolating nutrients is nasty, using solvents and chemicals. Many contaminants are found in "over the counter" supplements (this can be seen easily by urine analysis of the patients).

- Another reason is that the human body is a highly regulated and optimized system. Anything in the wrong place can be harmful. At this point, the system is too complex for us to go and pick our nutrients; we must eat whole real food.

There are, of course, cases when a supplement might be appropriate, and this is when proper nutrients are not provided by the food that is available:

- Some isolated communities don't get enough iodine in their diet. Iodine supplements could be appropriate to prevent against low thyroid and other iodine related illnesses.

- Some older people cannot produce enough thyroxine; supplements may be appropriate in their case.

- Some men have low testosterone that does not respond to exercise; testosterone supplementation could help them.

- If you have a cold, a zinc supplement may accelerate recovery.

- If you lack the ability to absorb dietary B12 (the incidence of this problem increases with age), take under-the-tongue B12.

Virtually all the rest of the supplements either do nothing or do harm. Here are the effects now known for popular products:

- Vitamin A is linked with a 18% increase in cancer risk.

- Vitamin B3 (Niacin) was promoted for heart benefits. In reality no benefits were found, and the risk of internal bleeding and gastrointestinal problems is increased.

- Vitamin B9 (Folic acid) significantly increases colorectal and prostate cancer.

- Vitamin C is promoted for use against colds, etc. Results vary, and no benefit has been consistently shown.

- Vitamin D, if used excessively, may increase risk of pancreatic cancer and problems with balance.

- Vitamin E is promoted for heart disease. The reality: no benefit for heart disease, and a slightly higher overall mortality.

- Multi-vitamins are clearly a bad idea in view of the above.

- Resveratrol supplements showed no benefits.

- Calcium, with or without vitamin D is promoted to fight osteoporosis. In reality, it slows down osteoporosis but increases the incidence of heart attacks by 20%.

Sweeteners

"The artificial sweetness will disrupt the neuroendocrine system that regulates hunger and activity."

While there is currently no proof that commercially available artificial sweeteners are more harmful than sugar, or that their long term consumption is linked to diseases, artificial sweeteners do have side effects on our body (even though they contain no calories).

Taste

Taste and nutrition have a strong relationship.

If the body likes an ingredient, it usually means that the ingredient has a function. For example, we discovered that diazepam makes people relaxed. Later we discovered that our brain has an exact receptor for it. There is a mapping of what's out in the world with what's essential in us.

Tomatoes

"The cancer protection property has only been observed with cooked tomatoes."

The only large clinical trial that looked at the effects of various foods on cancer and heart disease found that it was ONLY the cooked form of tomatoes that was protective. Some similar results were found in the GISSI Italian based study, one of the main studies cited as showing benefit from the Mediterranean diet. Therefore, there is a fair amount of epidemiological data on the benefits of cooked tomatoes.

Trans fat

Although trans fat has been identified as dangerous since the mid 90's, the FDA started looking into it only much later.

"Natural trans fats from properly sourced dairy and meat have beneficial metabolic effect."

- Palm oil, a natural trans fat, is perfectly safe.

- Trans-palmitoleic acid, naturally occurring in dairy, has been associated with many health benefits.

- Saturated fat in butter is not only safe, it is healthy as well.

"Consuming man-made trans fats, which our body isn't equipped to deal with, leads to serious problems."

It is an established fact that replacing traditional natural cooking fats by man-made trans fats caused serious problems and increased the incidence of heart disease.

The man-made molecule has an altered shape, compared to the natural molecule. Since the body doesn't know what to do with that new molecule, the triglycerides made with them aren't readily taken up by the cells, and so the particles containing them shrink as they continue to circulate. This causes heart problems. If the cells do take them up and try to use them as cell wall material, defects result. This has been well known for a long time.

"Grass-fed, grass-finished animals contain healthy fats with a high ratio of long-chain omega-3 and very few trans fats."

Long-chain omega-3 fatty acids are important to our metabolism: they must mostly be obtained through our food since our body's capacity to manufacture them is limited.

We don't actually have a lot of information one way or the other concerning the effect of animal trans fats. (The exception is trans-palmitoleic acid, which is definitely associated with positive health effects.)

A tidbit of technical information: "trans" is a lower bond energy state then "cis." This explains why some naturally occurring trans configurations require heating to convert them to the "cis" state. One more reason to cook foods.

Trans-palmitoleic acid

Trans-palmitoleic acid is uniquely dense in dairy and beef. It is associated with improved blood pressure, reduced diabetes and improved insulin sensitivity. Many studies show that dairy fat is beneficial.

Triglycerides

There are not a lot of free-floating fatty acids in our system. The majority of fats generated by the liver are in triglyceride form. They are circulated in the blood bound up in lipoproteins (VLDL, LDL, etc.).

Paradoxically, eating a lot of fat doesn't cause high levels of triglycerides. Eating high amounts of carbs does: insulin goes up, telling the cells to use glucose; the cells stop using triglycerides, which accumulate in the blood (and eventually get stored in fat cells).

It is undesirable to have high triglycerides for many reasons:

- The liver packages triglycerides into VLDL particles consisting of a cholesterol core surrounded by a thick layer of triglycerides. If triglycerides are high, more VLDL particles are produced. Since the available cholesterol stays the same, each particle has a smaller cholesterol core. After the particle has circulated and its triglycerides have been picked off by cells here and there, what is left is a much smaller cholesterol core (LDL particle) that can get stuck behind the artery walls.

- When there are a lot of triglycerides in the blood, triglycerides are broken near the cells by the cell enzyme lipase (LPL), and the resulting free fatty acids are taken in. As a result, the cells get clogged with free fatty acids, mostly in the mesenteric section of the body, that is, inside the muscle wall of the abdomen: triglycerides are more prone to deposit there (maybe because it's the first place they get to after leaving the liver, or because of our hormonal distribution). This results in abdominal fat rather than subcutaneous fat.

This mesenteric fat is the least healthy fat because this tissue has a particular signaling role for the entire body in terms of energy behavior; it secretes a whole array of hormones and can be viewed as an organ: for example mesenteric fat produces more leptin than subcutaneous fat does.

The way to lower triglycerides is to cut down on sugar, starch and alcohol.

Vitamins

Vitamins are not totally unrelated to macronutrients: for example, some vitamins are synthesized from fat. Note that the efficiency of vitamins can be affected by the rest of our diet: for example, glucose inhibits the uptake of vitamin C by competing for the same resources.

"By focusing on vitamins, we expose ourselves to the serious consequences of deficiency in the other nutrients."

"Vitamins are linked with short term disease. They don't take into account nutrient deficiencies with long term consequences."

The causal mechanism between vitamin and disease is not always clear, but the time lapse between deficiency and disease is always relatively short (by definition of vitamins). For instance, scurvy was associated with vitamin C deficiency a long time ago by observing British sailors.

Epidemiological facts linking diseases with nutrients not classified as vitamins take longer to establish, but they are statistically significant as well:

- Deficiency in long-chain omega-3 is statistically related to a higher incidence of stroke, heart attack and cancer.

- We know that people who have diets higher in sulforaphane, over time have a lower incidence in cancer.

Because these effects have a longer time scale, the role of sulforaphane or omega-3 is obscured, and they are not classified as a vitamin.

Vegans

See also *Further Reading - Veganism*.

It is frequently claimed that veganism (not eating any animal product at all) prolongs life. The fact is that vegans and vegetarians are usually health conscious individuals.

Some studies show that both health conscious vegetarians and health conscious non-vegetarians have the same mortality rate, and that it is significantly lower than for the rest of the population. While vegans also have a lower mortality than the general population, their mortality is higher than that of the average health conscious person. The only conclusion to be drawn is that it pays to be health conscious.

Some important components we need are mostly found in animal products: vitamin B12, vitamin D, omega-3 oils... It is possible to take supplements but the real problem is that we don't know how many substances are necessary: it could be 5,000 or 5,000,000, at this point we don't have a list. In fact, nutritional science makes advances by looking at the effect of deficiencies in vegans.

Weight Loss

See also *Weight Loss* section.

Weight loss is a real health need for part of the population. However, the obsession with thinness is also unhealthy:

The Body Mass Index (BMI) is an estimation of body fat based on a person's height and weight. It is often used as a health indicator: for a woman a "normal" BMI is between 18.5 and 25; a BMI higher than 25 is considered overweight. But in fact, several studies show that people with a BMI that would classify them as overweight live longer. Thinner is not necessarily healthier.

Index

(Bold characters are used to highlight the recipes.)

Illustrations

Table of Contents